Architecture
and the
Corporation

Architecture
and the
Corporation
The Creative Intersection

Thomas Walton

Studies of the Modern Corporation
Graduate School of Business
Columbia University

MACMILLAN PUBLISHING COMPANY
NEW YORK

Collier Macmillan Publishers
LONDON

Macmillan Publishing Company
866 Third Avenue, New York, N.Y. 10022

Collier Macmillan Canada, Inc.

Printed in the United States of America

printing number
1   2   3   4   5   6   7   8   9   10

Library of Congress Cataloging-in-Publication Data

Walton, Thomas,
    Architecture and the corporation: the creative intersection/
Thomas Walton.
        p.   cm.—(Studies of the modern corporation)
    ISBN 0-02-933931-6
    1. Architecture—United States—Decision making—Case studies.
2. Communication in architectural design—Case studies.   3. Architects and
patrons—United States—Case studies.   4. Office buildings—United States—Planning—
Case studies.   I. Title.   II. Series.
NA1996.W35 1988
    720—dc19   88-13062
                                                                                            CIP

(LT)
NA
1996
.W35
1988

STUDIES OF THE MODERN CORPORATION
Graduate School of Business, Columbia University

The Program for Studies of the Modern Corporation is devoted to the advancement and dissemination of knowledge about the corporation. Its publications are designed to stimulate inquiry, research, criticism, and reflection. They fall into three categories: works by outstanding businesspeople, scholars, and professionals from a variety of backgrounds and academic disciplines; annotated and edited selections of business literature; and business classics that merit republication. The studies are supported by outside grants from private business, professional, and philanthropic institutions interested in the program's objectives.

GUILIO PONTECORVO
Director

Dedicated to

My Father
and
My Patient Teacher

Clarence C. Walton

Contents

Preface

THE message of this analysis is directed to corporate executives as well as to the facility managers and professional designers involved in building decisions. Its theses are twofold. The first is that architecture and interior design are valuable corporate resources that executives can and do deliberately use to achieve organizational goals. The second is that adversarial relationships—endemic to joint enterprises where experts from different disciplines interact, including managers and architects—can be transformed into cooperative alliances through carefully structured decision-making processes.

The first hypothesis is supported by research that makes it clear that prestige and improved return-on-investment are only two of several ways creative design contributes to corporate success. Beyond these traditional benefits, it can be demonstrated that quality architecture and interior design can also have positive effects on productivity, corporate culture, values in the work force, cost control, planning flexibility, and social responsibility. A discussion of these important issues is the focus of chapter one.

The second chapter and the case studies that follow explore ways to achieve effective design decision-making. Effectiveness in this area is a significant challenge because experience suggests that conflicts are inevitable when experts from various fields engage in a single project. Within corporate organizations, financial guardians clash with advertising personnel, productivity teams differ with marketing strategists, and human resource directors confront corporate counsel.

That antagonisms intensify when outside professions interact with management is dramatically demonstrated when businessmen and scientists are engaged to solve common problems. Anthropologist Frank Dubinskas, currently at Boston College, for example, has tracked relationships between scientists and managers in twenty-five new bio-tech companies and found these differences: managers like order where scientists live in chaos; managers foster impressions of being in command while scientists appear bemused or confused; executives surround themselves with elaborate furniture while scientists labor in messy laboratories; managers respond to short-term market pressures whereas scientists accept long lags before breakthroughs as inevitable.[1]

When it comes to architects and executives, the adversarial stance is less pronounced because both recognize their common stake in a common venture. Nevertheless, even this natural community of interest can be eroded when the architect's willfulness becomes the client's waste, or when the client's wants do not meet the client's needs. In the first case, the architect asks too much, and in the second, resists too little. In addition, no major building is ever completed without unanticipated problems and neither architect nor executive is the prime mentor in what is, of necessity, learn-as-you-go experience. Optimal solutions come only when client and architect work together *before* construction begins to establish decision-making processes and communication networks. Once this is done, the prospects for using design as a business tool are greatly enhanced.

The detailed motives behind such cooperation and the pitfalls and successes in this type of relationship are especially evident in five original case studies. The selection was made to illustrate a variety of corporate situations and courses of action. The story behind the Lockheed Missiles and Space Company office in Sunnyvale, California, is significant because it suggests that a building can help change a corporate culture and because it clearly demonstrates that research can make valuable contributions to the design process. The studies of the Hercules and Beneficial headquarters offer insights into design management for companies that build only occasionally. Interestingly, the same narratives also provide important contrasts. One describes the construction of an urban officer tower for chemical engineers; the other outlines the development of a rural corporate campus for lawyers and financial services experts. In these cases, the comparative analysis in the last chapter identifies similarities *and* critical differences in goals, priorities, and management procedures.

The evaluations of Herman Miller and United Technologies discuss approaches useful to firms that have ongoing building programs. Being aware of future needs and assuring that construction is economical, flexible, and responsive are key objectives. Another feature of this type of company is that building becomes part of the corporate culture. In the first instance, architecture is used by Herman Miller to express its "covenant" with employees and its Design (with a capital D) leadership in the systems furniture industry. In the second, United Technologies adapts problem-solving techniques used by its many engineering businesses to make sure there is a close fit between facility needs and architectural results.

Obviously, these choices mean that others—which might have served equally well—have been ignored. Enormous interest, for example, has been generated by the Equitable skyscraper in New York, the Pittsburgh Plate Glass complex in that city's Golden Triangle, the new office towers on the San Francisco and Dallas skylines, and TRW's headquarters in Cleveland. The list could be multiplied almost indefinitely. Perhaps the projects actually selected reflect the old aphorism *de gustibus non est disputandum,* and there may be disagreement concerning the aesthetic merit of individual designs. At the same time, the five cases explain the two theses of this research simply and directly and in this way amplify the essential notion that, in today's competitive environment, design is a corporate resource too precious to be squandered.

Acknowledgments

FEW of life's odysseys are completed alone and it is quite appropriate, therefore, to offer thanks for help and encouragement received during the journeys. Several people are particularly deserving. Richard Eells, highly regarded as teacher and author, has been a special inspiration. The example of his own work and the generous gifts of time and insights have seen this project from conception to its final form. Giulio Pontecorvo, Columbia University professor and director of the Program for Studies of the Modern Corporation, and Elizabeth Parry, editor for this volume, have carefully watched over the details of this effort. My family—and I single out my father and my wife for service well beyond the call of duty—have read and reread the manuscript, sharpened my ideas by contributing reactions, and taken me beyond discouraging moments when progress seemed nonexistent. This is small gratitude for giving that can only be described as love.

There have also been numerous individuals who have freely and generously provided information and assistance with the case studies. Many I may never have seen or have only met briefly. I am sure, then, that this list is not exhaustive, but it does recognize a few in the large cast of characters that have made this book possible: Lee Windheim (Leo A. Daly) and Art Hubbard (Lockheed); John Greer, Ed Lacy, Elizabeth Ronat, and Carolyn Miller (Hercules); Sandy Hance (Beneficial), and John Pearce (Hillier); Tom Wolterink and Kathy Pruden (Herman Miller); and Drake Rowe (United Technologies) and Steve Kirk (SH&G).

1

The Rationale for Rational Design

"I like the thought," mused Philip Johnson, philosopher and *enfant terrible* of the architectural profession, "that what we are here to do on this earth is to embellish it for its greater beauty, so that oncoming generations can look back to the shapes we leave here and get the same thrill that I in turn get in looking back—at the Parthenon, at Chartres Cathedral . . ."[1] Johnson's credo would likely be embraced by the bulk of architects, who see themselves as a most interesting breed: inventive, important, and justifiably egotistic. They are, on occasion, as tyrannical as the legendary Frank Lloyd Wright, whom colleagues described as "always frank and always right."

Innovation, originality, and high self-esteem are equally visible in the business executives who, not unlike the archons managing the political affairs of ancient Athens, preside over today's vast organizational complexes.[2] While the jurisdiction of these contemporary archons differs from that of the ancients, their own domains offer as many opportunities for creativity as the city-state did to men like Solon (639–559 B.C.), who shielded liberty in an Athenian world seemingly bent on its own destruction. In the diverse arenas of commerce, finance, and industry, there are some Solon-like archons who produce not new political systems but new products for new markets and new buildings for new towns. When the energy and skills of business leaders interact positively with the energies and skills of architects and designers, the results have been beneficial both for the partners and for the larger community. Validation for this somewhat sweeping generalization comes from history itself.

In Mantua, Italy, there are many enduring and beautiful examples of the positive interaction between archons and architects. Although the city was waterlocked by lakes and rivers and threatened by decay, during the fifteenth century the Mantuans outperformed their rivals and transformed their provincial town into one of the artistic capitals of the world. Under the leadership of the Gonzagas, a landed family of peasant origins, Mantua attracted the painter Andrea Mantegna, the court composer Claudio Monteverdi and, especially interesting for the purposes of this book, the architect Leon Battista Alberti. Alberti and his followers made the lack of marble quarries nearby into a virtue, exploiting brick and stucco with such enormous originality that their influence is still felt. The grandeur of Venice provides a second illustration. St. Mark's and its piazza, the churches by Palladio, and the multitude of fine palaces along the canals continue to serve as both architectural models and as an expression of the economic vitality of that region's glassworks, textile shops, shipyards, and trading companies.

There is, of course, a dark side to the story. At times, architects have pursued their solitary course, indifferent to the client and to the environment. Business archons have behaved the same way when they ignored worker needs or plundered the landscape. When architect and archon, refusing to interact, have walked stubbornly along parallel lines, the outcome has been bleak. Few paintings have captured more effectively the loneliness of individuals and the starkness of the urban Hades of smoke-laden cities than Charles Sheeler's *American Landscape*. Sheeler's photograph-like expression of the contemporary industrial world—a serpentine machine defoliating the garden of Eden[3]—suggests that the present-day archon has made a bargain with Faust, "swapping his soul for a summer cottage and a second car," and leading others into the same miserable contract.[4]

Despite the artist's gloomy image, which reflects the hostility of many to modern cities, the metropolis has always been—and still is—a magnet for creative people. While there have been long epochs of dominance by agrarian societies, modern history is largely an urban story. In Europe and in the Middle East, places like Athens and Alexandria, Rome and Constantinople, Florence and Venice, and Paris and London have been the foci of industry and culture. In America, Boston and New York, Pittsburgh and Chicago, St. Louis and Detroit, San Francisco and Los Angeles have had parallel roles. It might be truly said, then, that as the city goes, so goes the nation, an axiom reaffirmed by developer James Rouse when he pointed out that

> . . . nearly one-half of all the people in the United States in the year 2000 will live in dwelling units that have not been started and on land that has not yet been broken. . . . Every month in the United States we are adding roughly 300,000 people, a city the size of Toledo. Every year we add a new Philadelphia. In twenty years we will double the size of Los Angeles and the San Francisco Bay area. We will add 6,000,000 people to the New York Region in the same period. . . . Such are the dynamics of our urban growth. It has been said that in the remainder of this century we will build, new, in our cities, the equivalent of all that has been built since Plymouth Rock. What opportunities this represents! Opportunity for business, for jobs, for the development of new and better institutions to serve our people. And the opportunity to plan and develop this new one-half of our American cities free of the mistakes of the past, responsive to the needs of the future.[5]

In this expansion archons and architects play leading roles. Contrary to a rather common assumption that urban vitality is chiefly due to geographic and historical advantages, entrepreneurial factors must be given equal recognition. Historian Charles Glaab made the point explicit when he wrote how simple it is to explain New York's rise to metropolitan dominance in terms of superior natural advantages such as a magnificent harbor and the reasonably level terrain sweeping westward across the state which permitted construction of the Erie Canal with relative ease. But, he notes, "it is also possible to point to organizational and entrepreneurial action on the part of the city's business community that earlier helped to insure the city's success."[6] The conclusion is as significant as it is obvious: as the American metropolis continues to spread across the landscape, the isolation and grimness depicted by Sheeler must yield to the models provided by Renaissance Mantua and Venice—all products of the creative partnership between successful business leaders and talented designers.

When there are problems in such partnerships, it is because, as one corporate analyst put it, "the artist and businessman march to different drummers. Practitioners of the fine arts ideally set their own standards of performance, personally and without reference to absolutes. The manager's work (eventually) is measured with tangible yardsticks, graduated in established units. Until there is a conversion scale by which we can compare aesthetics and coin of profits, managers and artists will pass through the forest on different trails."[7]

This inquiry suggests that conversion scales are possible, and that such scales tend to validate the thesis advanced in a pioneering study by Richard Eells. Viewing art as a mirror of society and as an indicator of future trends, Eells argued that art (and by implication architecture) had considerable significance for policymakers in the modern corporation because "the survival and growth of the great corporations depend upon a constant instream of knowledge from every available source, and one of the still unrecognized sources of valuable knowledge is the domain of art."[8]

Architects and the members of related design professions are part artists, part businessmen, and part city builders. Expanding on Eells' hypothesis, this study seeks to demonstrate that, while there is no precise way to measure the benefits of quality architecture and interior design in terms of profits, there is a relationship so fundamental that architects and corporate clients must give it attention. A necessary first step, however, is to understand the operations and the motives of the two major actors in the drama.

History

Forty years ago, economist Walton Hamilton hypothesized that government regulatory bodies established to control corporations were actually under corporation control. The only way to comprehend business and government relations was, in his words, to strip away the fiction "by piercing the corporate veil," a difficult challenge since the art of veiling had "reached such perfection so that by comparison Salome, with her seven veils, was a somewhat naked lady."[9] Fortunately, the veil that mantles business and architecture needs no piercing. A gossamer material allows interested persons to see what has been going on within the relationship between business and architecture over the past century and a half. During that time, the prime motives of archons were profitability and prestige. For architects the driving forces were willingness to serve and hunger for recognition. Examples tell the story and, since western Europe was the pacemaker, the continental experience becomes America's mentor.

In 1840, at a time when muddy paths were more common than sidewalks, a group of Belgian businessmen conceived the idea of a classical, glass-roofed arcade in Brussels which they decided to name the Galeries

St. Hubert. It was to be a retail center that would "in its opulence equal anything similar in Paris or London." Prestige and civic pride, however, were not the only forces behind this grandiose enterprise. To titillate investor interest a prospectus proclaimed boldly that

> . . . no operation has ever been more straight-forward. For some shareholders it may be speculation, but it is, above all, the most solid of investments. . . . There will be a theater, a concert hall, restaurants, and cafes. A theater brings with it twenty businesses which must be located nearby. All such shops are a constant attraction for pedestrian traffic and, as we have established, plentiful pedestrian traffic is the very lifeblood of retail trade.[10]

Long after its completion, the Galeries St. Hubert remains a beautiful and economically successful landmark in the heart of Brussels.

The United States has had variations on the St. Hubert story. During the last two decades of the nineteenth century, Chicago provided a testing ground for wedding profitability and design. For the city's business community architects created a new and lean aesthetic, free of ornament and expressive of the latest in technology. Most buildings were offices and some rose an impressive fifteen stories or more. Their chaste facades paralleled the strength and spareness of the steel frames within; wide windows and bays filled interiors with light and offered expansive display space to ground floor shops. Both public and critics applauded the new skyline. Architect John Welborn Root even anticipated the impact such designs would have on future builders when he commented that "by their mass and proportion, [they] convey in some large elemental sense an idea of the great, stable, conserving forces of modern civilization."[11] The prophesy was fulfilled when the so-called Chicago Style became the prototype for office structures during subsequent decades.

Like the Brussels arcade, however, the beauty and durability of this building type was intimately tied to an economic purpose. When architectural critic Montgomery Schuyler asked what would happen if a successful designer sacrificed one or more stories of a building for various embellishments and classical details, the response was blunt: "Why, the word would be passed, and he would never get another to do. No, we would never try those tricks on our business men." The creative process for these pioneering architects was straightforward: "I get from my engineer a statement of the minimum thickness of the steel post and its enclosure in terra cotta. Then I establish the minimum depth of floor beam and the minimum height of the sill from the floor to accommodate what

5

must go between them. These are the data of my design."[12] Like office construction today, one objective was to maximize return and the obvious way to achieve this was to build as much rentable space as possible. The particular talent of the Chicago architects was their ability to blend efficiency and function with a style that captured the imagination of both the business and the design communities.

In exploiting design as a business tool, a constant companion to the profitability motive has always been prestige, and a clear and early expression of this situation can be observed in the development of Renaissance Florence. During the fifteenth and sixteenth centuries, the Medici, Pazzi, Rucellai, and Strozzi families were among the most successful bankers and merchants in Europe. Florentine silk and wool were exported throughout the Continent; over thirty thousand people earned a living in the more than two hundred textile plants that flourished in the area; loans from Florentine banks, and their branches in Lyon, Geneva, Avignon, Bruges, and London, affected the fate of popes, kings, and princes. Yet later generations remember these Renaissance entrepreneurs less for their economic influence than for their lasting impact on art and architecture. With humble beginnings in rather mundane work, petty merchants formed partnerships with artists and architects; in time the small businessmen became like the classical archons because of their deep concern over the vitality and ambience of their cities. And ultimately such relationships brought about the patronage system that enabled Donatello to produce *David* and Botticelli to paint the magnificent *Birth of Venus*. As another sign of stature and concern, wealthy individuals commissioned imposing palaces noted for their beautifully proportioned rooms and courtyards. What is now the Uffizzi Gallery can perhaps be considered Europe's first corporate headquarters since it was the center for the many business interests of the Medici. Beyond their homes and places of work, individuals and guilds funded the construction and renovation of many civic buildings and squares in images that found inspiration in the greatness of ancient Greece and Rome.

To make sure that these edifices brought their builders the desired recognition, conspicuous details often included a "signature" for all to see. A common trick was to adapt a motif from the family coat of arms to the decoration of capitals, a practice that had no known precedent:

> Capitals abound with such conceits as the balls of the Medici, . . .
> the dolphins of the Pandolfini, and the griffin of the Rustici. . . . The
> personal device of Giovanni Rucellai, the sails of fortune, run all along
> the front of his palace, and they appear on the facade he financed at
> Santa Maria Novella.[13]

The art of "signature" has not been lost. Modern corporations have often used architecture to express both civic pride and the prestige of the organization. New York's Pennsylvania Station is a case in point. Styled after the Baths of Caracalla, it was a lavish Beaux Arts landmark for the city. In addition, the design was a model of efficiency, employing the most up-to-date building techniques and a sophisticated multilevel circulation system to handle the complex mix of train, automobile, subway, and pedestrian traffic. But at the time of construction, company executives also knew that the grand interior halls and Roman details of the station would be a constant reminder of the prestige, power, and vast resources of the corporation in an era when the Pennsylvania Railroad was considered one of America's invincible giants.

Another example is Chicago's Tribune Tower. This Gothic skyscraper, designed by John Howells and Raymond Hood, was selected as the winning entry in a $100,000 international architectural competition in 1922 because of the way it celebrated "three fourths of a century of amazing growth and brilliant achievement" for the newspaper. In the eyes of its owners, it was "the most beautiful office building in the world."[14] However, among all the structures influenced by the desire for prestige, New York's Chrysler Building, begun in 1928 by Walter Chrysler, has possibly the most fascinating story. The design was substantially changed after much of the construction had been completed because of the auto magnate's determination to have his monument capture the title "Tallest Building in the World." When newspaper accounts revealed that the Bank of Manhattan building in the Wall Street area would surpass his own tower in height, Chrysler informed his architect, William van Allen, that the situation was unacceptable and demanded that the plans be modified. The response was ingenious. Secretly van Allen had an aluminum-clad spire fabricated within the elevator shafts of the skyscraper and in the spring of 1930, only a month after the Bank of Manhattan had opened, the components of this gleaming crown were hoisted heavenward to surpass the height of its Wall Street rival by 119 feet.[15] It was a great moment for Chrysler. His building dominated the New York skyline. His signature, like that of the Florentine merchants, was there for all to read, for he, too, had personalized his monument—in this case, with giant aluminum hub and radiator cap motifs.

As the anecdotes suggest, using architecture as a business resource is not a new phenomenon. The process continues. In its inner-city shopping places at Harborplace in Baltimore and Faneuil Hall in Boston, the Rouse Company mirrors the attitudes of those who built the Brussels arcade, using design to enhance the quality of its urban projects and to improve the return-on-investment. The Rouse philosophy is significant because it articulates the value of the archon-architect relationship and it is, therefore, worth quoting in some detail:

- Each market is different from all others. Design begins with a sensitive understanding of what makes each market special. Innovation and freshness derive naturally from the history and tradition of an area. Good design fits easily with respect for the environment and established patterns of life in a community.
- Architecture seeks to emphasize merchandise and merchants. The shopping place facilitates the relationship between customers and that which they might need, wish for or discover. Beyond satisfaction, customers should derive enjoyment and delight from the shopping experience.
- Individual details matter in reinforcing the feeling of festival that should be part of the successful shopping environment—landscaping, benches, fountains, courts, light, banners, graphics, signs, merchandise, merchants—the entire center must be seen as a total environment designed to add to the fun of shopping.[16]

This sensitive approach reaps significant economic rewards. For example, in its first year Baltimore's Harborplace had "sales well above $300 a square foot, more than double those of a typical suburban mall."[17]

Developers Edward J. Minskoff and Gerald Hines, well known for their office and commercial ventures in New York and Texas, also carefully calculate the impact of design on their investments. Minskoff observed that a "building that is of high quality in both design and materials will prevail. It will have that standout quality ten, fifteen, twenty years down the road. And the quality will generate higher rentals even then."[18] Hines commented that his innovative design for Houston's Pennzoil Place "paid off in rents that command a premium of $3 to $4 per square foot."[19] Former Citibank chairman Walter B. Wriston discovered the same principle when an analysis showed that space in Manhattan's new Citicorp Center could be leased at 20 percent or more above the going rate. Wriston then decided to use most of the office floors for paying tenants rather than move himself or many of the bank's divisions into the structure.[20] In a sense, by associating the company's name with the building's award-winning design and subsequently renting the space, he had the cake of corporate prestige and was able to eat it as well.

As the last illustration suggests, beyond producing income, image has been an important motive for architectural projects during the past two decades. Although the scenarios are not as dramatic as that of the Chrysler Building, like the stories of Renaissance bankers in Florence and turn-of-the-century speculators in Chicago, they reveal how pride and personality are blended in distinctive and sometimes controversial design. In initiating a new headquarters project for American Telephone & Telegraph, then chairman John deButts had a simple mandate: "The world's greatest skyscraper for the world's greatest corporation."[21] The final costs were high (more than $230 per square foot), but the design's granite facade, Chippendale pediment, and triumphal arch entry were so unique and unprecedented that the building became an instant landmark. Indeed, it has even been compared to Alberti's church of Sant'Andrea in Mantua. In all likelihood, Philip Johnson, the corporation's architect, would be quick to admit that Alberti, who died in 1472, was one of the authentic fathers of modern architecture. And the builders at AT&T would probably be happy to align themselves with the Gonzagas in their mutual determination to unite aesthetics and function in a single structure.

The nexus between quality architecture and image is also evident in Humana's new Louisville headquarters tower, a monument the Kentucky-based hospital management firm consciously exploits as a prestigious and recognizable corporate symbol. Construction was not even complete when, in late 1984, Humana chairman David Jones and president H. Wendell Cherry used the building as a backdrop for an interview concerning heart transplant patient William Schroeder. In a similar way, Pittsburgh Plate Glass's Gothic-inspired complex is a stunning three-dimensional showcase for the company's energy-saving products.

Critic Joseph Giovannini has written that buildings such as these may have restored faith in "signature" design as an approach that can both satisfy corporate needs and improve the quality of urban life. Philip Johnson makes the point that, "the people with money to build today are corporations—they are our popes and our Medicis. . . . The sense of pride is why they build. Nietzsche would call it the will to power, the French would call it *la folie des pierres,* and developers call it good business."[22] And when good business translates into profitable and prestigious architecture, then contemporary business archons can and do contribute significantly to civic pride, community joy, and the reawakening of American cities and towns.

Some New Dimensions

One of the most respected students of corporate financial policies, A. S. Dewing, concluded that the gradual evolution of business organizations through centuries of changing economic circumstances required that their leaders project purposes "beyond the limits of a single human life."[23] Like human beings then, corporations only achieve a certain immortality by carefully tending to their needs and by appropriately adapting to new situations. That profound changes are coming to contemporary society is a truism. That there are spillover effects from such transformations into the business-architecture relationship is less obvious but equally true. In the past, the prime motives for businesses to use quality architecture were to increase return-on-investment and to create a symbol of corporate prestige. Changes came about through scientific management of the Taylor variety and through technological innovation of the Edison kind.

Within the last two decades, however, concerns have emerged which suggest corporations should include design as a facet of a larger and more comprehensive business strategy. The economic realities of the 1980s open new possibilities for architecture and interior design to address such issues as white-collar productivity, corporate culture, changing values of the work force, cost control, planning flexibility, and social responsibility. A brief examination of these points reveals why each has an important design corollary.

Productivity

Commonly known data make it obvious that the composition of labor in America is undergoing a major shift. Blue-collar jobs are declining and women are now a majority in the work force. As corporations move production outside the country, union membership drops so drastically that labor representatives bargain as aggressively for job security as they do for wages and benefits. At the same time, employment in the service fields continues to expand at a rapid pace. Offices, once regarded as passive support mechanisms for the manufacturing process (tracking sales, recording inventories, and monitoring production) are today "increasingly concerned with the generation and communication of ideas."[24] Vast data bases and analytical models have replaced paper as a medium and the once labor-intensive assembly line is now becoming the domain of robots and computers.

Not unexpectedly, change has been accompanied by a growing focus on white-collar productivity. The first scientific research on office management, begun in the early twentieth century, complemented Frederick Taylor's famous management studies of factory production. Investigators like William Leffingwell and Harry Hopf stressed organizational and technical procedures to improve the flow of work, and Leffingwell even endowed an award for the "outstanding accomplishment of practical value in office management."[25] Today, emphasis is on information technology—word processing, teleconferencing, microcomputers, and sophisticated reproduction techniques—and even traditionally conservative developers are responding to these techniques for enhancing the output of white-collar employees. In collaboration with builders, United Technologies is incorporating its Techloop Data Highway into "intelligent" offices. Advertisements for this sophisticated electronic system promise access to simultaneous voice/data communications, personal computing, word processing, electronic mail, outside data bases, management decision modeling and analyses, and much more.

This "hardware" approach, however, does not address equally important, albeit much softer, issues. John Naisbitt has urged managers to remember that the complement to "high tech" is "high touch" because corporate success is dependent on both elements: "Whenever new technology is introduced into society, there must be a counterbalancing human response—that is, 'high touch'—or the technology is rejected. The more high tech, the more high touch."[26] The design implications are significant. Ultimately, to improve white-collar productivity, a quality work environment is an essential complement to quality tools. Considerable evidence supports this conclusion. In a 1982 study conducted by the New York Stock Exchange Office of Economic Research, well over half of the forty-nine thousand firms surveyed subscribed to the idea that better design and better productivity went hand in hand. Specifically, the study found that "structuring plant and office space" was rated as "very successful" in enhancing productivity by a third of all the companies surveyed, and "somewhat successful" by nearly a third of the remainder.[27] A two-thirds batting average is an arresting statistic.

Another relevant study, undertaken by a team from the University of Michigan for the National Office Products Association (NOPA), was called "The Future of the Office Furniture Industry." Noting that office expenses had reached almost 50 percent of the overall cost of doing business and were climbing at the rate of 15 percent a year, the researchers reported that 90 percent of these costs were for direct personnel expenses. Given this fact, companies must address the physical, social, and psychological needs of workers to have a positive result from their investment in technology. A new field known as ergonomics is investigating the relationships among furnishings, equipment, and human comfort, but there are other issues relevant to managers and architects. As the NOPA study states:

Evidence is mounting that working in an automated office poses potential health hazards, and job satisfaction among workers in automated offices tends to be low. Dealing satisfactorily with this situation means countering not only the problems inherent in automation—the mechanization and the routinization of work, and the consequent boredom, fatigue and stress—but the potential hazards associated with these developments. Computerized scheduling, registered electronic mail that lets a sender know when a message has been read, the ability to monitor and measure productivity electronically—these and other outgrowths of office automation have resurrected a host of issues traditionally associated with the dehumanizing environment of the factory: worker alienation, surveillance, invasion of privacy, job elimination and decline in physical and psychological health.[28]

The challenge to leaders in the business, building, and design communities is obvious. The Buffalo Organization for Social and Technological Innovation (BOSTI) has identified aspects of the workplace that require particular attention. In 1983, this organization isolated four design elements that directly affect job performance: (1) the quality of lighting, (2) control over visual access to a space, (3) control over physical access to a space, and (4) participation in the design process. In addition, nine environmental factors were cited as influencing job satisfaction: floor area, temperature and air quality, lighting, safety and security, noise, ease of communication, comfort, participation, and flexibility. What makes this research especially valuable is that the authors translated design-related improvements in job performance and job satisfaction into dollar figures. They estimated that over an eight-year depreciation period "the present value of good design for (each) manager/supervisor is almost $7500; for (each) professional technical worker over $8000; and for (each) clerical worker over $2000."[29] The numbers become part of the conversion scale linking business and design that, until recently, was lacking.

The Corporate Culture

While academic and managerial interest in the nature of corporate cultures has not led in the past to systematic examinations of this phenomenon, it is increasingly evident that a strong culture has invariably been a driving force behind continuing success in American business. Illustrating this thesis with lively personal accounts from well-known companies like IBM, AT&T, General Electric, Procter & Gamble and National Cash Register, Terrence Deal and Allan Kennedy perceptively recorded five factors that nurture a healthy culture:

- A clear understanding of the business environment,
- A shared and well-articulated value system,
- The presence of corporate heroes,
- Rites and rituals to guide behavior, and
- An informal network to transmit values and mythology.[30]

Understandably, their concern is with people and events; but they might have explored the issue of architecture because buildings can both express a culture and facilitate changes in it.

Quality architecture, though not emphasized by students of corporate cultures, is obviously an aspect of the Naisbitt thesis that high tech requires high touch. Two other well known students of corporate culture, Thomas J. Peters and Robert H. Waterman, Jr., concluded that "all the stuff managers have been dismissing for so long as intractable, irrational, intuitive, and informal can be managed." Such management recognizes the profound importance of the allegedly "soft stuff."[31] Unfortunately, Peters and Waterman did not take the next step to point out the significance of the physical environment as the context within which the "soft stuff" becomes meaningful.

That the physical aspects of corporate culture have been understated by theorists can be shown in a few examples where business executives and architects have worked together to give serious responses to a serious concern. In Santa Clara, California, the headquarters for ROLM Corporation boasts a million-dollar sports pavilion complete with Nautilus equipment, jacuzzis, a gymnasium, and a tanning parlor. At Tandem Computers in Silicon Valley, employees gather with President Jim Treybig every Friday afternoon for a party around the company swimming pool; at other times, they relax in the exercise room or on the company golf course. In both cases, the management philosophy is that first-rate facilities foster high-level creativity and loyalty—attributes essential for success in the quick-paced, competitive, high-tech industry.[32] The Beneficial Management complex in Peapack, New Jersey, reflects a different culture. The wooded campus is a semiformal composition of low-scale, red brick buildings organized around several exterior plazas. While the arrangement and office designs suggest the hierarchical and conservative nature of this financial services firm, the shared dining, recreation, and outdoor spaces stress the notion of community and recognize the contributions each individual makes to the corporation's success.[33] In this instance, a potential tension between authoritarian and democratic values has been reconciled through an architectural dialectic.

The recent history of Levi Strauss & Company provides a telling example of why the design component of a corporate culture cannot be taken for granted. After going public in 1971, the apparel company grew so rapidly that it needed a prestigious office to replace the casual but over-crowded headquarters that had been its home for sixty-eight years. In 1974, the firm signed a long-term lease for twelve floors of a major San Francisco skyscraper. The address was perfect. The space was not. Levi Strauss' personable chief executive officer, Walter Haas, reported being isolated in his twenty-eighth floor office: "My style is pretty informal. . . . I like to barge in on people and keep up with what's going on." There were other problems as well:

> Executives stepped from a shopping arcade into one elevator bank while nearly everybody else used another set of elevators. There was no lobby the company could call its own. For some employees, getting a cup of coffee required a ten-floor elevator trip. . . . Executives hated the fishbowl effect of glass-walled private offices, complaining that if they pulled the venetian blinds for privacy, rumors spread that something hush-hush was afoot. Lower ranking employees missed what Howard Friedman, for three decades Levi's chief consulting architect, calls "the old Levi spirit: 'Good morning, how's the baby?' "

In many respects the experience of Levi Strauss was the very opposite of Beneficial Management: its culture was democratic but its new home encouraged authoritarianism. Thus, while the offices looked "right," they were incompatible with the company's style. The very year Levi Strauss moved into the building, it began to explore possibilities for constructing its own facility. After seven years of complex negotiations, an extended and careful design process, and a $35 million investment, the mistake was corrected. Its headquarters today is the highly acclaimed Levi Plaza, a low-scale complex of relaxed and warmly decorated offices. More impor-tant to employees is the fact that this facility nurtures the company's culture. As CEO Walter Haas happily noted: "At last we're back together again."[34]

Employee Values

Whereas management seeks consciously to create a culture, the values of workers seem to change almost whimsically. Shifts in demographics, education, fashion, and attitudes regarding family, leisure, and entertain-ment are among the items that influence the motivation and priorities of employees. In this respect, the third area in which quality architecture and interior design influence corporate success is found in how effectively they respond to the changing values of the work force. During the past two decades employees have become more affluent, better educated, and less job-dependent. Well educated youth, taking for granted the security their parents strove so hard to achieve, emphasize "creativity, autonomy, rejection of authority, self-expression ahead of status, pleasure seeking, hunger for new experiences, quest for community, participation in decision-making, desire for adventure, closeness to nature, cultivation of self, and inner growth."[35]

How different this new model is from the "organization man" described by William Whyte, Jr., in 1956, when fulfillment came from total dedication to the firm: workaholics were common; neglect of family was widespread; success was spelled out in statistics and dollar signs.[36] For the present generation, work is only one facet of a satisfying lifestyle. In managerial positions, younger employees wish "to be dealt with as nonconforming individuals, rather than as members of a group;" they seek "a clear mission, creative and cooperative co-workers, open communication, and a fair division of duties."[37] They are not particularly interested in traditional corporate concepts such as strong leadership, clear lines of authority, or exact directions.

In light of this new work ethic, an Aspen Institute study suggested four steps businesses should take:

1. Link rewards closely to performance. Most Americans believe there is little relationship between how hard they work and the recognition they receive. When individuals receive equal rewards regardless of effort, the message from management is clear: "We don't care about extra effort."
2. Develop programs that enhance human relations *and* productivity. Too often managers focus on efforts that make work more agreeable without taking actions that improve performance. Job holders need both satisfaction and motivation.
3. Enforce high standards of quality. Nothing undermines dedication more than a perception that a company is indifferent to quality. Conversely, a strict, even harsh, emphasis on the highest standards of quality reinforces the conviction that work is meaningful.
4. Flatten the hierarchy. Reexamine the status and authority system in the firm. Rigid distinctions between managers and employees tend to reduce motivation. Bureaucratic organizations put layers of formal distance between those who do the work and executives who make decisions and set goals.[38]

Any comprehensive implementation of these strategies requires understanding of the role design can play. As previously noted, simple things like lighting, control over access, and participation in the design process can enhance productivity. In addition, environmental factors can be a significant tool in countering the corrosive effects of declining loyalty.[39]

Design decisions allow firms to demonstrate their commitment to employees in distinctly visible ways. Convenient location and a workplace free from dirt, noise, and pollution translate into more satisfying jobs. These concerns, for example, were evident during the mid-1970s when Union Carbide studied a move from New York City to Danbury, Connecticut. In making its announcement, company officials wrote employees that while they recognized New York's many advantages, "the long-term quality of life needs of our headquarters employees were the overruling factors in arriving at this conclusion [to relocate]."[40] Had such a philosophy been extended to blue-collar workers at the company's plants in Bhopal, India, and Charleston, West Virginia, the world might have been spared tragedies and the corporation would have avoided costly and time-consuming suits.

Company executives routinely decide on matters that affect worker safety, productivity, and satisfaction. And designers have the skills to make genuine contributions in these areas. With respect to these issues, then, there is every reason for the architect to become the archon's counselor. Today, there is a growing awareness that employees are conspicuously underutilized resources and that "striking a balance between cost considerations and human values . . . is not altruistic; it is astute management and makes bottom line sense."[41]

Olivetti, the Italian office products and high technology concern, deserves recognition for its leadership in this area. For more than seven decades, its products, graphics, and showrooms have set the standards others follow and have made the firm an international success. During the 1950s the corporation's approach to design was even an inspiration to the fledgling IBM. But while the company has creatively pursued its economic objectives, it has also sought to provide a satisfying lifestyle for its workers. Adriano Olivetti, son of the organization's founder, spent much time preparing a proposal for an ideal community which he described as "a happier place where tomorrow the factory, nature, life— brought once more into spiritual unity—may succeed in giving a new conception of dignity to a new conception of man."[42] To give substance to the ideal, Olivetti has expressed this sense of responsibility in an architectural tradition that is truly extraordinary. Not only are its retail outlets, offices, and manufacturing plants well designed, but similar talent, energy, and resources have been invested in creating housing, daycare centers, and recreation camps for employees. The company's nursery at Borgo Olivetti, constructed in 1942, remains a joyful retreat of gardens and classrooms for youngsters. In 1976, this commitment was again demonstrated in a multi-use structure in Ivrea, Italy (site of the company headquarters) that contains an array of living and social areas, including fifty-five mini-apartments, a restaurant, movie theatre, a restored Roman/ medieval street, and a swimming pool as well as numerous shops and bars.[43]

For those businesses that regard these efforts as extravagances, it is well to re-emphasize the point that architecture has very real impacts on quality control, corporate culture, and the respect, hence legitimacy, accorded companies by the public. Without being lavish, a well designed and efficient office or factory can set a standard that, along with other commitments to excellence, enhances the pride individuals have in their work and the products they create. With regard to hierarchy, an interior layout can be so developed that individuals have privacy and a sense of place while, at the same time, feeling they are responsible parts of the organization. Such an approach was important when Procter & Gamble looked into the construction of new facilities. In this company, products are initiated by competing brand teams. The concept of "creative competition" led a consultant to recommend an imaginative "cluster" design that encouraged communication and cooperation and allowed status to evolve from superior performance rather than from superior office location, titles, or certain other amenities.[44] To summarize, if management genuinely believes that its most important asset is its people, then this belief system must be reflected in its design philosophy.

Cost Control

It is axiomatic that profitability is related to cost containment. The homely observation that "a penny saved is a penny earned" has particular meaning for large organizations, where even slight increases in cost have staggering negative effects on the bottom line. Conversely, decreases in cost add substantially to the bottom line. This obvious generalization was at work when Republic Airlines decided to build a new reservations center in Livonia, Michigan. Since its completion, economies in staffing, reduced leasing and rental fees, and improved passenger service all enhance profits.[45] With respect to buildings other cost factors also have to be considered, especially the escalating price of construction and high interest rates on loans. These constraints make it essential to develop facilities within budget and on schedule, and in this area architects and interior designers can have their most immediate and tangible effects on the bottom line. The opportunities fall into three general categories which deal with: (A) design and materials selection, (B) energy conservation, and (C) project management.

17

Design and Materials Selection

In most cases, a building can be so planned that, with a knowledge of local practice, it takes advantage of standard construction techniques and commonly available or mass-produced components. This approach generally saves both time and money, without sacrificing quality. The Herman Miller Seating Plant in Holland, Michigan, which opened in June 1980, is an example of this sensible and "centsible" approach. The decision to use simple bar joists, steel columns, and prefabricated wall panels permitted completion of this facility within fourteen months. A quality work environment was created by suffusing the interior with natural light; employees are never far from a window and a relaxing vista. Finally, the streamlined facades, accented with bright colors, give this building an air of distinction—a visual statement of the corporation's commitment to the community and to design excellence. All this was accomplished at a cost of about twenty-five dollars per square foot, an average price for an above-average structure.[46]

Over the long term, the selection of materials with respect to life cycle costs, rather than initial expenditures, is another way designers can save money. In this approach, maintenance, repair, and replacement costs are included in the evaluation of price. An item is not chosen because it is initially cheap but because, after upkeep and future changes are considered, it is cost-effective. With the complex technology that is part of almost every building, communications and electrical wiring are areas where this method is particularly useful. In one analysis, engineer Gary Hall noted seven alternatives to the wiring problem: poke-through, flexible plug-in, modular plug-in, cellular floor, flat cable, access floor, and under-floor duct. When he combined these with various lighting and office work-station arrangements, he developed an array of twenty-one design solutions, each having different implications with regard to price and flexibility.[47] A final determinant is how the client will use the building. When, for example, Lockheed Missiles and Space Company in Sunnyvale, California, was constructing a staff office, it selected a raised access floor as the optimum wiring system so that engineering teams, who were required to move frequently, could rearrange their spaces quickly without assistance from professional electricians.[48]

Energy

Since the oil crisis in 1973 energy conservation has become a significant variable for designers and businesses. Available techniques range from simple, passive devices that reduce energy-loss or heat-gain to sophisticated active systems that recirculate energy and solar collectors that heat or cool a building and its water supply. In Boston, the Massachusetts Department of Transportation Building provides a relevant illustration. Roof-mounted collectors generate 82 percent of the structure's hot water needs; heat pumps transfer energy to the perimeter offices during winter and store excess in three 250,000-gallon water tanks in the basement for use at later times; in addition, the water tanks also keep chilled water to reduce summer cooling loads. While the initial costs may have been high, these strategies allowed engineers to "reduce the amount of mechanical refrigeration from 2000 to 1200 tons and eliminate a backup heating system altogether."[49] The Lockheed office, mentioned above, is also a case in point. Here, an atrium design and a carefully detailed fenestration and lighting system reduced the annual electricity needs for ambient illumination by 70 percent.[50]

Project Management

The efficient management of projects is a third requirement for controlling costs, and the most common techniques are: (1) construction management, (2) value engineering, and (3) fast-track construction. The construction manager is an individual who oversees the programming, design, and development of a building on the owner's behalf. This coordinator not only makes sure that the design will serve the client's needs but also suggests cost-saving measures and strategies for construction. For companies that build infrequently (or for those undertaking a new project type), such expertise can be quite effective. Value engineering is the incentive built into construction contracts that encourages the builder to suggest alternatives for saving time and money without sacrificing quality. Essentially, if such proposals are accepted by the owner and implemented, the contractor is rewarded with a percentage of the savings.

Finally, there is "fast-track construction," a process where foundation and site preparation begin before all the contract drawings and specifications are complete. In theory, this speeds work since documents for later stages of the design can be finished while construction is actually going on. If the project is straightforward and well managed, this approach can be quite successful. But certain drawbacks have to be weighed by the client and the architect since final costs are generally not fixed until late in the process and expenses can grow if the commission is an unusual building type or if unexpected site conditions arise. For these management techniques and other methods of cost control, what is most important is for executives not to substitute outsiders' recommendations (from architects, engineers, or consultants) for a clear, in-house understanding of corporate needs and for good communication among all members of the design and construction team. Only in this way will officers be able to balance price with other corporate design objectives.

Planning Flexibility

On a General Motors assembly line, it once took up to forty hours to retool the dies used to stamp out automobile parts; in Japan, this job has been reduced to two hours. This flexibility problem is a design issue. Architecturally, it is a crucial element because plant and office configurations must be able to change rapidly in response to the development of new products or new management goals. During the past two decades, open office landscaping has been the traditional solution to this problem. Interiors are designed with movable panels and furniture components that, at least in theory, can be easily rearranged. Interestingly, this concept may have had its roots in a headquarters project developed by the German architect Peter Behrens in 1912 for the Mannesmann Tube Company in Dusseldorf. Frustrated by the directors' inability to agree on a functional program, Behrens devised a modular scheme based on the unit of a typical six-person team. This "cell" was used to create structural and spacial divisions. At the dedication ceremony, the architect pointed out the inherent flexibility of his design because the building was "arranged like a big hall in which you can partition off rooms as you like to meet your requirements that may arise at any moment."[51] The statement provided one of the earliest definitions of the "open systems" approach.

Still, such a concept may not be for everyone. Open systems have been criticized on grounds that: (a) they are not genuinely flexible since changes require extensive planning, time, and technical assistance; and (b) the work spaces are impersonal and lack privacy. In light of these comments, it is worth noting how Union Carbide's headquarters achieved flexibility by using enclosed offices. Since all rooms are approximately 182 square feet, operations can be moved with relative ease; at the same time, employees have opportunities to personalize these otherwise uniform areas by selecting chairs, desks, rugs, and cabinets from among four different furniture styles. This relative freedom, combined with views from every office of the forested site beyond, has created a relaxing and productive environment. In the words of one financial officer, "I can sit in this room and do in eight hours the work I did there [in New York City] in ten."[52]

Beyond planning at this micro level, design can also address flexibility issues on a larger scale. The pinwheel plan of the Herman Miller Seating

Plant in Holland, Michigan, was developed and sited so that the manufacturing facility could readily expand to three times its present size without sacrificing its high-quality work environment.[53] For Westinghouse Electric Corporation, the Pittsburgh architectural firm, Archiris, analyzed such things as production, distribution, sales, and marketing goals to prepare a five-year facilities plan. The designers specified four prototypes and made recommendations for phasing in twenty-three buildings across the country. The architects noted that the approach provided "our clients with a plan that is directly pertinent to their business goals."[54] The long and the short of flexible design is this: while serving immediate needs, imaginative and careful planning helps a company meet future objectives.

Social Responsibility

A retrospective view of corporate social responsibility indicates that the earlier definitions were somewhat limited. While the meaning of the term was implicit in many of the old classical writers—John Maurice Clark was one of them[55]—its scope tended to be restricted to corporate philanthropy by the famous *A. P. Smith Manufacturing Company* case of 1951. The tiny New Jersey company, selected by several large businesses to test the principle that corporate giving to higher education was lawful, made the court's narrow definition a headline and a constant.[56] Recent societal pressures, however, have induced corporate officers to go beyond philanthropy toward what some analysts have described as the "artistic model" of corporate social responsibility. Here, the organization is summoned "to fulfill a larger vision of man and society" by becoming a servant "in the cause of a higher civilization and culture."[57]

While this altruistic self-image is rare among businesses in the United States, there is evidence that the corporate vision of social responsibility is expanding and that architecture helps express this commitment. An early and classic example is Prudential which, through its then chief executive, Orville Beal, made a decision in the late 1950s to build in Newark when skeptics saw the site and the city as looming disaster areas. Today, as travelers approach along Amtrak's northeast corridor, they can see that Prudential's tower has not only enhanced Newark's skyline but also has acted as a magnet around which other attractive buildings cluster. The circumstances were similar in 1978 when New York City officials were deeply concerned about the "corporate flight" to the suburbs. In this case, AT&T gave the metropolis the much needed vote of confidence by announcing a new midtown headquarters:

We are convinced that this city's greatest days as a center of commerce and culture—and of communications—still lie ahead. In short, we believe New York City is destined to set the pace among the great cities of the world far into the future. And we want to be a very positive part of that future.[58]

The company certainly is an exciting part of Manhattan's future. Its controversial pitched-roof skyscraper contributes a dynamic alternative to traditional office design; a handsome street-level arcade includes elegant shops and its landscaped interior offers a tranquil interlude to the hectic pace of Madison Avenue.

Some firms have specifically acknowledged architecture as a moral imperative in their corporate social responsibilities, reflecting the conviction of one observer who believes that institutions are "the bridges that link architecture to civilization, that allow formal order to symbolize moral order."[59] Alexander Giacco, the chief executive of Hercules Corporation (a Delaware-based chemical firm), reflected this attitude at the dedication of the company's headquarters in 1983: "This building represents the revitalization of downtown Wilmington and the spirit of cooperation between private industry and government that has led us to this rebirth. . . . We are pleased to have been the catalyst to help bring Wilmington back to life."[60] And "back to life" meant not only jobs but a beautiful city center hallmarked by a riverfront park, the renovation of several historic buildings, and the construction of additional offices and stores. A second dramatic example is Pittsburgh Plate Glass, which has developed a complex of gleaming towers in that city that have helped restore a major town square. Still other companies include retail, entertainment, or recreation facilities within their office buildings as a way of enhancing the community. Whatever the form, there is little doubt that quality architecture is a significant expression of good corporate citizenship which, as part of a broadened definition of social responsibility, is making cities and towns more livable, more enjoyable, and even more lovable.

The Challenge: Full Utilization of Resources

Looking at the American past is to see the evolution of different kinds and styles of management to meet changing needs. Small merchants served colonial patrons adequately but were ill suited to manage the more complex enterprises of the post–Civil War period. In response, businessmen evolved into what might be called "entrepreneurial capitalists"—individual leaders who knew how to attract large groups of workers with the aid of generous immigration policies and how to exploit this labor force with modestly effective organizational techniques. But these companies could not solve the problem of capital formation. Firms, especially the railroads, needed more machinery, equipment and hardware to keep growing, a demand that was eventually met by a new resource known as "finance capitalism." Investment houses such as J. P. Morgan; Kuhn, Loeb; and A. M. Kidder began selling and trading securities in railroads and other industrial concerns. This was the era when Andrew Carnegie's steel holdings led to U.S. Steel and when John D. Rockefeller made Standard Oil a standard for ruthless efficiency.

But there were limits, the most significant of which was the inability of managers to coordinate satisfactorily the many activities of a large business. To deal with this issue, during the 1920s and 1930s yet another resource was added: the executive who knew how to decentralize a firm's operations into a multidivisional organization based on patterns successfully pioneered by General Motors, DuPont, and Sears.[61] Streamlined production, managerial accounting, product distribution, and advertising techniques facilitated even further corporate growth. Today, experts continue to fine-tune these resources with new approaches to management efficiency and technology. Matrix decision-making and Theory X and Theory Y are just a few of the recent theoretical alternatives.

What many of these specialists ignored, however, was the fact that, as larger numbers of people became dependent on sophisticated machines to do their jobs, one of the critical challenges was to improve relationships among workers (from factory personnel to executives), their tools, and their environment. *This interface is precisely the problem designers are trained to solve.* Needed, therefore, is a kind of artist-executive whose canvas is a montage of both old and new approaches to business. As in the past, markets must be created; capital must be acquired; organizations must be built and rebuilt. But the successful executive will also have a designer's eye that can see the significance of corporate building. And the architect, in turn, will have an archon's eye to read what the firm and the society require. In this analysis, then, the marriage of archon and architect is not merely a convenience but an absolute necessity.

Historian James Allen has documented one aspect of this link by investigating the motives and methods that led Walter Paepcke, former chairman of the Container Corporation of America, to found the Aspen Institute of Humanistic Studies and the International Design Conference in Aspen in 1950.[62] Observers have noted that the altruism of this early effort has evolved into more pragmatic ties in which corporations recognize that the arts help them "realize key marketing and sales objectives, involve them with audiences they wish to reach, and give them the kind of public image that is critical to success."[63] When the *Wall Street Journal* reported that "real estate—the buildings and land owned by companies that are not primarily in the real estate business—accounts for at least 25 percent of most American corporations' assets,"[64] it indicated one way to measure the value of architectural arts to the business community. But the corporate-design partnership offers even greater opportunities. Architects and interior designers are underutilized resources unless asked to address the issues of productivity, a firm's culture, values in the work force, cost control, planning flexibility, and social responsibility. While no panacea, design is an important aspect of successful business strategies, the crucial theme of this analysis.

2

Maxims to Maximize Results

AWARENESS of opportunities to exploit design is one thing. Taking advantage of them is another. As with all significant undertakings, effective action blends creativity and rationality, hallmarks of both successful architects and successful executives. Creativity conjures up images of invention which translate into innovation and superior performance. Rationality suggests the capacity to select appropriate means to achieve appropriate ends. Nothing appears more sensible than to see the two as natural allies, as any "walking-of-the-fingers" through a dictionary illustrates. How experts in wordsmanship relate these concepts is seen in their definition of mind: "that thinking and perceiving part of the consciousness which expresses itself in rational powers."[1] Thinking and perceiving are, therefore, two sides of the same coin. Rational thinking is the engine for creativity, and creativity reciprocates by enriching the thought process.

Yet what seems eminently logical to lexicographers and abundantly clear to designers and businessmen individually, often becomes confused when ambitious architects and strong-willed corporate administrators interact. While these professionals can share the same vocabulary, the meanings they associate with "rational" and "creative" can differ significantly. In addition, when diverse decision-making styles are appended to the language issue, it is evident that every engagement between architect and executive—if it is to be successful—must respond to important differences.

In ways analogous to economic theory, which establishes laws to explain producer and consumer behavior (the law of diminishing returns and the law of enlightened self-interest, respectively), it is possible to improve understanding of relationships between architects and executives by postulating "laws" to account for their respective expectations. Perhaps, more accurately, these should be referred to in the very broad sense employed by the famed Joseph Schumpeter when he spoke of "the law of creative destruction" to describe how capitalism, by producing new products, destroys old ones.[2] Creation and destruction mean tensions in societal decisions. They mean the same thing to businessmen and designers when a building is under consideration. Ideas surface which are eventually discarded in a process that can, unless it is well managed, leave bruised egos and damaged reputations. In the case of archon-architect interaction, the laws are better described as maxims, that is, a series of counsels which, if followed, maximize results. Four are worth stipulating because they provide a conceptual basis for using design effectively as a business resource:

1. Integrate Multiple Perspectives;
2. Emphasize Casting;
3. Sift for Relevant Facts; and
4. Manage Pluralistic Decision-Making.

Maxim One: Integrate Multiple Perspectives

While reference has been made to language barriers in general, it is necessary to flesh out specific implications of this issue in the corporate building process. Everyone involved in a project favors "good design," but interpretations of this goal may differ sharply. For managers, it can imply efficiency and both short and long-term cost effectiveness; for employees, it may signify privacy, the ability to personalize a space, or an office with a view. For architects, good design means a structure that is functional and aesthetically pleasing. Ludwig Wittgenstein has referred to the diverse connotations of similar words as a "language game." Differences emerge because a person's mind acts like a camera lens, focusing on reality with unavoidable distortions. Once a situation is expressed in words, it is necessarily exaggerated by personal circumstances and attitudes so that alternative perceptions are always possible and generally probable.[3] It is similar to the well-known diagram that is both the profiles of two people facing each other and the silhouette of an elaborate urn.

Regarding the ability to exploit the full potential of corporate architecture, it is critical for companies to recognize and integrate diverse perspectives. The archon's expertise is business whereas the architect's is design. But since both have some knowledge of the other's field, each makes contributions to the building process. Seemingly on the periphery, yet still very important, are worker expectations. Thus, while it seems bland to say that those involved in the building game must be sensitive to subtle differences in outlook among participants, failing this, key players have been known to move blindly in opposite directions. The successful approach to design begins with a dialectic that enhances cooperation, spurs creativity, and generates a shared vision.

A story from twentieth-century physics illustrates this concept. Albert Einstein and Niels Bohr, both titans in the field, were researching the behavior of subatomic particles.[4] Einstein's perspective was shaped by the principle of causality, so he looked for a system that would simultaneously describe the location and momentum of a particle. Bohr's perspective, on the other hand, was influenced by the law of probability, and consequently he thought it impossible to know both location and speed at the same time. His quantum theory merely identified "fields" where the presence of particles were likely, the explanation eventually accepted as the norm. After a brilliant scientific debate, the best that could be done was not unlike the uncanny estimates of a bookie.[5] The practical lessons from the episode are that expertise and a common vocabulary in no way guarantee agreement and that consensus only comes through respectful dialogue.

In design it is especially crucial that this exchange occur early since correcting mistakes can be expensive or even impossible. The history of urban renewal during the 1950s and early 1960s suggests the price paid when the integration of different perspectives fails to occur. After World War II, planners and architects, convinced that their work would generate an enduring vitality in American cities, began tearing down the old and enthusiastically laying out new highways, superblocks, mass housing, and cultural and civic centers. In 1961, however, when Jane Jacobs looked at these developments, she concluded they were the very things responsible for destroying the metropolis:

> Low income projects that become worse centers of delinquency, vandalism and general social hopelessness than the slums they were supposed to replace. . . . Cultural centers that are unable to support a good book store. Civic centers that are avoided by everyone but bums. . . . Commercial centers that are lack-luster imitations of standardized suburban chain-store shopping. Promenades that go from no place to

nowhere and have no promenaders. Expressways that eviscerate great
cities. This is not the rebuilding of cities. This is the sacking of cities.[6]

Like Einstein and Bohr, intelligent people evaluated the same facts yet
reached significantly different conclusions. Both the planners and the
critics saw decay and both wanted to reinvigorate urban America. But
although committed to a common objective, the professionals believed
in a knock-down, build-up technique whereas Jacobs favored a gradual,
add-on process that was sensitive to the existing city fabric and open
to diverse functions and building styles. Unlike the physicists, though,
who could adapt their theories to new evidence without much expense,
the architectural debate took place years after much of the construction
had been completed. The damage was done before there was agreement
on the facts and their physical, economic, social, and aesthetic meanings.
Eventually, officials accepted and implemented many of the principles
espoused by Jacobs, but this often translated into abandoning or totally
rehabilitating earlier projects. The case of the Pruitt-Igoe apartments
in St. Louis is relevant and poignant. Constructed in the 1950s as a
housing project for three thousand low-income families, this complex
of thirty-three buildings received awards and high praise when it first
opened. But after design flaws, neglect, and racial tensions caused endless
problems, the first of the eleven-story slabs was blown up in 1972. Authorities had decided that the structure was not even worth renovating.[7]
While tragedies resulting from failure to follow the maxim of multiple
perspectives are seldom this dramatic, the story does highlight why corporations investing large sums of money in facilities should probe what
officers and employees say they want in order to discover what they
really need. And to be effective this must be done early in the design
process. It is appropriate, therefore, to detail the tasks that help integrate
different perspectives.

The Managerial Perspective

During the initial stages of a project the primary burden falls on
executives to fulfill three tasks: (1) define objectives and priorities, (2)
establish standards of quality, and (3) articulate corporate values. The
expressed need for new facilities can emanate from a manager who
determines more space is necessary for continued operations, from the
director of strategic planning who feels it is time for expansion, or from
the chairman of the board who decides that officers and staff should be
located in new headquarters. Regardless of the source, once a project

is under serious consideration, it is the responsibility of corporate officers, with assistance from in-house experts and consultants, to identify and enumerate the purposes the building should serve.

Define Objectives and Priorities

At the starting gate nothing can be taken for granted. While motives for a new structure are multiple—prestige, productivity, image, culture, cost control, energy efficiency, flexibility, and social responsibility—only the executive can establish priorities. The CEO must then summarize reasons for the decision and have the statement studied and endorsed by the board. If this first step is taken carelessly, it can necessitate major revisions in plans, create continuing confusion and uncertainty, and result in lost time and money. If taken carefully, it becomes an invaluable tool for matching corporate goals with the talents of those who will be working on design and construction. In short, step one outlines critical components of a building before architects and contractors are even hired and reveals the owner's attitudes about quality and budget.

The Dravo Corporation, an international industrial firm headquartered in Pittsburgh, provides a good example of how to initiate an architectural project. In 1978, the firm outlined the objectives for its new headquarters in these terms:

1. *Presence*—The building will be called the Dravo World Headquarters Building. It should have a presence through its siting and design that gives Dravo an identity as one of Pittsburgh's major corporations. The building should be the central feature of a major development complex that will be identified with it.
2. *Relationship to Site*—The Dravo building should be a good neighbor and a good corporate citizen. Pittsburgh's Golden Triangle is unique and this building should relate at its edges to the existing fabric of the city. It should relate to the city's street pattern, scale, and character unless changes are in the form of enhancement as perceived by both the architects, city fathers, and neighbors as well.
3. *Access and Egress*—The site should be developed with an understanding of where Dravo's employees come from and are likely to come from in the future. It is essential that adequate parking be provided for Dravo's move-in and future requirements. Also loading and service facilities should provide ample room for deliveries of all types.
4. *Marketability*—The Dravo building should project the aggressiveness, excitement, and sophistication of its prime tenant. It should rise beyond the image of an average engineering building alone and reflect Dravo's full personality.

5. *Amenities*—The Dravo building and its development area should be more than just a place to work. It should contain shops, restaurants, and public spaces integrated into the site and the city as discussed above.

6. *Cost*—The Dravo building must reflect the efficiency and reasoned attitude toward long-term economy that characterizes Dravo's own engineering activities. This first-class building must be developed on the basis of the programmed move-in space requirements and must be organized to maximize productivity and operational efficiency. All major systems in the building should be designed with energy conservation and operating efficiency as primary concerns, while incorporating interior systems of standard modular design to minimize renovation costs. Labor efficiency, cleaning maintenance and security are of prime importance.[8]

Obviously the Dravo executives had done their homework. Image, corporate responsibility, convenience, corporate culture, and budgetary factors were all described. The result has been a handsome tower that enriches the Pittsburgh community as well as the company.

Establish Standards of Quality

Cost is vital in any architectural undertaking. It is not uncommon, however, to deal with this variable simplistically by calculating an average price per square foot, and then mandating a maximum figure for the new project. While this may provide a target, several other factors should be explored. If a structure is a "first" for a company—or otherwise unique among its facilities—a tour of comparable buildings is appropriate. This permits officials to evaluate the quality of space needed and to set standards for finishes and furnishings. It also helps executives determine in advance what are acceptable trade-offs between higher initial prices and later maintenance and energy costs. Becoming familiar with codes and ordinances, as well as with local construction practices, are other techniques that can have positive effects on quality. Such a review expedites the design process and helps assure firms they are getting the most for their money.

Articulate Corporate Values

Besides statements concerning objectives, priorities, and quality, corporate officers must also begin a design commission by deciding how their proposed building can articulate the company's culture. The legendary Apple Computer whiz kid, Steve Jobs, for instance, had a modest open office surrounded by his staff to reflect a culture that was relaxed and not particularly status-conscious. Another example is provided by

Stanley Stahl, a New York City real estate developer who puts together sites for major downtown office buildings. Stahl has two spacious executive suites, each identically furnished. One, cluttered with papers, is the real center of business; the other, impeccably neat, is only used for client meetings.[9] In this case, two spaces are needed because, while the creative work is messy, the culture is conservative and hierarchical. Based on a firm's mission statement, on surveys and interviews, and on personal experience, officers need to outline those values critical to company operations. In some fields teamwork and open communication are essential; in others quiet and privacy are necessary. Some corporations regard themselves as large families; others so stick to business that they are impersonal. In some offices location and amenities are emphasized; in others these have little meaning.

The caveat in expressing culture through design is to avoid preconceptions. Thomas Watson, Jr., former Chairman of IBM, discovered how assumptions can lead to counterproductive results at the Endicott production facility in New York State. There, as part of a larger renovation, an elegant, multilevel, landscaped dining room was opened for employees, but people seemed reluctant to use it. After a few interviews, it turned out that assembly-line workers believed they would get it dirty, and the lavish space had to be simplified.[10] Another illustration involves a suite of five Senate offices on Capitol Hill. Before design changes, individuals paraded past other areas to reach their own desks; after the "improvements," they entered each room separately from a public corridor. While physically the new scheme appeared logical, psychologically it was flawed. Workers felt isolated and uninvolved and the result was lower morale and reduced employee commitment.[11]

The Employee Perspective

The IBM and Capitol Hill anecdotes suggest why, in addition to understanding management's perspective, it is also important to analyze employee attitudes. Although worker concerns may appear less weighty than those of corporate officers, research has demonstrated they are vital to project success. Consultants at Citicorp, for example, discovered that staff who did not participate in renovation efforts were much less satisfied with results than those that had a voice in the decisions.[12]

Seek Employee Participation
Since satisfaction can affect productivity, user involvement is essential. This is particularly true because over a ten-year period, in an owner-

occupied office, personnel costs are 85 percent of the total operating expenses.[13] Since even small increases in productivity substantially enhance long-term results, attention to employee concerns becomes a *sine-qua-non* in the architectural planning process. To exploit these opportunities, the project team can use surveys and interviews to determine what workers say they want. Reactions to materials samples, the chance to develop preferred spatial arrangements with scale models, and the testing of mock-ups give an even clearer indication of employee preferences. Interestingly, as one expert found, the information generated by these techniques sometimes runs counter to traditional design choices: "White, grey, beige, marble, chrome, steel, baked enamel on metal—many of the colors and materials commonly specified by architects in recent decades—are roundly rejected (by employees). . . . Wood and wood-grain laminate are preferred for work surfaces and desks. No matter what any architect may have been taught about honesty in materials, fake wood is better accepted than forthright metal."[14] Data such as these should become part of the design objectives and criteria.

The Architectural Perspective

As a last critical component of maxim one, corporate managers must compare company goals, style, and needs to the strengths and skills of various architects. When tyrannical professionals are mentioned, a story told by Samuel Johnson, chairman of S. C. Johnson & Son, inevitably comes to mind. He once described a conversation his father, Hibbard Johnson, had with Frank Lloyd Wright concerning Wingspread, the family's elegant estate near Racine, Wisconsin. One evening, when they were dining with important guests, heavy rain poured through a leaking roof. After water started to stream down on the elder Johnson's bald head, the host telephoned Wright to complain furiously. The designer responded simply, "Well, Hib, why don't you move your chair?"[15]

Look for a Compatible Marriage with the Architect

The anecdote makes an important point for corporations, namely, that firms should make certain that they are compatible with their architects. They must seek designers that can translate corporate values into quality projects. This is a challenging task. All architects will insist they can do the job, but each has different talents. Some are large, interdisciplinary firms, while others are small, specialized organizations; some excel in designing prestigious offices, while others are recognized for their engineering and energy-conscious designs; still others are highly regarded for their responsiveness to tight budget and time constraints, while others feel that extra money can always be found. Final judgments should be based on a match between corporate priorities and the architect's perspective.

Compatibility is significant in another way. Project directors should question the designer's role within the larger team. As the building process becomes more complex, it is vital to coordinate architectural contributions with those of other professionals. Some design offices work best if they are in charge; others operate effectively under the direction of a construction manager, space planner, or consultant. The issue is to make sure that the corporation's proposed delegation of responsibilities and lines of communication are consistent with the architect's own management style. A mismatch here causes time-consuming arguments, unnecessary debate and, often, escalating mistrust.

By way of summary, this diagram outlines the key components in the initial phase of an architectural project:

Integrate Multiple Perspectives	*Corporate Tasks*
The Managerial Perspective	Define Objectives and Priorities
	Establish Standards of Quality
	Articulate Corporate Values
The Employee Perspective	Seek Employee Participation
The Architectural Perspective	Look for a Compatible Marriage with the Architect

Maxim Two: Emphasize Casting

Within the last ten years, the processes for effectively using design have become more complicated, and more complicated processes have meant more performers in the building drama. In the past, corporate building involved a limited number of people—key executives, an architect, two or three consulting engineers, a contractor, and perhaps an interior designer. Once a decision to go forward with a project had been made, a list of technical and space needs was developed. This might first be done in-house and later refined by the architect or engineer. Building proposals were prepared in consultation with structural and mechanical engineers and this was followed by cost estimates and continued adjustments to the design. As work progressed, an interior designer was often employed to choose finishes. After a final budget had been determined and construction documents prepared, the job was sent out for bids. Normally, the project was built under the architect's supervision. The process was essentially linear and limited to a small number of decision makers. Communication was relaxed and responsibilities were clearly understood.

A Multitude of Actors and Roles

To deal with the many architectural issues that arise today (white-collar productivity, corporate culture, worker values, cost control, planning flexibility, social responsibility, as well as the traditional concerns of improved return-on-investment and prestige), the design process is necessarily more intricate and involves expertise in an expanding range of disciplines. Choosing the right actors for the right roles, then, is a significant assignment. The following suggest talents that, depending on the corporation, the complexity and the location of a project, are required for success. Four steps are involved:

1. Appoint the in-house players
2. Hire outside managers
3. Select the design team
4. Work with key public actors

1. Appoint the In-House Players

The CEO oversees the project to see that economic, planning, social, and aesthetic goals are met, so that architecture becomes an effective corporate resource.

A Construction Manager/Project Manager supervises the design and construction process and facilitates communication among all decision makers. If a firm builds frequently, the job may be handled by a construction management team; when, however, a firm builds only occasionally, a person with strong organizational skills and a basic knowledge of construction must be chosen for this task.

A Facility Manager translates company and employee needs into the spatial and technical program that is the starting point for design, facilitates employee involvement in the design process, and analyzes the suitability of architecture and interior design proposals.

Corporate Lawyers prepare and review various contracts that are part of the design process as well as interpret statutes and regulations that affect a project.

34

2. Hire Outside Managers

A *Construction Manager* is especially important for companies that build infrequently. This consultant has expertise in building costs, local construction practices, and management techniques and is competent to oversee the design, budget, contracting, and scheduling of a project, and analyze decisions and other issues related to a client's objectives.

A *Real Estate Consultant,* with expertise in the areas of land costs, zoning, transportation, and building services, assists in the selection and acquisition of a site.

A *Financial Adviser* recommends alternatives for financing a project, helps find mortgage and construction loans, and/or sets up a limited partnership for investing in a building program.

3. Select the Design Team

A *Space Planner* studies existing interior configurations, forecasts future needs, and develops alternative spacial arrangements which promote efficiency and flexibility. A constant task is to refine the design program in light of new developments.

The Architect is responsible for the building's design, for the preparation of construction documents, and may coordinate input from engineers and consultants.

Engineers deal with a building's structural, mechanical, and electrical systems.

The Interior Designer recommends furnishings and finishes and develops alternative layouts.

An Environmental Consultant analyzes the impact of a project on natural resources and the neighboring community and recommends strategies to avoid environmental problems.

Other Consultants include experts in such fields as transportation, human behavior, energy, lighting, acoustics, wire management, communications equipment, and security.

Directing these many actors and making sure all have mastered their lines is difficult in the building drama because, in many ways, it is like a play written by the actors themselves where improvisation is the norm rather than the exception. This kind of talent is in short supply, and selecting and motivating these individuals become even more challenging when, as happens, the best actors are prima donnas who need equal amounts of stroking and scolding. Adding further complexity to the job of casting is the fact that some actors are selected by others, coached by others, rewarded by others. Because these players often have important roles, managers must pay close attention to cues coming from this group.

4. Work with Key Public Actors

Government Leaders can give critical support to a project. Their endorsement is especially necessary as communities become increasingly concerned about the impact of buildings on services, the environment and the economy.

Municipal Review Boards have their own agenda and those responsible for design must find out in advance what issues are most important to these groups.

Zoning and Building Code Officials interact with the design team by enforcing the ground rules for design and construction.

The Public is, in some real sense, the ultimate judge of the success or failure of a project. Executives and designers should frequently take the pulse of this group because the public's heart beat can change suddenly, dramatically, and sometimes for what appear to be unimportant reasons.

Assembling the Cast

With so many "influence centers," an effective design team is only possible if the participants themselves recognize with management that a process, once linear, is now layered and circular. Responsibilities often overlap and communication can be arduous. Under these circumstances, making effective role assignments depends on several issues.

Determine the Mix of In-House vs. Outside Services

Large companies having an ongoing building program solve some problems with an in-house design operation. At IBM, for example, the Real Estate and Construction Division (RECD) is one of the biggest corporate organizations of its kind with a staff of about a thousand people. It manages site acquisition, architect selection, design and construction for all operations in the United States, and serves as an advisor to IBM's international projects in Italy, Japan, Brazil, Sweden, and other countries. It supplies the firm with high-quality laboratory, manufacturing, and office space, and has special departments responsible for energy management and environmental issues.[16]

Another illustration is California-based Syntex Corporation, an international pharmaceutical, health and personal care products company that has put its rapidly growing office and research complex under the direction of a Corporate Facilities Planning group. Using master plans prepared for each of two large Silicon Valley sites, this twelve-person team supervises programming, engineering, design, and construction. It updates annually the company's three-year projection of facility needs and main-

36

tains an ongoing working relationship with the architect it has used since 1968 and the construction manager it has employed since 1980. This organization—and the company's commitment to quality—have resulted in buildings that reflect the desired corporate image and are completed efficiently and cost-effectively.[17]

In small companies that cannot afford in-house groups or when larger organizations encounter unique design programs, outside expertise is necessary. Fortunately, the need is so common that consulting firms and special educational programs are now available. One pioneer, the Facility Management Institute in Ann Arbor, Michigan, will not only analyze a firm's particular problems, but also offers courses to help facility managers take a stronger and more effective role in strategic planning. Seminars like Managing Effective Workplaces and Long-Range Facility Planning relate building design to fundamental business objectives. After completing the sessions, executives can respond to questions such as these:

- How does the proposed site relate to the work force, suppliers, corporate image, energy delivery?
- How does the particular architecture relate to image, work processes, materials?
- How do technical systems—heat, electricity, acoustics, ventilation, air conditioning, energy—relate to profits, work processes, workers?
- How does interior layout facilitate communication, work flow, employee satisfaction, group cohesiveness, productivity?
- How do facilities relate to changes of departments, work processes, personnel, management style?[18]

Another approach to these issues is provided by the Philadelphia architectural firm Ewing, Cole, Cherry, Parsky. To serve clients unfamiliar and ill prepared to cope with the building process, it has structured itself into multidisciplinary teams called "design centers" which manage projects from conception to occupancy. The principals believe this type of organization contributes significantly to efficiency and quality control. In one case, for instance, the designers were able to provide White Hall Laboratories, Incorporated, with a new research and development facility in just twenty-four months.[19]

Stress the CCC Syndrome: Commitment, Communication, and Competence

Beyond balancing in-house and outside expertise, three additional elements can greatly enhance prospects for success. The first is to make sure all senior managers are committed to using architecture as an authentic business resource. The second is to develop an open communications network where design alternatives and economic facts are evaluated by those ultimately responsible for the building and the budget. The chief executive should appoint a liaison with the project team who is knowledgeable about the benefits of design and familiar with the construction process. With this link, it should be possible to analyze architectural choices from the perspective of long-term contributions to the company and technical efficiency as well as first cost and aesthetics.

The third component is the special competence found in leadership: who among the project team can optimize corporate objectives? If, for instance, prestige and visibility are vital concerns, then the architect might be in charge; if productivity and efficiency are most important, then space planners and interior experts should be considered; if cost is crucial, a construction manager could head the team. While this choice is critical so, too, are the resources made available to the leader. In this regard, experience is a necessity. When corporate managers are well acquainted with a building's proposed location and type, or when they are constructing a specialized production facility, they can depend more on in-house talents. On the other hand, if a geographic area is unfamiliar or if the project is unique, it is beneficial to have assistance with concerns ranging from zoning and building ordinances to help with energy conservation and the selection of office equipment. In sum, maxim two includes these steps:

Emphasize Casting	*Corporate Tasks*
A Multitude of Actors and Roles	Appoint the In-House Players
	Hire the Outside Managers
	Select the Design Team
	Work with Key Public Actors
Assembling the Cast	Determine the Mix of In-House vs. Outside Services
	Stress the CCC Syndrome: Commitment, Communications, and Competence

Maxim Three: Sift for Relevant Facts

In ambitious undertakings, participants become obsessed with their own domains: the part is the whole, the single is the totality. Frustrated when other specialists suggest the primacy of their assignments, experts take defensive strategies, overstating the importance of their own work. Distortions result and a careful sifting is essential to determine the relative importance of facts. Like casting, however, this is easier said than done.

Design Research

Architects are immune neither from their own fantasies nor from adopting those of other designers who have achieved momentary fame. Tom Wolfe, often the object of criticism himself, has lambasted early twentieth-century architects and the coldness of contemporary design; he is equally skeptical of the recent preoccupation with revivalism and historical allusions. Rather than depending on sheer technology or some flimsy reinterpretation of the past for inspiration, he challenges architects to create spaces that celebrate life and the activities within a building: "We now have a large educated public able and willing to meet architecture half way. . . . Architects have to be able to embrace the public from the heart. It cannot be a game."[20]

Turn Facts into Options

But to get beyond fads, the factual terrain must be expanded. Decisions must be based on the analysis of client needs, and problems must be stated in ways that promote creative investigation.[21] Designers can learn from psychologists Daniel Kahneman and Amos Tversky who questioned subjects about a single scenario phrased in two different ways. In the first instance, individuals were asked to address a situation where two out of six people might die; in the second, the group made choices concerning the same circumstances where four out of six might live. What Kahneman and Tversky found was that reactions to the case depended more on wording than on facts.[22]

For architects, too, how a problem is posed has a significant impact on what facts become important. The most effective approach is a statement that demands investigation from several points of view. But in a building project preconceptions can make this impossible. If, for example, a client has commissioned an office and asks for open-landscaped interiors, that will probably be the result. If the same need, however, is expressed as a desire for productive working environments, the designer must explore other, and perhaps more beneficial, alternatives.

Admittedly, the schedule, budget, and complexity of a job place limitations on the extent of fact-finding, but even in a modest-sized commission, the evaluation of options can be rewarding. The design of a Tower Record

Company retail outlet in New York City provides such an illustration. Before 1981, the firm was strictly a California operation. In that year, with the increasing success of its music and video retailing business, owner Russell Solomon decided that it was time to expand to the east coast. It was a bold move since the market was fiercely competitive. Solomon, however, believed that he could woo loyal customers with a strategy that blended shopping, entertainment, and massive inventories. He acquired a four-story loft in Manhattan's Greenwich Village and decided to decorate it with the "pipe racks," posters, and music that had attracted his California patrons. The businessman knew his old clientele and assumed that what had worked in the west would also work in the new location.

But New York architects for the project, Harold Buttrick and Ted Burtis, wisely investigated other ideas. After studying techniques that made shopping an event rather than just a purchase, and after analyzing the circulation and lighting requirements of the site, they concluded that there were other ways design could stimulate sales. Neon murals, special graphics, and reflective finishes were used to orient and move shoppers through the large, multilevel store. Attractive social settings were created to allow people to linger and watch visiting celebrities or the resident disc jockey. These changes enlarged the sights and sounds customers experienced, and thus encouraged buying. In this instance, the architects examined the businessman's traditional west coast operations and developed nontraditional alternatives to enhance them. Although their effort meant additional time and money, the costs appeared consistent with the risks of moving into a new market. Rewards from the designers' analysis were impressive: two years after its opening in 1983, the Tower Record outlet attracted over six thousand customers daily and had become the most profitable in the Solomon chain. Not unexpectedly, Buttrick and Burtis now have commissions to develop other sites in New York, San Francisco, and Washington, D.C.[23]

On a larger scale, there is the story of Prudential Insurance Company's Enerplex complex in Princeton, New Jersey. Two talented firms—Skidmore, Owings & Merrill (SOM) and Alan Chimacoff—were selected to meet the same challenge: develop a 130,000 square-foot office building incorporating prototype strategies for energy conservation. Each was given a site adjacent to the other in Princeton. Each created an innovative structure that was comparable in size, shape, and cost. Yet, because each firm emphasized different approaches in the research phase of the project, the concepts and technical aspects of the two buildings vary in significant and interesting ways.

40

SOM discovered that, contrary to traditional beliefs, by incorporating certain active solar techniques, they could design sleek glass facades and still have an energy-efficient structure. In this case, they used roof-mounted collectors and a sophisticated ventilation system that, by blowing air between double-paned exterior walls, is able to heat the building in winter and cool it during the summer. By contrast, Chimacoff's office, which is detailed with limestone panels and quasi-classical motifs, evolved from a thorough study of passive conservation. Again, for its size and type, the building achieves unusual efficiency by combining well-insulated walls with an interior atrium that acts as a thermal buffer, and with light shelves and transoms that help illuminate perimeter spaces. Ultimately, while the two schemes are distinct, they both success-fully addressed the issues and demonstrated the unsuspected breadth of facts related to cost-effective and energy-conscious design.[24] The clear lesson is that fact-finding and the careful sifting of facts are essential in developing innovative solutions to architectural problems.

Critical Topics

Where, however, should the corporate design team focus its efforts? Buildings include so many components that possibilities seem endless. Materials selection, construction techniques, furnishings, lighting, acous-tics, and mechanical systems are only the beginning of the litany. While it is true in a very general sense that particular research depends on the type of facility and the company's objectives, it is also true that three areas possess almost universal value. Each requires comment.

Study Technology, Layout, and Image

Technology has been a critical item since the mid-1970s when energy and the high-tech office and production line became increasingly impor-tant to corporations. Today, options continue to expand and trade-offs between first and long-term costs are quite complex. In such a climate, designers, consultants, and company officials must carefully evaluate a multitude of available systems. Certain decisions regarding an office for the Lockheed Missiles and Space Company in Sunnyvale, California, suggest the kind of technological choices design teams confront. Because Lockheed's engineers moved frequently, a raised floor was selected for the project. Although the initial price was higher than those represented by other approaches, it paid for itself in terms of efficiency by making relocation of people, computers, and communications equipment a rela-tively fast, simple, and inexpensive task.[25] In the same building a sophisticated day-lighting strategy was implemented after testing by the architect showed that it would reduce the annual amount of electricity for general illumination by 70 percent.[26] In Sheboygan, Wisconsin, the energy package designed into the new offices of the consulting engineering firm, Donohue & Associates, saved that company about forty thousand dollars a year and should recover expenses even faster than the originally anticipated six years.[27] The point of the illustrations is that, under most circumstances, the thoughtful analysis of technology is a useful tool in balancing present costs and future savings.

A second major consideration is interior layout. The concern here is to avoid a simplistic interpretation of a firm's management and space needs. Designers sometimes base proposals on information gleaned from organization charts, but these graphic representations of a company often differ substantially from day-to-day operations. Given this situation, a project team must study how work is actually carried out in order to develop a design that provides for private and group functions, improves the working environment, flexibly accommodates change, and realistically reflects the strategy and tactics of the corporation.

While this kind of investigation is essential in complex organizations, it can also enhance modest and small-scale undertakings. A medium-size (14,500 square-foot) office for the Federal Aviation Administration in Atlantic City, for example, had the supervisors' offices, conference rooms, laboratories, snack bar, and library located along the edges of the space, with staff work stations neatly arranged in the remaining central area. On paper, the plan appeared eminently logical. In reality, the layout was ineffective and confusing: circulation was random, noise extreme, and privacy nonexistent. In 1979, a government research group studied the conditions and prepared a scheme that divided the floor into three subspaces. After the renovation was implemented, the environment was more efficient, attractive, and quiet and, at the same time, served the functions with less square footage than the original.[28]

A company's image is a complicated thing—even for the corporate image-makers themselves. In architecture, misunderstanding of what it is—or is intended to be—results in a caricature rather than a portrait. In this respect, two questions need probing: How can a new facility enhance the corporate profile? And how can it complement the life of the surrounding neighborhood? Effective research on the first issue was carried out by the Beneficial Management Corporation. After analyzing their random mix of offices in Morristown, New Jersey, executives decided that the construction of a campus-like complex in nearby Peapack would not only satisfy growing space needs but would strengthen employee loyalty and reflect the company's idea of itself as a community. In another example, O. M. Scott & Sons used a modern interpretation of barn lofts for its new headquarters in Marysville, Ohio, because the form suggested the firm's leadership in the grass and lawn care business. In terms of the second concern—namely, enhancing the environment—Hercules Incorporated in Delaware has been especially successful. In this instance, the company explicitly determined to make its tower the centerpiece in Wilmington's downtown revitalization.

A final case relating to image is the General Foods headquarters in Rye, New York, which was hailed by one critic as "an eye-stopping, gleaming white . . . Beaux-Arts palace with two equal wings flanking a central rotunda." While the company's director of communications downplayed the superlatives by saying that the building merely showed pride and professionalism ("it's like our food—clean and white"[29]), it nevertheless goes beyond that. Surely the General Foods building is more lavishly exciting than a General Foods product wrapped in a General Foods carton. The product sells. The building speaks. Obviously, the same care that went into product research had to go into building research. Package appeal and building appeal, whether directly or indirectly related, depend on solid investigation. Major aspects of this analysis process are summarized in the following diagram:

Sift for Relevant Facts	*Corporate Tasks*
Design Research	Turn Facts into Options
Critical Topics	Study Technology, Layout, and Image

Maxim Four: Manage Pluralistic Decision-Making

By now it is abundantly clear that using design as a business resource involves complex decision-making. The goal is a quality building project. The process leading to the goal demands a successful synthesis of many viewpoints, many talents, and many architectural options. There is a temptation to interpret the pluralities as unmanageable and competing domains and to approach them with a skepticism not unlike the one that greeted the famous 1904 Entente Cordiale when England and France ended centuries-old rivalries to join together against a growing German menace. Suspicions remained but gradually a partnership that began in necessity was transformed into a constructive alliance as, over time, the two nations saw other benefits emerge from their plans for common defense. In a similar fashion, when archons and architects forge an entente of necessity and potential conflict, that, too, can have positive results through the effective management of pluralistic decision-making.

Principles related to this important issue were first authored by Henri Fayol (1841–1925).[30] His contribution was welcomed by industrialists who had learned that the market's invisible hand could be guided by the visible arm of the executive. The effectiveness of the grasp, of course, depended on decisions that were correct and timely.[31] Since Fayol's time, others have elaborated on steps to improve the decision-making process.[32] The various diagnoses have yielded several common elements—identify options, assess consequences, give priorities to the results, and select and implement a course of action. Another shared conclusion is that, while individual decision-making is difficult, group decision-making poses a far greater challenge. More expertise comes from the two-heads-are-better-than-one premise, but the process is slower. Consensus sometimes becomes more important than correctness and extended communications often result in distorted impressions.[33]

Elements in Design Management

When membership in the corporate design team grows, diversity becomes both problem and opportunity. As in most creative ventures, pluralism is especially evident in the intellectual arm-wrestling that occurs before final agreement is reached. It has been noted how executives can perceive enclosed parking as a luxury, whereas architects deem it an aesthetic necessity; senior managers and staff may have different views on office layout, privacy, and interior furnishings. Such debates, and others more complicated, are encountered in almost every building project. Fortunately, most are resolved by following a few critical decision-making procedures.

Emphasize Goals, Not Positions

Architects and corporate clients usually hold positions which force both to bargain. Typically, negotiators take a hard attitude and butt heads with the hope of discovering a solution. A more fruitful approach, however, avoids discussing positions and instead stresses shared goals and the circumstances that must change to achieve them. Rather than insisting on agreement or victory, the more productive stance acknowledges that both sides desire a wise outcome reached efficiently and amicably. In

addition, negotiations are more productive when personal issues are sepa-
rated from substantive concerns. Making concessions to cultivate a relationship (or demanding concessions as a precondition of a relationship)
may satisfy the ego, but are ultimately counterproductive.[34]

In design, this process means that the project team must make choices
that fulfill corporate objectives rather than satisfy aesthetic preferences
or preconceived ideas of form and function. The approach seems to restrict
the architect's creativity but, as the Pittsburgh Plate Glass (PPG) buildings
demonstrate, it can generate spectacular results. Months before hiring
Philip Johnson to design the complex, the corporation had established
its priorities: prestige, first-class design and construction, energy conservation, an efficient and flexible layout, interiors that would enhance
communications and productivity. With these goals already prepared,
Johnson could devote his experience and talent to translating the mandate
into a series of glass-gothic towers that are an exciting display of the
company's products and a downtown landmark that has added substantially to the city's pride and image.[35]

By contrast, if an architect or client is committed to a particular style
or design before a project is even initiated, or if it does not use corporate
priorities to test viability, the results may be an expensive disappointment.
Or there may be no results at all! Architect Leon Krier is an example
of one who dogmatically insists that classicism is the only answer to
modern design. His proposals have remained at the theoretical level
because, as critic Paul Goldberger put it, "Mr. Krier is a polemicist and
a moralist . . . and until someone is willing to build Mr. Krier's classical
world precisely as he sees it, he would rather draw instead."[36] So while
the Kriers of the world keep galleries and publishers busy, they are
unable to keep contractors busy because they emphasize positions rather
than goals. This points out the need for trade-offs in the design process.

Develop Consensus

Compromise is rarely neat and tidy. It is, however, typical of American
society in general and of the business-architecture interchange in particular. Since a company's facilities simultaneously serve the needs of management, staff, community leaders and the public, success involves consensus. Thus, while this form of agreement seldom satisfies everyone
to the same extent, it is vital because it responds to the concerns of all
major participants without totally alienating any of them.[37]

Confronted with dilemmas, members of a project team may be hesitant
to air internal differences. Executives and designers, however, should
insist on an open forum, for it is clear that when people are encouraged

to speak freely and share different perspectives, they make better and more innovative decisions.[38] Hercules Incorporated in Delaware employed these techniques in the late 1970s when the chemical products company considered relocating its Wilmington headquarters. After extended conversations with the mayor and other officials about the liabilities and advantages of remaining in the city, both sides found a way to cooperate. The firm was given financial concessions to help underwrite the higher costs of staying in Wilmington, and the city received a prestigious office tower as part of its effort to reinvigorate downtown.[39]

There are, on the other hand, examples of flawed decision-making procedures. One involved the development of Lockheed Missiles and Space Company's Building 157. In this case, the architects designed an innovative office that, once completed, received high praise from Lockheed executives, staff engineers, and critics who valued the structure for its outstanding working environment and impressive energy efficiency. In spite of these accolades, the corporation has yet to give the designers another commission. This is largely due to the fact that, during design and construction, communication among senior corporate officers and the architect never produced a consensus about the benefits and costs of the building.[40]

Integrate Decision-Making with Culture

This last case suggests that pluralistic decision-making must complement the style and culture of the corporation. This integration comes naturally to firms such as Herman Miller Inc., whose progressive philosophy encourages discussion and the exchange of information. It is more difficult in hierarchical companies such as International Telephone & Telegraph where shared decision-making was less common under executives like Harold Geneen. Further, it is well-nigh impossible to achieve consensus in businesses marred by internal strife—such as General Motors during the late 1960s and early 1970s. In this instance (if John DeLorean can be believed), there were neuroses among many of those at the headquarters: "Festering hostilities among members of upper management became open wounds. . . . The same guys who were slapping each other on the back and shaking hands in public were going after each others' jugular in private."[41] While the description may be exaggerated, the point is clear: in conflict-ridden organizations, the motives behind choices are seldom objective because they reflect personal ambition over corporate welfare. Since designers cannot cure a sick culture, rather than naively setting forth as crusaders the project team must assess the context for its work. This imposes limitations; it also helps to identify, then manage, the decision-making avenues with the most potential. Again, a chart summarizes the focus of this maxim.

Manage Pluralistic Decision-Making	*Corporate Tasks*
Elements in Design Management	Emphasize Goals, Not Positions
	Develop Consensus
	Integrate Decision-Making with Culture

Towards Specifics: Case Studies and a Scorecard

Together, the four maxims describe strategies that allow corporations to exploit design as a business resource. Results will be maximized when firms address the issues of multiple perspectives, casting, research, and management. But enough has been said in theory. It is now appropriate to shift from generalizations to specifics in order to illustrate how different corporations and different architects have applied the maxims. Case studies include companies that build frequently and those that build infrequently; the construction of headquarters, office buildings, and manufacturing facilities; and the use of design in both large and medium-size organizations. They examine issues ranging from budget controls and worker productivity to interaction with community leaders and consultants.

Within this diversity are two common threads: (1) the cases focus on structures that are architecturally distinguished and owner-occupied, and (2) they outline processes that lead to success. A brief introduction to each explains the rationale for building and the relationship of certain activities to the project's significance. After a somewhat detailed narrative, each case concludes with a summary and scorecard measuring the effectiveness of the design and decision-making. In the last chapter, these evaluations are synthesized into practical guidelines that promote an enduring and fruitful partnership between archon and architect.

A typical scorecard follows to clarify the evaluation system. Each maxim is rated separately and the "Maximum Subtotal" suggests the relative contribution of that maxim to project success. The two most critical areas, multiple perspectives and decision-making, each represent a maximum of fifteen points out of a possible fifty; casting and research are worth slightly less contributing a maximum of ten points each to the total. The performance of each corporation is rated "Excellent" to "Poor"

47

which is, in turn, associated with a multiplier to arrive at an "Actual" score. The multipliers are:

Excellent	1.0
Superior	0.8
Average	0.6
Below Average	0.4
Poor	0.2

"Actual Subtotals" and "Actual Totals" are provided, but two caveats must be noted. First, a low rating in one category does not indicate failure, but points out where the design process can be improved. Second, two cases with the same "Actual Total" can have important differences in their strengths and weaknesses. Comparisons, therefore, must be based on the evaluation narrative as well as the scorecard. In a very general way, "Actual Total" values on the scorecard indicate these overall ratings:

45–50	Excellent
35–45	Superior
25–35	Average
15–25	Below Average
0–15	Poor

Maxims to Maximize Results

CORPORATION AND BUILDING NAME					

MAXIM		CORPORATE TASKS	MAX PTS	RATING	ACT PTS
MULTIPLE PERSPECTIVES	The Managerial Perspective	Define Objectives and Priorities			
		Establish Standards of Quality			
		Articulate Corporate Values	7.5		☐
	The Employee Perspective	Seek Employee Participation	5.0		☐
	The Architectural Perspective	Look for a Compatible Marriage with the Architect	2.5		☐
		MAXIMUM SUBTOTAL	15.0	ACTUAL	☐
CASTING	A Multitude of Actors and Roles	Appoint the In-House Players			
		Hire Outside Managers			
		Select the Design Team			
		Work with Key Public Actors	2.5		☐
	Assembling the Cast	Determine the Mix of In-House vs. Outside Services			
		Stress the CCC Syndrome: Commitment, Communications, and Competence	7.5		☐
		MAXIMUM SUBTOTAL	10.0	ACTUAL	☐
RESEARCH	Design Research	Turn Facts into Options	2.5		☐
	Critical Topics	Study Technology, Layout and Image	7.5		☐
		MAXIMUM SUBTOTAL	10.0	ACTUAL	☐
DECISION-MAKING	Elements in Design Management	Emphasize Goals, Not Positions			
		Develop Consensus			
		Integrate Decision-Making and Culture	15.0		☐
		MAXIMUM SUBTOTAL	15.0	ACTUAL	☐
		MAXIMUM TOTAL	50.0	ACTUAL	☐

3

Building 157— The Lockheed Story

LOCKHEED MISSILES AND SPACE
SUNNYVALE, CALIFORNIA

PROJECT INITIATED: 1979
PROJECT COMPLETED: 1983

Summary

BOB Fuhrman, President of Lockheed Missiles and Space, referred to the company's new office in these terms: "Employees have been our most valuable asset in reaching this success. Accordingly I'm glad that we can provide such a pleasant work environment . . . and concurrently accomplish new highs in working efficiency and economy."[1] The statement suggests the multiple motives behind the decision to construct Building 157, a facility for three thousand staff engineers. Executives felt a new engineering office would allow them to handle a growing volume of contracts more productively and with greater flexibility. The staff and operations personnel saw it as an opportunity to address certain qualitative aspects of the work environment as well as the quantitative issues which motivated senior management. The architects thought they could do all these things and, at the same time, provide a structure that would become a model of lighting and energy efficiency.

In the end, Building 157 met these many objectives. Unfortunately, because the goals were never synthesized into a single program endorsed by top officials, when the project ran into construction management and budget problems, compromise was difficult and painful. The Lockheed case offers three lessons: (1) it is essential to articulate and integrate different perspectives; (2) it is criticial to recognize when in-house expertise must be supplemented by consulting talent; and (3) research can make significant contributions to efficiency and design innovation.

Background

Design innovations to Lockheed mean developments in technology and engineering. The corporation has a staff of over seventy-two thousand worldwide, with production and support facilities in the United States, Central America, Western Europe, and the Middle East. Its products include "heatshield" tiles for the space shuttles, transport ships for the Navy, supersonic aircraft for the Air Force, and research assistance for the federal government's dioxin clean-up program. The physical environment for this diverse array of work ranges from sterile laboratories to heavy construction plants to white-collar office space. And the major criteria for building are pragmatic—security, flexibility, speed, and low cost. Not known for distinguished architecture, then, management was surprised when one of its new offices was featured in a widely read architectural magazine.[2] The structure was Lockheed Missiles and Space Company's Building 157 in Sunnyvale, California, forty miles south of

(Courtesy Lockheed Missiles & Space Company, Inc.)

51

San Francisco. While the Lockheed name was undistinguished in architectural circles, this new facility was not only aesthetically superior but
incorporated many innovative energy-saving features. In addition, a history of Building 157 yields important lessons regarding research, design,
construction, and white-collar productivity.

Lockheed Missiles and Space Company (LMSC), a wholly owned subsidiary of the Lockheed Corporation, was responsible for $2.7 billion of
the parent company's $6.5 billion 1983 sales. Although LMSC is develop-
ing a site in Austin, Texas, to accommodate growth, the majority of its
operations are headquartered on the 555-acre tract in Sunnyvale. There,
three divisions (Advanced Systems for Research and Development, Missile Systems, and Space Systems) employ twenty-three thousand people
who work in a variety of offices, laboratories, and warehouses. The oldest
building dates from 1956 and others were constructed between that
year and the early 1970s. In the mid-1970s, in response to major fiscal
problems, the company reduced staff and renovated structures to meet
changing needs rather than undertake expensive new construction. By
1979, with renewed financial health and an increasing volume of contracts, LMSC once again recognized that it was time to build.

From the outset, various expectations surrounded the project. For
executives, the new office would improve efficiency and save money.
For managers, the building would bring three thousand "desk and board"
engineers and their department heads under a single roof, enhancing
communications and facilitating team assignments. For the engineering
staff, the proposed facility would provide an improved working environment and allow vacated spaces to be used for more appropriate functions
such as shop and lab work.

Starting the project in accord with traditional LMSC policy, engineering
managers consulted with the vice president for operations and the group
responsible for facilities to develop a proposal for a 500,000 square-foot
office. This in-house approach expedited the design because of the staff's
familiarity with general program requirements and the stringent security
measures needed. After the specifications were complete and a preliminary cost estimate had been determined, four architectural firms were
invited to bid for preparation of contract documents. Three responded
and in June 1979 the San Francisco branch of Leo A. Daly (an international planning, architecture, and engineering concern based in Omaha,
Nebraska), was selected, primarily on the basis of price. So far, nothing
in either the process or in the selection of the architect suggested that
the new project would be any different from Lockheed's older ones:
buildings should meet a specific need within a specific cost range.

The Plans Change

The job was proceeding on schedule when several events occurred that transformed an ordinary commission into a unique design opportunity. The first indication of change was a casual conversation between Lee S. Windheim, senior vice president of Daly/San Francisco and project officer for the Lockheed work, and Wayne Shannon, who was special assistant to the vice president of LMSC's Advanced Systems division. The two men were professional colleagues and, in the past, had collaborated on several research projects. In July 1979, they met to renew their association and started discussing the new office. Before the friendly chat ended, Windheim had posed an intriguing question: "If we could design a building for Lockheed that would use half as much energy as the one it's planning to build, would the company be interested?" Shannon could not give a formal response but he felt Windheim should share his ideas with Lew Ericson, LMSC's Manager of Plant Engineering.

At this later encounter (during August), Ericson asked for more information. Seven days later, Windheim gave the Lockheed executive the so-called Quick Study. This presentation described how 40 to 50 percent of the total energy in an office building was used for lighting and for the removal of heat generated by lighting, and how, by substituting natural for artificial light and by integrating an efficient heating, ventilating, and air conditioning system into the design, a corporation would realize major energy savings. Windheim also made clear that a daylight environment, in conjunction with appropriate interior design and space planning, would enhance worker comfort and productivity.

The proposal clearly reflected the philosophy of the Leo A. Daly company: "To provide the best possible design solution at the lowest possible cost in the least possible time is firm wide. . . . Daly professionals bring all their knowledge and the latest technology to the constant and exciting challenge of satisfying human needs through excellence in design."[3] Having worked for Daly since graduating from Iowa State in 1949, Windheim had been coordinator of environmental systems, executive architect for the innovative Children's Hospital in Washington, D.C., and the individual responsible for opening the San Francisco office. With this rich experience, he was able to translate the company standards into a personal theory of design management, concepts he has expressed verbally in these terms and visually in the diagram that follows (see figure 1):

> The global concerns of design are both ARTFUL (subjective) and SCIEN-TIFIC (objective). Designs originating ideas spring from human PHILOSO-

PHY—the aspects of effectiveness—while ECONOMICS provide boundaries—the aspects of efficiency. Good design must integrate all of these.[4]

He then defined quality as the balance between human satisfaction and return-on-investment, and identified three specific questions to measure a structure's success:

1. Does the design reduce operating costs?
2. Does it increase the personnel's productivity?
3. Does it symbolize the organization's values and principles?

To implement this approach Windheim always made certain that his designers and staff were well versed in the latest energy and technology research. In addition, they were required to keep up to date with the growing body of literature dealing with the relationship of interior office design to worker satisfaction and productivity. Finally, when the San Francisco office dealt with clients, it established links not only with executives and the operations or facilities officer, but also with contract

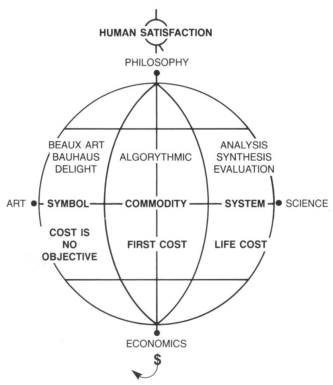

FIGURE 1   Lee Windheim's Design Philosophy (Courtesy Leo A. Daly)

and procurement managers, any in-house space planners and designers, and with the office employees and users themselves. This arrangement, with its parallel lines of communication, sped the design process and helped to assure compatibility between the building and those whose needs it must serve.

After reviewing the Quick Study, Ericson was impressed with the alternative scheme. The appointment of a new LMSC vice president for operations, Arthur L. Hubbard, however, and Sunnyvale's unexpected moratorium on construction—to give city officials time to update the building code and municipal services to accommodate the growing number of tall buildings—made it difficult to take immediate action. Fortunately, after a few months, circumstances had improved and, at Ericson's request, the Daly team put together a more detailed set of drawings and a perspective sketch of the energy-efficient office concept. In the plan, the service core was located at the ends of the structure and an atrium in the center provided natural light to interior spaces. Lockheed managers reviewed the proposal in early 1980. During that same spring Sunnyvale ended its building moratorium. The time for decision had arrived. On May 23 Hubbard made a bold decision. Responding to Daly's creative and bottom-line orientation, he convinced LMSC's senior executives to scrap the 1979 project and offer the architectural firm a contract for a new design.

Hubbard's own background suggests why he was receptive to Windheim's proposal. Having been with Lockheed since 1944, including several years as facility manager for the Missile Systems division, he had witnessed the growing concern of employees for their environment. In 1972 there was an unsuccessful attempt to unionize the company's salaried personnel and poor-quality office space was among the reasons cited for dissatisfaction. In response, a Quality of Space Committee was established with a mandate to improve working conditions at LMSC. Within a short time, departmental representatives and the engineers in charge of design outlined a new palette of interior colors and alternative schemes for office layout and furnishings. These were disseminated to managers and staff, and over the next few years were implemented as people moved and spaces were renovated. In high-technology firms, where it is essential to keep skilled and highly specialized engineers from transferring to other companies, such programs contribute to employee loyalty. This is certainly true in the case of LMSC which, in 1982, had a turnover rate of 4.3 percent, about a third less than the national average, a track record the company was anxious to maintain.[5]

What had started as a nondescript building in 1979 had become a

---

PRIMARY MOTIVES FOR BUILDING

- The Need for Space
- Planning Flexibility
- Cost Control

SECONDARY MOTIVES FOR BUILDING

- Response to Changing Values
- Productivity
- Reflection of the Corporate Culture

FIGURE 2   Lockheed Missiles and Space—Building 157

genuine architectural challenge by June of 1980. LMSC was breaking with tradition. It was exploring new ways to enhance efficiency and productivity and, for the first time, it seemed interested in aesthetic issues. For its part, Daly was exploiting an extensive knowledge of systems and technology and wanted to provide Lockheed with the most advanced, flexible, and cost-effective office (see figure 2 summarizing the motives for building). Hubbard and Windheim were both sensitive to the design issues. The archon and architect shared a common goal and a common vocabulary, and it appeared that there was great potential for an exceptional project.

Design Perspectives and Casting the Project Team

Within the first week the scope of the project was established and responsibilities defined. While basic functions remained the same as the original commission (essentially a flexible, secure office space for three thousand engineers), Lockheed added a 30,000 square-foot computer facility to the program. Beyond this change, five major topics were identified in discussions between Hubbard and Windheim as critical to success:

1. A design that used natural light for most of the building's illumination;
2. Acoustics that allowed small groups to work together without being overheard by their neighbors;
3. A heating, ventilating, and air conditioning system that quickly exhausted excess heat and made effective use of Sunnyvale's mild climate to cool the building;
4. A wire management system that accommodated extensive telecommunications and computer equipment and permitted easy access

when changes were necessary (LMSC employees move an average of once a year); and
5. An open interior plan that offered a variety of office and conference space configurations, each of which could be developed from a few basic components.

Given these goals, Building 157 posed intricate design problems, a situation further complicated when management set August 1980 as the deadline for a major review. To meet the schedule and to promote communication, Hubbard suggested a "free-looping" system consisting of two parallel teams, one within LMSC and one within Leo A. Daly. Tasks were precisely assigned and, in addition to formal biweekly meetings, individuals were encouraged to contact the appropriate team member when information was needed.

Because of the numbers of people involved in decision-making, it is well to identify each. For Leo A. Daly, Windheim and Kyle Davey coordinated overall design, and Adolph Makurak, Bob Riegel, and Samir Mondle were designated as engineers. The Lockheed counterparts to this group were Hubbard, his associate Dave Hobs, and the LMSC Facility Design department. Daly's space planning and interior design experts included Windheim, Davey, and acoustical consultant Richard Hamme. Adrian Blaighlock was Lockheed's representative in this area. Construction and contract documents were the responsibility of Willis Schmeeckle at Daly and of Lew Ericson and Jack Manss at Lockheed. Finally, Jim Fitch at LMSC worked to assure that the design would meet all government and industry security standards. (Figure 3 summarizes the organization of these teams.)

With well-stated objectives and with the partnership arrangement in place, energies were devoted to refining the project. At each major decision point Daly, after careful analysis of LMSC's requirements, presented and discussed its solution. In many cases necessary changes were defined and incorporated at these meetings; if a situation demanded further research or specific expertise, the group determined how and when this would be done. Over the four-month design process (from June to September 1980), this system kept back-tracking and costly modifications during construction to a minimum.

Design Research

The consensus for the conceptual design of Building 157 was based on two sources: (1) the atrium scheme presented to Lockheed executives

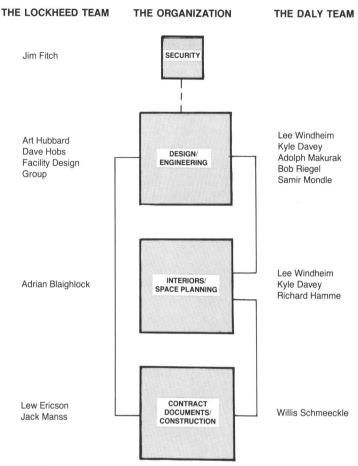

FIGURE 3   Organization of the Lockheed and Daly Project Teams

in early 1980, and (2) principles developed during the 1950s when schools made extensive use of daylighting (with high ceilings and the careful orientation of large windows). Drawing on these precedents and recent scientific data, Windheim quickly outlined two alternatives for the more complex, multistory Lockheed office. In the proposal that was adopted, core services and the computer facility were located to the east and to the west, and windows faced north and south where lighting conditions were relatively constant and controllable. After assuming a height limit of ninety feet for a five-story structure, the designers estimated openings should be fifteen to twenty feet tall in order to illuminate spaces deep within the building. Still, with the vast square footage required, there remained a dark interior without views. To address this problem a large glass-roofed court was used to open up the central offices.

While both Lockheed and Daly generally agreed on this approach, significant questions remained. What were the optimum widths for a typical floor and the atrium? What shading devices were most effective, especially on southern exposures? Should interior ceilings be sloped or flat? What was the best ventilation and cooling system? How much artificial light would be necessary and how should it be controlled? Since many of these issues were interrelated (a sloped interior ceiling, for instance, might work best with one kind of shading device and a flat interior ceiling with another), the architects decided, before making their recommendations to LMSC, to test various design combinations. Renowned for its energy research, the Lawrence Berkeley Laboratory at the University of California was ideal for this work because of its recently completed "artificial sky." With ⅛″ scale models this simulator could indicate the quantity of natural light reaching a specific point in the proposed building under different weather and seasonal conditions. Under the direction of Michael Shanus, Leo A. Daly experimented with floor widths from 80 to 100 feet and atrium widths that varied between 40 and 120 feet. After this, ⅜″ scale models were built to analyze fenestration and ceiling configurations. Skylights and windows using clear, diffuse, and transluscent glass were tested; horizontal louvers and large "lightshelves" were studied as potential shading strategies. Various ceiling options were explored: a flat ceiling, a ceiling sloping down from the windows and atrium to the center of each floor, and a ceiling sloping down to the third points in each floor and flat in the middle.

This intense and intricate work was completed in a little over three months. Based on these findings and research on open office planning, Windheim developed a specific design. The floor width was set at ninety feet and the court or "litetrium" (Lockheed preferred this more functional name) width at sixty feet. Windows would be fifteen feet high with twelve foot deep horizontal lightshelves dividing them into two areas. The lower portion would have tinted glass while the upper would employ clear glass. The ceiling would be sloped to the center of each floor and the lightshelves would shade the work areas below and reflect natural light on to the ceiling above. On the south side of the building an exterior louver would provide additional shade (see the architectural drawings in figure 4).

Throughout the testing and design process Windheim and his research associates repeatedly applied a Department of Energy computer program

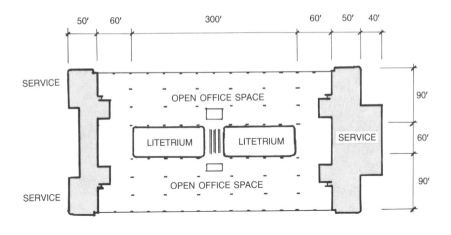

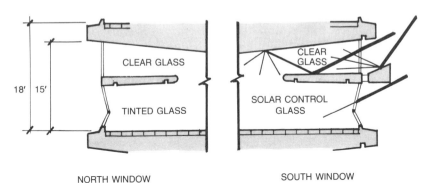

NORTH WINDOW   SOUTH WINDOW

FIGURE 4   Typical Plan and Section of Building 157 (Courtesy Leo A. Daly)

and other analysis techniques to project the building's energy use. After all the refinements had been incorporated into the calculations, including an automatic dimming system for the fluorescent lights, the result was a 70 percent annual reduction in the amount of electricity needed for general illumination.[6] The analysis had also demonstrated that insulation in the walls and roof and insulating glass would be counterproductive. Even with such traditional energy-saving features eliminated, Windheim noted with pride that the LMSC office would "consume only 45 percent of the allowable energy budget" stipulated in California's energy code.[7]

After the large-scale aspects of Building 157 had been defined, the next assignment was to prepare proposals for the interior. Although the aerospace firm had been using an open office system for some time, Hubbard asked representatives from Lockheed and Daly to explore alternatives. In particular, he wanted components that were easier to rearrange than those currently in use. To this end, the designers worked with a newly reconstituted Quality of Space Committee (composed of twenty-four representatives from LMSC's main operating divisions), and interviewed a cross section of managers and engineers to find out what people did, how they did it, and what they wanted in their new offices. To facilitate discussions small-scale models were made so that workers would point out potential problems and rearrange components for optimal efficiency and comfort.

The interview findings proved interesting. Managers insisted on enclosed offices even if the trade-offs meant distance from their staffs, windowless space, and used furnishings. At Lockheed the managerial positions were coveted and privacy was an important reflection of this prestige. Engineers, on the other hand, represented a different culture. They were accustomed to open offices where each person had a desk or a drafting board. Beyond this essential work area, their concerns were with space, flexibility, and lighting. While they wanted privacy, they often needed to discuss problems with neighbors and were, therefore, grouped in clusters. In addition, they required small and conveniently located conference rooms for more formal reviews. With regard to lighting, control over table and drafting lamps was crucial, as well as protection from glare and direct sun when using computer terminals.

In a continuing dialogue between the Lockheed and Daly teams, this information was used to create an effective interior design for Building 157. Private spaces for managers and LMSC executives were located beside the east and west core areas. Only the four corner offices on each floor had windows. A prototypical work station was designed which, in good engineering fashion, Windheim dubbed the "utility module" to suggest its universal application and flexibility. Whatever the name, it had 68-inch high, sound-absorbing panels surrounding three sides of the desk, fluorescent task lights under a closed shelf, file drawers, and a multi-use, adjustable-height table near the main work surface. Special two and five-drawer padlocked file cabinets were designed for secure storage and an adjustable arm chair was specified (see figure 5). When combined with other utility modules, Lockheed could accommodate clus-

FIGURE 5   Typical "Utility Module" (Courtesy RoseJohnson Inc.—Photographer, Len Allington)

ters of from two to four engineers and conveniently arrange these into the groups of up to about fifteen people who reported to a supervisor.

Dispersed among the work areas on each floor were a minimum of twenty-eight conference spaces. Most were for meetings of six to eight people, although one could serve up to a hundred. In addition, a three-hundred-seat auditorium and a hundred-seat conference room were located on the ground floor. For privacy, conference spaces were enclosed by 80-inch partitions and a gentle "white sound" was transmitted throughout the building to mask noise. Diffusing and tinted glass windows protected against glare from the sun. Auto-dimming fluorescent lamps, employed to augment the daylight system and for night work, pleasantly illuminated offices by reflecting light off the ceiling. Complementing this was a 10-inch raised floor which provided maximum flexibility for the layout of engineering areas. By removing a few carpet tiles and screws, telephones, computer terminals, and power lines could be shifted quickly without professional electricians.

The research that contributed so substantially to the initial design of Building 157 was also used in one of the last phases of the process. To make certain that the structure's many elements would function harmoniously, a full-scale mock-up of a thirty by forty-five foot office section was tested at the Owens-Corning Fiberglass Technical Research Center in Granville, Ohio. The acoustics, daylighting, artificial lighting, and wire management systems all checked out. Daly and Lockheed also took this opportunity to decide on finishes. Simulated wood veneer was chosen for the tops of desks and bookshelves and vertical panels were covered with fabric. On the advice of LMSC's interior experts, Russell Robinson and Ingrid Leister, a color scheme of beiges, tans, and dark green accents was selected for panel covers, furniture upholstery, and carpeting.

Interestingly, the most noteworthy result from this simulation involved air conditioning and ventilation. Daly's engineers had detailed a sophisticated network of ducts to supply and exhaust air. What they found, however, was that this could be greatly simplified without any loss of environmental comfort by substituting a fiberglass air tube for the conventional system. Once in place, this single modification was responsible for over $500,000 in construction savings and more than paid for the full-scale prototype and testing.

Security and fire code issues rounded out the major decisions made by the Lockheed and Daly design teams. At first Jim Fitch, LMSC's security manager, was concerned about the openness of Building 157 and the potential for people to see classified material. But after extensive debates among Lockheed managers and the architects, everyone was satisfied that the important and pleasant litetrium did not pose an exceptional risk. Employees would enter the building through guarded turnstiles activated by their own magnetically coded identification badges. They would wear these badges whenever they were in the building and, as a matter of policy, they were continuously cautioned to conceal and lock up classified documents, and to report any unusual behavior or visitors.

The fire safety plans were finally approved after construction. The architects had incorporated ceiling sprinklers, smoke detectors and alarms, four exterior exit stairs, and an air system, monitored around the clock, whose pressure could be adjusted to localize a fire in any section of the structure. While these met or exceeded Sunnyvale's requirements, some of the individuals concerned with this area wanted to enclose the litetrium in glass. Because this would have substantially reduced the efficiency of Daly's approach to daylighting and environmental control, the architects argued that the present precautions were ample. The fire marshall was cooperative but took a wait-and-see attitude. Once Building 157 was finished, an elaborate test showed that the designers were correct and the office was approved for occupancy.

Final Decisions and Construction

During late July and early August 1980, facts and figures were compiled and drawings and charts were prepared for a complete presentation to Lockheed management. Renderings revealed the office's sleek lines, clear organization, and attractive court; plans were made for the ground and typical upper level floors; diagrams explained the building's unique daylighting and mechanical systems; photographs showed the "utility module" and cluster arrangements. Nevertheless, the most impressive points were made by cold statistics: major savings through significantly reduced energy consumption, a simplified air system, and elimination of the need for insulation and insulating glass. The construction estimate indicated that there was about a $3 million premium for the lightshelves, sloped ceilings, and automatic dimming system. Because of the efficient approach to energy, however, this would be recaptured in less than ten years. For a company familiar with the concept of long-term return, this reasoning made eminently good sense.

In reports written during August and September 1980, Windheim wished he had noted another potential benefit of the Daly design—improved productivity—but Hubbard was reluctant to broach this issue with Lockheed senior management because specific data were hard to come by. Still, referring to studies by the Buffalo Organization for Social and Technological Innovation and other corporations and research groups, the architect believed that thoughtful interior planning could increase productivity from 5 to 15 percent.[8] Seven factors had to be considered:

1. Sufficient personal space;
2. Comfortable furnishings and efficient layout;
3. Controlled temperature and air quality;
4. Sufficient and glare-free ambient light and control over task lighting;
5. Some access to windows and views;
6. Visual and speech privacy; and
7. Ease and support of communications.

Windheim was sure the interior design of the Lockheed office addressed these concerns and that LMSC could, over the long run, anticipate returns well beyond those outlined in the construction and maintenance analysis. He called attention to studies by the Government Services Administration and IBM that calculated the total operating costs of an office over a thirty-year period (see figure 6).[9] The breakdown was 2 percent for the

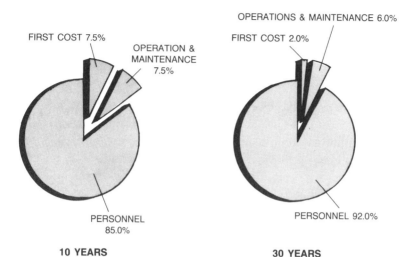

FIGURE 6   Total Owning and Operating Costs for a Building (Courtesy Leo A. Daly)

capital costs of site, building, and equipment; 6 percent for operation, maintenance, and reconfiguration of space; and 92 percent for personnel salaries. The designer kept hammering home the same point: since employee expenses were by far the largest portion of operating an owner-occupied office, even a small increase in productivity translated into dramatic savings. On the other hand, quantifiable improvement in the future output of white-collar workers is a notoriously elusive figure, and it is a special challenge to convince management to spend time and money without hard facts. Nonetheless, Windheim's argument did suggest that effective design could properly be regarded as among the least-cost investments to enhance productivity.

Even without a discussion of this issue, it was a V Day for Lockheed when corporate officers approved the design in fall 1980. Daly's office immediately began to develop the contract drawings and specifications, a job it divided into three parts: sitework and foundation; steel framework and shell; and finally, mechanical systems, finishes, and interiors. As each step was completed, the documents were turned over to Lew Ericson, LMSC's Manager of Plant Engineering, who was coordinating the building process. With its personnel in place and a target cost of $66 per square foot (established by analyzing the price of recent corporate offices in the area), Lockheed selected a contractor. The foundation was begun early in 1981 and the design team was cautiously optimistic that all would go as planned.

Initially, everything appeared to be working out. The site was inspected at least twice a week; invoices were carefully reviewed; and Daly's office provided design interpretation. In July 1981, only a few months into construction, however, most of the steel was up, but so, too, was the estimate for the job. To expedite the building process, Lockheed had used a "fast track" system in which bids were solicited as phases of the drawings and specifications were completed. While this saved time, it did not allow the company to "lock in" a final price until the structure was almost finished. Several other factors compounded this uncertainty and suggested why the initial estimate may have been low. LMSC had added 100,000 square feet and a computer facility to the program; the lively pace of construction in Silicon Valley kept quotes from subcontractors unusually high; and inflation seemed to be getting out of hand.

Having identified the problems and knowing that, at this point, it was already committed philosophically, physically, and economically to the new design, Lockheed was determined to get the project back on track. With its growing number of contracts, the corporation needed Building 157 to improve efficiency. But it also wanted to reduce costs. In this respect, the project team reviewed all aspects of the structure and decided to redesign certain features: an underground passage to neighboring laboratories was postponed; a central fan for air conditioning and ventilation was substituted for twenty modular units; interior shading devices on the south side of the litetrium were deleted; and some finishes in the courtyard, lobby, and conference area were modestly downgraded.

LMSC also changed its management and contract procedures. For the last phase of Building 157, finishes and interiors, the company hired Hensel Phelps Incorporated as construction manager and general contractor. This firm worked for many corporate clients and had an outstanding reputation for controlling budgets and meeting deadlines. In addition to this expertise, the agreement with Hensel Phelps had two important provisions designed specifically to contain costs. First, the general contractor could do no more than 15 percent of the work. The rest had to be competitively bid, and the bids and the subcontractors' detailed billings were to be available for inspection by Lockheed on demand. Second, once the job was 60 percent complete, the builder had to make a commitment regarding price. Then, using a carrot-and-stick philosophy, the agreement stipulated that if final costs were under this amount, the contracting firm kept 30 percent of the savings; if over, it had to absorb the loss.

With these modifications and scrupulous line-item monitoring by Lockheed executives, work generally proceeded on schedule with an exception caused by the late delivery of windows. During the winter of 1982 office stations were installed and by April of 1983 engineers were at their desks. Final costs had come in at about $85 per square foot and, although the building experience had, at times, been harrowing, LMSC was satisfied it had spent its resources wisely. Dedication ceremonies, held in May, were highlighted by an evening reception attended by the entire city council and mayor of Sunnyvale. And on June 4, LMSC Family Day, enthusiasm for the design extended to an even larger group when fourteen thousand visitors toured the new office.

Beyond local acclaim, Building 157 has been well received nationally. In the Second National Passive Solar Design Competition it won an Award of Merit, and its energy and daylighting features were described as a model in the January 1984 *Architectural Record*.[10] A *Los Angeles Times* business reporter hailed the design with these words: "When 3000 engineers and other Lockheed Missiles and Space Company employees move next spring into a large new office building nearing completion here [Sunnyvale], they will be excused for blinking twice. . . . In a step backward from trying to overpower the natural order of things, Lockheed and other forward looking employers are rediscovering sunlight."[11] (See figure 7.) In a related vein, the *San Jose Mercury News* wrote enthusiastically of "Lockheed's Secret Garden," noting that "most people who have [previously] visited Lockheed Missiles and Space Company in Sunnyvale would admit that, aesthetically speaking, the facility has about as much charm as an Army barracks. That is why it is such a shock to stand in the middle of Building 157 and . . . look up at engineers working under natural light in open work stations behind balconies of cascading grape ivy."[12]

While praise for the beauty of the new office pleases LMSC executives, they continue to emphasize the functional and cost-effective aspects of the space. Hubbard himself has stated the structure's rationale quite simply: "Daylight is the best light to work by. Vision isn't as good under electric lights."[13] To outsiders, it may appear that Lockheed was somewhat embarrassed by its success, an accomplishment that did not fit in with its no-frills, no-nonsense tradition. This may underrate company pride. Although Hubbard and Windheim, in retrospect, wish that an outside construction manager had been included in the original project team, both believe that, in spite of the involved nature of the design and decision-making process, Building 157 may yet prove to be a most valuable prototype for Lockheed and other corporations.

FIGURE 7   Building 157's Atrium (Courtesy Lockheed Missiles & Space Company, Inc.)

Evaluation

Three important lessons emerge from the Lockheed case. First, it is evident from the development of Building 157 that while articulating different perspectives is always important, it is especially so in hierarchical organizations. Second, the project points out the need for a balanced relationship between in-house expertise and consultants. Third, it suggests the breadth of contributions that research can make to architectural design. Each issue becomes clearer when the office is evaluated in terms of the four maxims described previously.

Maxim One: Integrate Multiple Perspectives

A very significant feature of Building 157 was the wide range of motives behind the commission. Even among executives, there were several points of view. Senior corporate officers wanted a facility in the low to moderate-cost range that would handle the increasing volume of LMSC contracts and improve efficiency. Other levels of management supported this mandate but added other priorities. Arthur Hubbard, vice president for operations, desired better quality and more flexible office space for staff engineers. Lew Ericson, manager of plant engineering, was interested in an energy-efficient design. And mediating these attitudes was the critical assumption that the objectives for building could be as broad as anyone wished so long as they did not increase the budget.

From the perspective of employees (in this instance, "desk and board" engineers), Building 157 was designed to serve three major purposes: (1) improve the working environment, a continuing concern since the movement to unionize in the early 1970s; (2) respond to corporate culture by providing enclosed offices for managers and clusters of open offices and nearby conference spaces for staff engineers; and (3) enhance flexibility through the incorporation of furniture and mechanical systems that permitted rearrangement of project teams with minimum disruption to ongoing work.

Blending the goals of both management and staff, the focus of the Leo A. Daly architects was on the design of a high performance office structure, a workplace that was energy-efficient, productive, secure, safe, and adaptable.

The evaluation of how well these multiple perspectives were integrated is mixed. While executives articulated the reasons for building and certain qualitative aspects of the design, they failed by not more fully exploring the relationship between proposed budget and proposed objectives. This is important in every company and for every project. It is particularly essential in hierarchical organizations because change is difficult and decisions are made slowly. It is equally significant with regard to buildings that are to be used by staff rather than management. Budget and objectives are usually more flexible for a headquarters development than they are for general office space or manufacturing facilities. Thus, the further removed a building is from corporate officers, the more specific everyone should be about money and goals.

Another criticism of the Lockheed performance is absence of a careful review of construction procedures. Because LMSC had not built for some time, it would have been appropriate for executives to analyze how construction would be managed. If the company had done this itself, or if it had been suggested by the architects, the building process would have been streamlined and the potential for saving dollars and time would have increased. In the end, given these omissions, Lockheed receives an "average" rating (4.5 out of 7.5 points) for its handling of the executive perspective.

On the more positive side, employee perspectives and attitudes were thoughtfully examined. Both the company and architect worked together to discover staff priorities. In addition to interviews and questionnaires, those responsible for design asked individuals to arrange models into ideal spatial configurations, an especially valuable technique. This effort was so well handled that Lockheed deserves an "excellent" rating (5.0 out of 5.0 points) here, an evaluation supported by the fact that much of this information was translated into specific design proposals which have subsequently caused noticable reductions in absenteeism.[14]

The objectives of Leo A. Daly were comprehensive and innovative. They emphasized performance. The designers wanted—and knew how—to develop an up-to-date office. On the other hand, the architects' inability to integrate their scientific approach to Lockheed's decision-making, budget, and construction processes made later changes a difficult experience. While this perspective was marked by vision and good intentions, it was never completely accepted by the client and thus, in terms of compatibility, deserves a "superior" rather than "excellent" rating (2.0 out of 2.5 points).

Maxim Two: Emphasize Casting

Because it had been several years since Lockheed had commissioned a new building, both Hubbard and Windheim now realize that an independent construction manager should have been included in the original "free-looping" design team. This would have helped development of a realistic budget as well as contract coordination and scheduling. As it was, such an organization (Hensel Phelps Inc.) became involved only in the last phase of the project, too late to realize the full benefit of its expertise. Other than this missing component, however, Building 157 included a reasonable balance of in-house and design talent and, therefore, receives an "average" rating (1.5 out of 2.5 points) in the category of "Actors and Roles."

With regard to assembling the cast, the lack of an outside construction manager led to leadership problems. During the actual building of the

Lockheed office, architectural services were limited to design interpretation, leaving decisions in the hands of an incomplete in-house team. When, after several months, management executives finally decided to supplement the LMSC group with a consultant, budget problems had already become a reality. Resolving them was then an uphill battle.

It is important to note that these difficulties were not due to lack of commitment. Both the Lockheed and Daly participants were dedicated and knowledgeable. On the other hand, an inadequate framework for communications made it impossible to achieve optimum coordination of their talents. While Hubbard himself understood the expanded priorities of Building 157, there was no established mechanism to convey the full implications of this change to senior corporate officials. In a similar fashion, Windheim was never able to convince Lockheed managers that an emphasis on performance could be as cost-efficient as an emphasis on price. Situations like this highlight the necessity of establishing an approach to communications *before* design gets underway. In the Lockheed case, the rating for casting must be considered "average" (4.5 out of 7.5 points).

Maxim Three: Sift for Relevant Facts

Little needs to be said in the area of research. Building 157 is an outstanding example of how cooperation between archon and architect enabled the design team to get beyond preconceived ideas. The analysis here focused on technology and interior design, but it is worthwhile noting that the success of the Lockheed office has also enhanced the company's image. There is no doubt that the LMSC project merits an "excellent" rating (10.0 out of 10.0 points) in this category and that the Daly company must be commended for the breadth and competence of its approach.

Maxim Four: Manage Pluralistic Decision-Making

Not unexpectedly, when difficulties with the budget and construction schedule for Building 157 were obvious in mid-1981, Lockheed decision-makers decided that reassessments were in order. Ideally this process should maximize the architectural potential of a project, exploring the most economically efficient and expeditious ways of using design to serve corporate goals. But in this case, such an approach was not feasible because, to avoid conflict in the early stages of design, those involved with the LMSC office had not reached a consensus on the primary objectives. Headquarters executives felt money was the top priority; the divisional staff stressed flexibility and energy conservation; the architect emphasized employee and building performance.

Although a compromise was eventually reached, rather than a re-evaluation based on mutually determined goals, initial discussions focused on figuring out what went wrong and who was responsible. It was a classic case of seeking to censure individuals or groups while glossing over the inadequate processes that make problems a virtual certainty. Because there were no common standards for making judgements, when the dust had settled, Building 157 exceeded expectations—but everyone paid a price. The structure was more expensive than estimated. The reputation of the in-house construction management team was tarnished. The architectural firm has yet to receive another Lockheed commission, and public praise has not compensated for private lapses.

Two steps might have avoided the situation. First, a specific statement of goals and priorities, endorsed by both management and the design team, would have made it significantly easier to develop consensus throughout the design process. Instead, decisions were often made by mandate, and this precluded a complete understanding of the issues and exploration of potentially valuable alternatives. Second, Leo A. Daly could have prepared a strategy to better integrate the hierarchical organization and cost-conscious nature of Lockheed's decision-making with its own relaxed and experimental approach to design. Especially as the scope of the program changed, the architects might have suggested that a representative from Lockheed's central office be included on the project team and that the in-house construction manager prepare budget estimates for the new proposals. Since, as already noted, these shortcomings had important consequences, Building 157 receives a "below average" rating (6.0 out of 15.0 points) in the area of decision-making.

Conclusion

The scorecard summarizes results. In essence, fact-finding was exceptional and decision-making was weak. The two other maxims (multiple perspectives and casting) were in the average to above-average range. What becomes apparent, then, is that while research and innovation are critical to a building's success, the lack of agreement on goals and a framework for communications can make achieving that success a difficult experience.

Building 157—The Lockheed Story

MAXIM		CORPORATE TASKS	MAX PTS	RATING	ACT PTS
MULTIPLE PERSPECTIVES	The Managerial Perspective	Define Objectives and Priorities			
		Establish Standards of Quality			
		Articulate Corporate Values	7.5	AVERAGE	4.5
	The Employee Perspective	Seek Employee Participation	5.0	EXCELLENT	5.0
	The Architectural Perspective	Look for a Compatible Marriage with the Architect	2.5	SUPERIOR	2.0
		MAXIMUM SUBTOTAL	15.0	ACTUAL	11.5
CASTING	A Multitude of Actors and Roles	Appoint the In-House Players			
		Hire Outside Managers			
		Select the Design Team			
		Work with Key Public Actors	2.5	AVERAGE	1.5
	Assembling the Cast	Determine the Mix of In-House vs. Outside Services			
		Stress the CCC Syndrome: Commitment, Communications, and Competence	7.5	AVERAGE	4.5
		MAXIMUM SUBTOTAL	10.0	ACTUAL	6.0
RESEARCH	Design Research	Turn Facts into Options	2.5	EXCELLENT	2.5
	Critical Topics	Study Technology, Layout and Image	7.5	EXCELLENT	7.5
		MAXIMUM SUBTOTAL	10.0	ACTUAL	10.0
DECISION-MAKING	Elements in Design Management	Emphasize Goals, Not Positions			
		Develop Consensus			
		Integrate Decision-Making and Culture	15.0	BELOW AVER.	6.0
		MAXIMUM SUBTOTAL	15.0	ACTUAL	6.0
		MAXIMUM TOTAL	50.0	ACTUAL	33.5

4

A First New Home—The Hercules Headquarters

HERCULES INCORPORATED
WILMINGTON, DELAWARE

PROJECT INITIATED: 1979
PROJECT COMPLETED: 1983

Summary

WITH respect to corporate headquarters, to build or not to build often represents an arduous decision. For the international chemical products firm of Hercules Incorporated, however, the move was almost inevitable. By 1979, after the company had completed its reorganization to streamline operations, existing facilities were not only inefficient but leases on the space were expiring. Beyond immediate needs, Delaware's high income tax rates made recruiting difficult and the recently appointed chief executive was searching for ways to enhance visibility and prestige, and by so doing, broaden the opportunities to attract talent. But how should the company approach the problem? For nearly seventy years it had rented offices and the idea of constructing its own "official home" was an unsettling mandate.

To meet the challenge, three executives were appointed as a full-time project team to work with consultants and state and city officials.

Over a four-year period this group managed the design process so success-fully—from the description of spatial requirements through the dedication ceremony—that final costs were only 0.3 percent above the original esti-mate. The accomplishment was largely due to three factors:

1. Hercules clearly defined its goals and ordered its priorities;
2. There was a harmonious balance between in-house and outside talent; and
3. The communications framework encouraged consensus.

Background

What first captures the eye about the Hercules headquarters? To the north an attractive riverfront park, angled curtain walls, and a granite tower create the image of a gateway; to the south a landscaped plaza, a carefully detailed stone facade (designed to blend with the nearby town-houses), a central clock, and an impressive pedestrian entrance define this structure as an urban landmark. The building is an anchor for Wil-mington's River to River development, which runs fourteen blocks from the Christina River to the Brandywine Creek. Inside, two levels of retail space and a twelve-story atrium offer such amenities as restaurants, a bank, specialty shops, boutiques, natural light, and that "touch of class" that instills pride in the Hercules staff. John Morris Dixon, editor of *Progressive Architecture,* was so impressed that he said what countless residents feel: the Hercules building puts Wilmington "on the map, architecturally."[1]

The structure is not simply an architectural highlight. It is, as well, an historic highlight, for it is the first headquarters Hercules ever designed for its own use. For most of the years since its founding in 1912 (a spin-off from DuPont resulting from a federal antitrust suit), the chemical company had leased space in the Delaware Trust Building. But seven decades of growth and a changing economy necessitated change.

Revenues in Hercules' initial year of operations were $7.2 million, largely from contracts for explosives. During the First World War business expanded and by 1919 sales had reached $19.6 million. In the years between the wars, the firm extended its line to include naval stores (turpentine and resins), and the manufacturing of synthetics and organic chemicals.[2] By the mid-1970s, with a work force of twenty-five thousand employees, facilities included a multimillion-dollar research center in New Castle County, Delaware, as well as plants and offices in eighty

(Courtesy Hercules Inc.)

other locations in the United States, England, Belgium, West Germany, and elsewhere. In 1979, the year the decision was made to build, assets were $1.8 billion.[3]

More specific reasons for reviewing the headquarters situation included the 1973 OPEC oil crisis. Since petroleum, the base of significant numbers of products, had increased dramatically in price, the strict control of inventory and purchasing was critical and highlighted the need for streamlined operations. In addition, while the Delaware Trust Building had served with reasonable efficiency, expanding demands gradually required more and more space. Periodically, Hercules had persuaded

76

the building's owners to construct additions. Yet despite an accommodating landlord and rather ingenious *ad hoc* arrangements, problems remained. Three main entrances in the Trust edifice posed security difficulties; the small distance between columns and an array of enclosed offices reduced flexibility; communications were often awkward because of the physical separation among personnel. Finally, if building constraints interfered with attracting and holding high quality people, Delaware's state income tax (19 percent for the highest brackets) and the declining vitality of Wilmington itself, which had been characterized by decreasing population since World War II,[4] made the job even harder.

In 1977, when Alexander Giacco became Hercules president and chief executive officer, both internal and external forces were in place for major changes. The city needed the company. The company liked the city. But both had to act boldly if the city-corporate marriage was to survive.

Casting the Project Team and Defining Goals

Initially the company had considered an out-of-state move. Evidently, however, the corporate walls were porous because the General Assembly reduced the personal income tax rates. Mr. Giacco, then, determined to stay in Delaware and an announcement to that effect was made on July 2, 1979. The state was reassured. The city had to wait.

At the time there was no construction budget but an in-house team was soon appointed to work full-time on the project. Assistant Vice President for Administration and Public Affairs John Greer directed the effort. It was a wise choice. With forty years of experience at Hercules, Greer was not only knowledgeable in long-range planning but had also established many contacts in the public and private sectors. Edward F. Lacy, III, and Elizabeth Ronat assisted Greer. The former had a solid background in mechanical engineering as well as in facility and construction management. Ronat, an electrical engineer with computer expertise, was given responsibility for energy and space-planning issues. The trio, having a repertoire of skills that augured well for success, reported to Senior Vice President S. R. Clarke who, in turn, relayed information to Mr. Giacco.

Management's single mandate to the team was to keep the design and building process moving. The schedule was important for two reasons: first, the company's leases expired at the end of 1982 and second, everyone knew delay and changes translated into increased costs. And cost, like time, was a major concern!

Fifteen days after Hercules announced it would stay in Delaware, the firm hired Philadelphia's Interspace Incorporated to do an abbreviated space requirement and configuration study. With satisfied clients like ARCO and Cigna Insurance, Interspace had a reputation for quality research and analysis. Over the next three months the consultants interviewed a cross section of executives and department heads to gather essential data. The conclusions were that 425,000 square feet of offices (600,000 gross square feet) would be needed by 1984 and that, given certain functional relationships, two configurations were appropriate. A four-story suburban building was the more efficient solution, but only slightly less attractive was a twelve to fifteen-story urban office tower. In addition to these recommendations, the study included information on interior planning, flexibility, lighting, and acoustics.

While Interspace was doing its analysis, the project team investigated other concerns. Among the interrelated issues on its agenda, three were of major importance:

1. To construct a new building or renovate the Delaware Trust Building;
2. To meet only company needs or lease space in a larger structure built by a developer; and
3. To stay in Wilmington or move to another location.

Because renovation meant substantial disruption to operations, it was quickly determined to build a new structure. Greer, Lacy, and Ronat also decided that, in order to control design and enhance prestige, it was better to build only for its own requirements rather than share space with others. Because of its political and economic implications, the third question took longer to resolve.

The city, with support from then Governor Pierre du Pont, wanted to keep Hercules. Besides the 1500 jobs involved, Wilmington officials knew that it would be most unfortunate if an important corporate citizen left just as they were initiating major efforts to attract new businesses. The mayor's office designated its own liaison, Elliott Golinkoff, to the Hercules project. He surveyed the city for potential sites and, working with an architectural consultant, narrowed the choice from about fifteen to three. To make an even more persuasive case, Golinkoff invited Cushman & Wakefield and the Hines Group, two nationally known developers, to make presentations at a meeting attended by the governor, mayor, and the Hercules chief executive. Proposals were unveiled which demonstrated how a downtown office tower would enhance the company's visibility and prestige and meet its space, access, and long-term requirements as well as help the municipality.

Although impressed, the corporation felt an obligation to explore other options. One significant alternative was to build at its thousand-acre research center: construction costs would be lower; the parklike setting offered amenities such as a golf course and a recreation center; and expansion, when required, would be easier to accomplish.

To come to a final decision more information was needed. An in-house staff analyzed four types of financing: ownership, sale and lease-back, a joint venture arrangement, and selling the building to the pension fund. After carefully weighing tax implications, Hercules determined in 1979 that sale and leaseback was the best because this minimized investment, permitted the company to deduct rental expenses, and still allowed it to control design. The project team also wanted a clearer estimate of costs. To arrive at an accurate figure and monitor expenses, they hired a construction management company to evaluate design and construction decisions. Eight firms were reviewed for this role, and by the end of November, DiSabatino CM (DSCM), of Wilmington, was selected. Although not the largest firm, DSCM worked closely with the nationally known CRS Construction Managers, Inc., of Houston, a recognized innovator, had considerable experience with major projects, and was intimately familiar with the local trades. In short, Hercules' decision was based on favorable assessments of DSCM's mastery of the latest information, its competence, commitment, and familiarity with the area, and its rapport with area contractors and the corporation.

The project team had now expanded from the three Hercules representatives to include two from Interspace and one from DSCM (see figure 8). Having developed a good working relationship, this group visited a selection of recent offices to determine the quality level Hercules could demand in its new quarters. Considerable time was spent in Houston

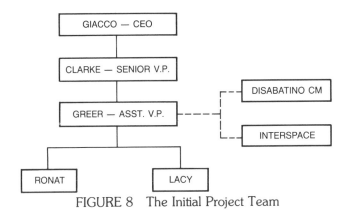

FIGURE 8   The Initial Project Team

visiting the work of Gerald Hines, a Texas developer, whose reputation rested on his ability to combine design excellence with a high return-on-investment. Examining twenty offices, the visitors gleaned insights into issues such as location and interior layout, furnishings and ceiling heights, building materials and hardware, maintenance and energy use, scheduling and flexibility.

On January 2, 1980, six months after Mr. Giacco's announcement, seven building goals synthesized efforts to this point:[5]

- EFFICIENT AND PLEASANT WORKSPACE DESIGNED FROM THE INSIDE OUT— one that would complement business functions and workflow patterns so that the office would suit Hercules' needs and expedite operations
- A QUALITY ARCHITECTURAL STRUCTURE THAT WOULD ENHANCE HERCULES' IMAGE—one that would establish Hercules' presence in Delaware and in the chemicals industry
- HIGH FLEXIBILITY IN OPERATION AND EASE OF REARRANGEMENT
- HIGH COST EFFECTIVENESS ON A LIFE CYCLE BASIS—one that would address maintenance and energy issues over the long-term
- READY ADAPTABILITY TO ADVANCED OFFICE SYSTEMS—one that would easily accept the latest word-processing equipment, voice-message systems and audio and video-conferencing
- HIGH LEVEL SECURITY
- USE OF HERCULES PRODUCTS WHERE APPROPRIATE—such as Herculon olelin fiber in fabrics and carpeting

Having set the parameters, and with the design program prepared by Interspace, it was now possible to make cost comparisons. After DSCM had prepared estimates for the four-story structure at the research center site and for the office tower in Wilmington, it reported that expenses would be $15 million greater in the city. Despite the certainty of staff turnover and Hercules' commitment to Wilmington, economic realities suggested it was time to leave. In early 1980 Goldman Sachs was engaged to work out details for financing the structure on the basis of a limited partnership/leaseback arrangement.

The company's move led the mayor and governor to redouble their efforts to keep Hercules in town. The city hired consultants to develop land use and traffic strategies; it coordinated discussions among parking authority officials and other department heads to discover approaches that would make an urban location more attractive; it considered subsidized loans and/or reduced land costs as added incentives. The intense effort paid off. In March 1980 Hercules stated its willingness to build in Wilmington if five conditions were met: the tract bounded by Market, Orange, 13th, and 14th streets near Brandywine Creek would be made available; additional parking would be constructed nearby; subsidized financing for the $15 million construction difference would be provided; plans for the park to the north of the site would be accelerated; and the property to the south would be developed in a way that would complement the Hercules project.

With little opposition because of the importance and prestige of the undertaking, the city agreed to these stipulations and applied to the Department of Housing and Urban Development for a subsidized loan. On April 30, after the company's board had approved an initial appropriation for the project, Hercules signed its part of the HUD Urban Development Action Grant (UDAG) application. The final arrangement called for Wilmington to sell the site to Hercules for a dollar and to lend it $12 million at 5 percent for twenty-seven years. The parking authority would build spaces for 125 cars under the headquarters and a garage for a thousand more across the street.

In the interim, with cost estimates and a design program in hand, DSCM had begun the architect selection process. An initial group of forty was screened to eight. Then, based on experience with the city's consultants and on discussions with other corporations—especially Union Carbide and Owens Illinois, which had recently built headquarters—the Hercules team added two more designers to the list. Accompanied by the building goals statement, a condensed program, and an outline of the roles DSCM and Interspace would play in the project, a "request for proposal" was sent out to the architectural firms asking them not to submit preliminary designs but to list similar projects they had done in both urban and suburban locations, and to describe how their offices operated, the design processes used, and the names, responsibilities, and biographies of key personnel who would be involved with Hercules. Eight of the ten firms responded.

When the submissions were reviewed by the Hercules project team, construction manager, and space-planning representatives, they eliminated one for lack of experience and decided to interview the other seven. From among these, they then chose four studios to visit before identifying three finalists. After each made a comprehensive presentation, the eight-person group (representing Hercules, DSCM, and Interspace) again visited the architects' offices and certain buildings designed by each. Throughout the four-week process, the project team kept Messrs. Giacco and Clarke fully informed because these two men would make the ultimate decision.

On March 1, 1980, the New York firm of Kohn Pederson Fox Associates PC (KPF) was selected. Like the other finalists they had a structure for working with Hercules, Interspace, and DSCM and for listening to and interpreting client needs. But KPF took several other steps. First, they assigned two principals to the project. Second, they proposed a methodology for creatively addressing both design and cost. Third, in a subtle and sensitive approach to communications, they made extensive use of models, a "language" very familiar to Hercules engineers who, in building manufacturing plants themselves, used models rather than drawings to assure that the complex routing of pipes and chemicals would work. Thus, what possibly seemed of secondary importance to other architectural firms turned out to be of critical positive value for KPF.[6]

Following selection of the designers, attention was focused on engineering services. KPF made suggestions which were reviewed by Hercules and DSCM. In less than nine days contracts were signed with Joseph R. Loring & Associates, Inc., as electrical and mechanical engineers, and with Severud-Perrone-Szegezdy-Sturm as structural engineers. Since both were located in New York City, they were convenient to the architects.

Managing Pluralistic Decision-Making

On March 10, 1980, the first full design briefing was convened in Wilmington. The session was very important. Although design decisions were not made, the lead characters established working relationships that transformed the group's independent talents and expertise into a highly effective "layered" team effort (see figure 9). Together they reviewed the program, budget, schedule and building objectives, outlined responsibilities, and clarified how decisions would be made. The engineers would work with the architects and make recommendations to Hercules through KPF. Interspace would critique the efficiency and flexibility of floor plans, prepare detailed interior proposals, oversee the testing, development, and selection of office components and finishes, and coordinate its efforts with the architect. DSCM, on the other hand, would exercise a more independent role, reviewing designs and reporting directly to Greer and his colleagues. Any changes would be conveyed to KPF and the engineers from Hercules in consultation with DSCM.

The arrangement worked particularly well in monitoring construction expenses and avoiding costly modifications. When completed in 1983 and in spite of an inflation rate as high as 20 percent, the headquarters was a mere 0.3 percent over the September 1980 estimate. And this

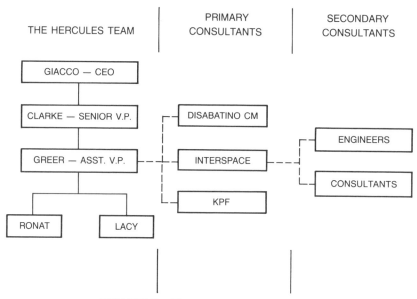

FIGURE 9   The Layered Project Team

included everything from furnishings and interior equipment to light-bulbs and chalk! Within this total, Hercules staff time, professional fees, and financing costs were under budget, while the construction management contract was larger than expected. The last item was a worthwhile trade-off because Hercules desperately wanted to control costs and avoid changes during construction. To achieve these objectives, more extensive analysis was required from DSCM than originally anticipated. In a volatile economy and for an important and unique project such as this, however, the higher fee was a modest price to pay for assurances that things were on track.

For the purposes of keeping the design and building process moving, the layered approach also functioned well. The DSCM staff reviewed plans immediately and discussed any alterations with Greer and KPF within ten days. These were generally based on a "value engineering" philosophy which, with its knowledge of local trades and material costs, allowed DSCM to modify design and construction in ways that saved time and money without sacrificing quality. In the case of the structural system, for instance, substituting thinner, lighter, and more open "stub girders" for traditional steel beams not only lowered costs, but better accommodated ductwork and reduced the floor-to-floor height. Overall, this was an effective and cooperative decision-making framework, and as experts were added for lighting, acoustics, security, and landscaping, they quickly became part of the team. On the very few occasions when Hercules requested consultants to make personnel changes, the situations were resolved through negotiation.

Assuming a positive response to the UDAG application, KPF architects Sheldon Fox and Arthur May used Interspace's conceptual layout and developed proposals for the Wilmington site. During this phase they met twice with Mr. Giacco to elaborate the seven building goals stipulated initially. The chief executive noted later: "We wanted an image that says we're out front, we want to be the best, [and] we don't want to be held down by convention."[7] To implement this mandate, surveys of the surrounding area, including an update on Wilmington's "River to River" master plan, were carried out to assure Hercules that its building would be "out front."

Within a short time, KPF had prepared four alternatives, three atrium schemes and one slab office tower. By the end of March 1980, Mr. Giacco and the project team had reached consensus on a single design and one month later details were being refined. The headquarters' U shape, dramatized by a skylit atrium (see figure 10), would open to a riverfront park on the north; facades would be made of granite and glass; retail

FIGURE 10   The Hercules Atrium (Courtesy Hercules Inc.)

space would be provided on the ground levels to serve both employees and the general public.

Over the next six months the Hercules executives worked tirelessly with the architects, engineers, interior designers, construction manager, and consultants on final specifications. With Greer coordinating this effort, Lacy was responsible for financial matters, contract administration, and relations with the city. He also acted as arbiter and peacemaker when disputes arose among company officials, designers, and the construction manager. His busy schedule was matched by Ronat's, who reviewed space planning and interior proposals and acted as liaison to the Hercules staff.

On a formal level, a full team meeting occurred monthly to review progress, resolve problems, and finalize decisions. At the macro scale, the group determined that a 30′ by 45′ structural grid would be used to provide flexibility and ease of change. In order to provide a comfortable and responsive environment, the building's systems would be divided into quadrants, each floor being regulated by four separate controls for heat, air conditioning, and light. Finally, thermal storage tanks would be built underground to reclaim, store, and recirculate otherwise wasted energy.

At the micro scale, the team made four key decisions: (1) the furniture and building module would be three feet; (2) 90 percent of the work stations would use open-office landscaping; (3) every work station would be compatible with computer and communications equipment; and (4) circulation would run along the perimeter. This last decree gave all employees an opportunity to enjoy views and was especially welcomed by secretaries who hitherto had occupied small inside spaces.

In early June 1980, Wilmington and Hercules received preliminary notice of a $16 million UDAG award. Since the city had already begun to acquire the necessary land, it now seemed certain that the headquarters would be constructed downtown. Still, it took months of negotiations before all parties agreed to a final contract. The issues of sharing the costs and benefits of the retail space and the order in which funds would be spent were particularly difficult to resolve. Timing got down to the wire. By September everything was readied for a presentation to the Hercules board. With meticulous care, a model was prepared, colored perspectives and plans were mounted for display, major features of the headquarters were outlined and final cost estimates were determined. On September 24, 1980, the board unanimously endorsed the venture. The team had proved its mettle.

Events now moved rapidly. A week later the city signed the UDAG contract with HUD. Closing on the land, construction financing, and leaseback arrangements took place on October 3, 1980. Some hundred documents were carefully reviewed and signed. Hercules would own the land and lease the building from an investor group known as Tarleton Associates; the state would build a park on the north side of the headquarters along Brandywine Creek; Hercules would construct a plaza to the south and donate it to the city; and the Wilmington parking authority would begin its thousand-car facility.

On a warm and sunny October 6, distinguished guests joined an enthusiastic crowd for the groundbreaking ceremony. A selected list of those present suggests the event's importance:

Philip M. Klutznick, United States Secretary of Commerce
Joseph R. Biden, United States Senator
Pierre S. du Pont IV, Governor of Delaware
William T. McLaughlin, Mayor of Wilmington
Thomas C. Maloney, Administrator for HUD
David S. Cordish, Director of UDAG for HUD
Alexander F. Giacco, Chairman, President and CEO, Hercules Incorporated
John E. Greer, Assistant Vice President, Hercules Incorporated

All knew that the headquarters would significantly enhance Hercules' image, provide a quality environment for employees and a magnet for visitors, and serve as a cornerstone in Wilmington's renewal.

Construction and Moving In

Excavation began on November 11, 1980. In addition to serving as construction manager, DSCM was also responsible for scheduling contractors, a particularly challenging task. To save time and money, Hercules used a "fast-track" approach which allowed construction to begin before all the contract documents were completed. But managing this process meant that reviewing drawings and design proposals, soliciting bids, tracking budgets, and supervising field work occurred simultaneously. In order to control costs, assure quality, and maintain schedules, Greer, Lacy, and Ronat arranged for daily site visits and gave immediate attention to the architect's recommendations and to continued input from DSMC. Formal updates were held weekly and the budget was thoroughly analyzed once a month. Informally, team members were in daily contact and no effort was spared to solve problems or disputes immediately, even if it meant working long into the night. In addition, materials and craftsmanship were carefully inspected by Hercules' management. The constant attention paid off since changes—such as the redesign of drywall details around the elevator core—were quite modest.

As the superstructure went up, detailed interior plans were developed. Marketing and leasing strategies for the ground floor retail area were in the hands of the Wilmington-based Bellevue Holding Company. Knowledgeable about local economic conditions, Bellevue suggested two alternatives: a high-profile galleria of thirty small boutiques or a more modest group of shops, open to the public but primarily meant to serve employees. Although it meant subsidizing certain rents, Hercules opted for the second scheme because it reinforced the headquarter image and improved security. Executives also believed that Wilmington's River to River master plan would attract growing numbers of people downtown and that gradually subsidies could be reduced or eliminated.

With the exception of the executive levels which were designed by a firm associated with KPF, Interspace was responsible for interior layout. To facilitate office relocation, Hercules used a poke-through wiring system and an open plan. To implement this decision, Interspace invited employees to test four different systems for an entire year. The results were a secretarial space and several work stations made of handsome oak and fabric-covered components that easily accepted computers and other communications equipment and that could be combined and modified to suit the needs of various staffs. The reaction of Hercules' lawyers to this approach was particularly interesting. Initially reluctant to surrender their private offices, this group, after seeing and using the mock-ups, was so impressed by the versatility and beauty of the furniture that they became supporters of the design. Finally, to further personalize space and give each level its own identity, the colors for elevator lobbies and corridors alternated between blue on even-numbered and maroon on odd-numbered floors.

Patricia Conway of Kohn Pederson Fox Conway interior designers was in charge of the eighth- and ninth-floor executive spaces. In addition to offices for the chairman, the vice chairman, and five vice presidents, this was the area for a conference room, boardroom, and executive dining room. A dramatic staircase connecting the two levels gives its own punctuation mark to the Hercules statement and enclosed offices ensure privacy and signal status. Mr. Giacco's space is tastefully appointed with traditional furnishings accented with marble and rosewood details (see figure 11) and offices for each vice president are similarly decorated. All enjoy a dramatic vista across the rooftops of Wilmington.

FIGURE 11   The Chief Executive's Office (Courtesy Hercules Inc.)

A final concern was with the interior atrium, the entrance plaza, and the park to the north. Although control over these areas was divided among Hercules, the city, and the state, all agreed to hire the Watertown, Massachusetts, landscape firm Sasaki Associates to design the spaces. Each has a distinct character. Although graced with benches and trees, the plaza is hard and urban; the atrium is lush and warm with a waterfall and dense planting; the park is relaxed and open with grassy mounds and winding paths. At the same time, because brick pavers and granite trim are used throughout, there is an elegance and unity to the scheme that, with less cooperation, might have been missing.

With its bright offices and modern equipment, the new headquarters was a positive and dramatic change for Hercules employees. Still, change—even for the better—can disrupt operations and make people restive. To smooth the transition, the design team, KPF, Interspace, and the public relations office published periodic reports in *Horizons*, the in-house newsletter, which outlined the construction and occupancy schedules and illustrated the open-space plan. In addition, two video tapes were produced to introduce employees to the project. Six months prior to the move, managers reviewed and finalized space assignments and responded to staff questions. And before the building was opened to the press and general public, there was a special tour for present and retired employees.

Spring brought excitement as everyone prepared for the move. Boxes were packed and numbered, and for three days trucks shuttled between the Delaware Trust Building and the new office, four blocks away. On May 31, 1983, Hercules Plaza was officially open for business. While there were minor frustrations, a "hotline" handled these immediate concerns and within two hours it was "business as usual." After a few weeks almost all problems were corrected and people began to feel at home.

Since about 1,350 people worked in a headquarters designed for 1,700, there was a cushion of flexibility. Combining this aspect with the building's prestige and visibility, its advanced facilities, and its quality furnishings, management considers Hercules Plaza an investment that will pay dividends in terms of both productivity and pride for decades to come. At the June 28 dedication ceremony, Mr. Giacco noted that with the new headquarters has come "a revitalized *esprit de corps*, a renewed sense of pride."[8] A year after the building opened, more tangible changes were apparent. Employees were dressing better; attracting talented staff and managers was easier; paperwork was reduced and communications improved.[9]

It should be added that the company now gives prominent attention to art. Over five hundred paintings, prints, posters and sculptures, many by local artists, grace office walls and the atrium bridges. Fifteen works were specifically purchased or commissioned for the building. A statue by Annabelle Eckels reflects the *Zeitgeist*. Titled *The Women of Hercules* (see figure 12), it has been placed in the visitors' lounge, and in a similarly visible location, the plaza fountain contains a fascinating piece composed of marble spheres rotating on a thin film of water.

A Note on Finances

As mentioned earlier, during a period of high inflation, final costs were only 0.3 percent above the 1980 estimate. Typical of the entire building process, this achievement was due to a thorough analysis of the financing and ownership options. Originally Goldman Sachs concluded that leasing was better than owning. Commercial paper was then sold by the Tarleton Associates Limited Partnership (one of the first times this was done) that, along with the UDAG loan, covered the mort-

FIGURE 12 "The Women of Hercules" by Annabelle Eckels (Courtesy Hercules Inc.)

gage. Alterations to the tax laws in 1981, however, made ownership more favorable, producing a savings of about $3 million. The drawbacks to changes were that Tarleton Associates had already made substantial financial commitments and that Hercules would have to pay $2 million in transfer taxes.

An ingenious solution resulted in a "sandwich" corporation known as Sector. Tarleton would lease the headquarters to Sector which, in turn, would lease it to Hercules for a predetermined and gradually increasing rent over thirty years. Hercules' initial cash flow would be very low. Further, with modest inflation and through wise investment of the money saved, the company could cover the cost of higher rents later on.

Obviously, financing is just one of many elements that distinguishes this case as a model of excellence. Beyond benefits to the corporation, the building has been a catalyst for significant urban renewal. Nearby, the first floor of the parking garage includes a fitness club, a drug store, dry cleaners, and a day-care center. To the east, Wilmington Trust recently completed an office tower incorporating a former U.S. Post Office as part of the design. The Waterworks Cafe revitalized an old riverfront building. Blue Cross and Blue Shield has renovated its structure, and a nineteenth-century flour mill has been restored as the centerpiece of a downtown housing development.

Hercules is proud of its headquarters and its continuing relationship with the city. The city, in turn, working with federal and state authorities, has reasons for its own pride. Big projects require big people. In this instance, the company, city, state, and federal government provided such people.

Evaluation

It is difficult to fault Hercules' approach to design and construction and many companies might wish to duplicate its experience. A critique of the process suggests that three points are particularly instructive. The first lesson highlights the value of early and clearly defined objectives and priorities as a basis for future decisions. The second demonstrates a method for assessing the talents and responsibilities needed to balance the project team, including input from public officials. The third illustrates how effective communication and design management make critical contributions to success. The maxims provide a framework for more detailed analysis.

Maxim One: Integrate Multiple Perspectives

From the moment Hercules determined to build, senior executives were explicit about the needs and objectives. Interspace was hired to investigate square-footage requirements and optimum interior layouts. DiSabatino CM prepared budget estimates and Goldman Sachs looked into financial aspects of the venture. Within the company, Alexander Giacco established the priorities of schedule and budget. A tour of similar facilities helped set quality standards and, working with this information, Greer and his associates were able to develop a list of specific architectural goals. It was a well orchestrated plan, resulting in a building program that not only saved time and money but complemented the firm's reorganization and its team culture.

The only missing elements were guidelines for the design of spaces for senior management. Discussions of this topic are sometimes avoided because they sound self-serving and even connote luxury and waste. In this regard, while Hercules' statements emphasize efficiency and quality, its actions suggest a broader range of motives. It is especially interesting that a second interiors firm was chosen for the executive levels where, in addition to function and comfort, prestige was important. Perhaps this was necessary because the design team did not explore the issue of image as thoroughly as it had other goals. Even with this omission, Hercules deserves a "superior" rating (6.0 out of 7.5 points) for its capable handling of the executive perspective.

Employee contributions to the headquarters were more modest. Hercules did only what most companies do. They interviewed a cross section of managers; they tested furniture systems; they briefed staff on progress. The new offices have been well received. This may be due more, however, to the improved amenities of the building and the sense of identity and cohesiveness it generated than to employee input. Here, the Hercules effort deserves an "average" rating (3.0 out of 5.0 points).

It is unusual for a firm as innovative as Kohn Pederson Fox and a corporation as cost and schedule-conscious as Hercules to have such compatible relationships. The happy marriage is all the more noteworthy since a space planner/interiors consultant and a construction manager were hired before the architects, a situation that often results in competition. Yet, with the exception of the executive offices noted above, members of the design team shared common goals, listened well, and spoke a language everyone understood. This facilitated cooperation and successful risk-taking. Aesthetically, Hercules was more daring. KPF allowed others to contribute to design process. Interspace pushed an approach that combined beauty *and* efficiency. In this case, the rating of the architectural perspective is "superior" (2.0 out of 2.5 points).

Maxim Two: Emphasize Casting

It is obvious that Hercules put together a highly qualified project team. This was possible because executives matched goals with talent. Having no precise definition of space and organizational requirements, the corporation hired Interspace to provide it. Knowing that budget and schedule were critical, the chief executive appointed a full-time in-house staff to manage those issues. Looking for designers who were simultaneously creative and disciplined—namely, able to work with limitations and as part of a team—Hercules interviewed until they found just the right combination of skill and commitment. Finally, open to the option of remaining in Wilmington, corporate officers told government leaders what they needed and cooperated with efforts to make it happen. It is apparent that Hercules dealt capably with many actors and roles and, therefore, appropriately receives an "excellent" rating (2.5 out of 2.5 points).

If finding talented people is difficult, casting them well is an even greater challenge. Guided by an honest assessment of its own abilities on a project beyond normal operations, Hercules made three of its own managers coordinators and left the rest of the work to consultants. It was an effective balance. All were assigned to the jobs they did best. DSCM watched the budget and construction; Interspace and KPF worked on planning and design; Goldman Sachs monitored financial strategies; Greer, Lacy and Ronat made sure all the pieces fit and were on schedule. Open and frank communication characterized the organization. Informal meetings were held several times a week; complete reviews occurred at least monthly; and daily visits to the site were the norm after excavations had begun. Substitutions in the team or additional help were rarely needed. Overall, Hercules' approach to casting was "superior" (6.0 out of 7.5 points).

Maxim Three: Sift for Relevant Facts

It is natural to assume that a chemical products company would place a premium on research. Such an attitude, however, was not evident in the Hercules case. It was more a process of gathering the latest gadgets without asking whether the gadgets actually improved the situation. Executives insisted on advanced technology including computers and communications equipment, closed circuit television, a production studio, and videoconference rooms. In addition, the structure has automated mail service, sophisticated security and alarm devices, and energy-efficient mechanical systems. Nevertheless, no one analyzed in depth how these enhanced productivity and efficiency. While it may have been too soon after a major reorganization for this kind of investigation, senior managers can still take advantage of this research with a thorough post-occupancy evaluation.

With respect to interior flexibility, the project team tested several different furniture systems and developed a structural bay that facilitated the layout of offices. Yet, with the exception of perimeter spaces that remained free so everyone could enjoy the views, the actual design was conservative and rearranging work stations will require a good amount of effort and expense. In the area of image, Mr. Giacco likes to note proudly that the new headquarters has made Wilmington a "two-horse town." While the assessment is true, it was achieved by selecting creative designers rather than by carefully weighing alternatives. This intuitive approach can yield success; it can also result in expensive and embarrassing failures. In general, the Hercules research effort was good if not particularly innovative and the company, therefore, merits an "average" rating in both the awareness and issues aspects of this category (6.0 out of 10.0 points).

Maxim Four: Manage Pluralistic Decision-Making

The bold design of Hercules Plaza suggests that image was the essence of the project. But an analysis of the order in which consultants were employed points to other priorities. In the chronology of events (see figure 13), the space planner, the construction manager, and the financial consultant were all hired before the architect. It was an unusual sequence, especially for a headquarters. In this case, however, where money, time,

October	1977	Alexander Giacco Appointed President and Chief Executive
March	1979	Rumors Hercules May Leave Delaware
July	1979	Hercules Will Stay in Delaware Interspace Hired—Programming and Interiors In-House Project Team Appointed
November	1979	DiSabatino CM Hired—Construction Manager
January	1980	Building Goals Announced Goldman Sachs—Financial Advisor
March	1980	Hercules Will Stay in Wilmington Under Certain Conditions Architect Selected and Hired First Full Design Briefing
April	1980	Application for UDAG Grant Schematic Design Approved
July	1980	Preliminary Notice of UDAG Award
September	1980	Approval of Design and Budget by Hercules Board
October	1980	Groundbreaking
November	1980	Excavation Begins
1981 thru	1983	Construction Interior Design Testing and Proposals
May	1983	Move to New Headquarters
June	1983	Dedication

FIGURE 13   Hercules Plaza—Chronology

and efficiency were as important as aesthetics, the process helped keep people focused on goals rather than positions. Participants knew that unrealistic proposals would quickly be rejected and that innovation and style would result from team brainstorming instead of individual inspiration. In this sense, the designers and engineers developed the building's form; the construction manager suggested modifications to the structure and materials; the interior and landscape consultants prepared schemes to enhance productivity and beauty. Here, success was due to everyone's contributions.

Inevitably there were differences of opinion, but the criteria for making judgements and the responsibilities of senior Hercules executives for final decisions were spelled out from the beginning. This encouraged consensus and, while it may have appeared to dampen creativity, it responded to the team corporate culture and assured that information reached the highest levels of management. Since there were many benefits to this system, Hercules deserves an "excellent" rating in pluralistic decision-making (15.0 out of 15.0 points).

Conclusion

With a total score of forty and a half, the design process for Hercules Plaza distinguishes itself as clearly above average. If there were any weaknesses, they were in research and the definition of image. The areas of management and casting were especially strong and worthy of emulation.

ARCHITECTURE AND THE CORPORATION

HERCULES INCORPORATED—HERCULES PLAZA

MAXIM		CORPORATE TASKS	MAX PTS	RATING	ACT PTS
MULTIPLE PERSPECTIVES	The Managerial Perspective	Define Objectives and Priorities			
		Establish Standards of Quality			
		Articulate Corporate Values	7.5	SUPERIOR	6.0
	The Employee Perspective	Seek Employee Participation	5.0	AVERAGE	3.0
	The Architectural Perspective	Look for a Compatible Marriage with the Architect	2.5	SUPERIOR	2.0
		MAXIMUM SUBTOTAL	15.0	ACTUAL	11.0
CASTING	A Multitude of Actors and Roles	Appoint the In-House Players			
		Hire Outside Managers			
		Select the Design Team			
		Work with Key Public Actors	2.5	EXCELLENT	2.5
	Assembling the Cast	Determine the Mix of In-House vs. Outside Services			
		Stress the CCC Syndrome: Commitment, Communications, and Competence	7.5	SUPERIOR	6.0
		MAXIMUM SUBTOTAL	10.0	ACTUAL	8.5
RESEARCH	Design Research	Turn Facts into Options	2.5	AVERAGE	1.5
	Critical Topics	Study Technology, Layout and Image	7.5	AVERAGE	4.5
		MAXIMUM SUBTOTAL	10.0	ACTUAL	6.0
DECISION-MAKING	Elements in Design Management	Emphasize Goals, Not Positions			
		Develop Consensus			
		Integrate Decision-Making and Culture	15.0	EXCELLENT	15.0
		MAXIMUM SUBTOTAL	15.0	ACTUAL	15.0
		MAXIMUM TOTAL	50.0	ACTUAL	40.5

5

Building the Company—The Beneficial Design Program

BENEFICIAL MANAGEMENT CORPORATION
PEAPACK, NEW JERSEY
PROJECT INITIATED: 1977
PROJECT COMPLETED: 1982

Summary

FOR more than sixty years, Beneficial Corporation could count itself among the majority of American firms that had little or no track record in design. In the late 1970s, however, this situation changed. Growth required expanded facilities and, with the appointment of a new chief executive, this need was translated into a mandate for a new headquarters. While first proposals for the project fell through, the financial services company's commitment to people and quality helped it persevere despite discouraging news. The delay also permitted architectural objectives to be refined, a process that ultimately resulted in an award-winning design.

During the three years it took to build Beneficial Center, executives learned more than just the "ins and outs" of construction. They became increasingly sensitive to the contributions design could make to other aspects of business. By the mid-1980s, additional decisions in this area included an extensive corporate identity program and the renovation of

(Architect: The Hillier Group)

hundreds of local offices—efforts that have begun to pay off in terms of reinvigorating employee pride, reconfirming consumer confidence, and improving financial vitality. Beneficial's approach yields several conclusions:

1. The full spectrum of design as a business tool exploits interiors, graphics, and products as well as architecture;
2. Effective use of design is a process that can be learned; and
3. Dedicated leadership and perseverance are essential to success.

Background

Imagine walking among the classical red brick buildings and intimate quadrangles of a small nineteenth-century college. Imagine further, just beyond the surrounding villages, a tranquil woodland setting alive with the music of a stream meandering through the hills and meadows. It is an ideal picture but, to a large degree, a happy reality for those who work at Beneficial Center. This is the main office of Beneficial Corporation, a financial services holding company with more than thirteen thousand employees and revenues of $1.8 billion in 1984.[1] It is also headquarters for several subsidiaries including Beneficial Management Corporation, Beneficial Data Processing Corporation, and credit insurance subsidiaries.

Located near the villages of Peapack and Gladstone, New Jersey, about fifty miles from New York City, the entrance to this campus-like complex is a tree-lined drive that leads to a clock tower and arcade. Past this symbolic center, a relaxed composition of Palladian-style offices are nestled into the landscape and related to one another around a piazza, a courtyard, fountains, terraces, and parks. Details such as copper roofing, dormer windows, and handsome chimneys reinforce the warm and human-scaled atmosphere. That this was to become a special place to work was noted in the American Institute of Architects' *Journal* when its critic commented that the "total effect is a satisfying and rare combination of grace and logic."[2]

Yet architecture is only part of the story. In addition to the buildings, the corporate logo and visual communications system have been redesigned, hundreds of loan offices across the country have been renovated, and an architect has been named to the parent corporation's board where he serves on its influential Strategic Planning and Evaluation Committee. Together, the actions highlight a conviction by company executives that design excellence is an essential facet of their business. For Beneficial Corporation, design is a critical interface between the firm and its many constituencies: its employees, the local community, its clients, the financial community, and the general public. Thus, while Beneficial Center is seen and used almost exclusively by those who work there, it is a sign of the organization's broader commitment to quality management and quality service.

The awareness of design's value matured slowly. Founded in 1914 as the Beneficial Loan Society, the company was established to serve workers, lending money based on wages rather than collateral. The rationale for the enterprise was straightforward: common laborers as well as the affluent needed access to loans. It was also successful. By the end of World War I, the enterprise boasted seventeen offices and within another decade the figure had mushroomed to more than two hundred. Expansion into Canada occurred in 1933 and a London branch was opened in 1959. Today, Beneficial Corporation and its subsidiaries offer consumer finance and insurance services to individuals in the United States, Canada, the United Kingdom, and West Germany.

Inevitably, more than seventy years of growth translated into changing facility requirements and, in Beneficial's case, led to headquarters in a variety of locations. Top management had worked in Elizabeth and Newark, New Jersey, and New York City. Today, because it is legally incorporated in Delaware, Wilmington is the home of the parent company. Yet from 1955 until the completion of Beneficial Center in 1982, central operations were in Morristown, New Jersey. Generally, space was leased. The company built one "neo-colonial" structure for its own use but the firm traditionally defined image in terms of people and services rather than in terms of architecture. It was more concerned with what it did than what its buildings said—a priority revealed in its nondescript mix of offices.

With the election of Finn M. W. Caspersen as chief executive officer in 1976 the situation changed. Mr. Caspersen, a lawyer from a prestigious New York firm, became associate counsel to Beneficial Management in 1972. In November 1975 he was named vice chairman of the board of the entire Beneficial Corporation and, less than a year later, chairman. Under his leadership, the company's assets rose from $2.7 to over $7.7 billion[3] and operations in Morristown expanded into twelve different buildings.

The impressive growth in no way diminished the firm's emphasis on people and on service. Mr. Caspersen himself set the example by volunteer work with a local school board and with a foundation created to aid diabetic children.[4] But the most visible corporate expressions of the chief executive's priorities were in the areas of architecture and graphics. Since the late 1970s, Beneficial has come to recognize that quality design not only responds to the physical and aesthetic needs of employees but also reinforces corporate values that stress attention to the customer as the surest guarantee of financial success. Pragmatism, more than idealism, underlies this business philosophy. In 1977 it was abundantly clear that customer satisfaction meant continued growth and that growth, coupled with expansion into new markets, would overwhelm the Morristown facilities. Projections indicated space and communication problems would become particularly severe by the end of the decade. Given these facts, Mr. Caspersen made a presentation to the board's Executive Committee which endorsed the search for potential sites during the summer of 1977. The single stipulation in the effort was that the move be within a twenty-mile radius of Morristown. Beneficial had a talented and dedicated work force and, by staying close to its old home, hoped to avoid unnecessary turnover.

The First Proposal

In early September 1977, all appeared to be moving according to schedule when the company secured an option on a 1500-acre tract in the nearby townships of Bedminster and Bernards. The land was ample and attractive. But during the next several months executives learned that it would take more than enthusiasm, acreage, and a reasonable design to get the job done. The surrounding communities were small, generally affluent, and especially sensitive to environmental issues. Indeed, in a rezoning process begun before Beneficial had shown interest in the area, many residents wanted the large parcel designated "open land," noting the adverse effects development might have on air, noise, traffic, schools, and the water system. And when asked specifically about the proposed corporate headquarters, the mayor of Bedminster stated simply: "It's not wanted here. . . . [It] would mean headaches for us."[5]

Beneficial was sympathetic to the communities' views and wanted to address their concerns. To this end, the company hired environmental consultants Jason M. Cortell and Associates, Incorporated (JMCA) from Waltham, Massachusetts. JMCA had done similar analyses for AT&T's complex in Bedminster and had a reputation for responding realistically and sensitively to this kind of situation. The commission to the firm was to:

1. Thoroughly evaluate the site;
2. Determine building approaches that minimized adverse environmental impact; and
3. Assist with the selection of architects.

To monitor and comment on progress, an in-house Building Committee was established. Gordon L. Wadmond, executive vice president with responsibilities for facility management and personnel, and Charles E. Hance, litigation counsel, co-chaired this group. Wadmond's twenty-three years with Beneficial gave him a unique familiarity with space needs, the operating styles of various subsidiaries, rates of growth and, most significantly, an awareness of what employees—from senior management to clerks—valued in their work areas and in their relationships to the company. Hance's talents complemented Wadmond's. Joining the firm in 1975, he had dealt with a variety of legal questions and, as this undertaking required complex contractural arrangements and the ability to sort out detailed zoning and environmental procedures, his skills were important. In addition, ten other representatives from key departments provided input and served as intermediaries with fellow workers.

A potential site in hand, the immediate challenge confronting JMCA and the Building Committee was selection of a designer. The consultant suggested six architects and five accepted the invitation to make a presentation. After a busy week of meetings, the choice was narrowed to two.

At follow-up discussions, the finalists gave complete profiles of their principals and the consultants working with them, outlined criteria for the optimal relationship with the Beneficial team, and described techniques for keeping the project on schedule. By the end of September 1977, the corporation chose the designers that seemed most responsive.

Work over the next three months was intense. No energy was spared in efforts to secure preliminary approval from the municipalities before a December 31 rezoning deadline. Models and plans were developed; environmental studies were completed; reports were written; applications were filed; meetings were held; and two distinct proposals were presented—the first to Bedminster and the second to Bernards. Still, while executives believed that the communities had much to gain from the company's presence, township officials concluded that traffic and housing problems, above and beyond the pressures created by AT&T's offices, would be overwhelming. Before year's end, it was clear that Beneficial would not receive the necessary rezoning. As one member of Bernards' Planning Board questioned, with all the potential difficulties, "How neighborly would it be for Bernards to permit a headquarters so near the municipal line, and permit the traffic to go through Bedminister?"[6]

While disappointment with such attitudes was keen, the community resistance was a great learning experience. To avoid further delay and uncertainty, corporate leaders made two decisions: (1) to look for land that was already appropriately zoned; and (2) to complete the detailed building program. The figures resulting from this latter mandate were impressive: the gross area totaled more than one million square feet with operations, broken down by company and division, occupying about 570,000 square feet and underground parking and remote garages adding another 478,000 square feet.

Fortunately, as the months passed, the Building Committee also grew more articulate about the character and image it expected in the new headquarters. In a series of significant discussions, for which there had been no time during the rush to complete the first design, the Committee learned that most employees enjoyed the red brick facades and the three or four-story scale of the Morristown offices; the staff felt comfortable with the intimate atmosphere provided by several smaller structures rather than a single large one. Having gathered these facts, Beneficial abandoned its original scheme, which had called for large floors and expansive terraces, and the Building Committee decided to hire another architect who would communicate better with executives and approach the project with a fresh outlook toward design.

102

A New Site and a New Design Team

Prospects for the project improved in spring of 1978 when Beneficial evaluated a 300-acre site (100 acres of which were zoned industrial) in a community known as the Borough of Peapack and Gladstone. Rolling meadows, a stream, and clusters of pine and hardwood trees made the land attractive; a location that straddled both sides of a state highway and close proximity to two interstates made it convenient; sufficient acreage to build and still preserve the natural beauty made it environmentally appealing. Such assets were powerful arguments for purchase and, once borough officials indicated their general enthusiasm for the headquarters, Beneficial bought the land in June. The first lesson from community rejection had been mastered: make sure the corporation is welcome *before* getting deeply involved in negotiations.

As they had done earlier, JMCA and the Building Committee now had to choose an architect. Before beginning a new search, they decided to review the firms considered the previous September—plus one new contender, The Hillier Group from Princeton, New Jersey. This last company was included for two reasons: (1) it was not far from Morristown, which meant the designers were familiar with the area; and (2) Mr. Caspersen, while attending a trustees meeting at Brown University, had visited a building the architects had done for Butler Hospital in Providence—and liked what he saw. It was a situation encountered many times by designers: clients prefer to see what architects have done rather than hear claims about what they can do.

Despite this recommendation, Wadmond and Hance remained keenly aware that Beneficial required a professional who listened well and could interpret the company's philosophy in spatial terms. This meant finding a firm that could creatively respond to certain objectives the Building Committee had distilled regarding environmental, functional, and aesthetic requirements. With this information and the memory of past experience, the two executives interviewed the Princeton architects to determine how innovative *and* cooperative they might be.

Not unexpectedly, discussions with J. Robert Hillier and his associate, John Pearce, focused on processes rather than buildings and, in particular, on the potential communications and working relationships among the architects, the consultants and the corporation. Citing examples of procedures it had used for companies such as AT&T, Allied Chemical, and W.R. Grace Company, The Hillier Group demonstrated how its approach would harmonize with Beneficial's goals. Hillier himself explained the

103

firm's philosophy: "I don't think of us as creators, but rather as translators of a client's ideas. . . . We adapt our designs to the client's needs, taste and budget. When a project is completed, it stands as a monument to the client, not to us."[7] The quote recalled the attitudes of architects during the Middle Ages and the Italian Renaissance, and the Beneficial managers were impressed. After Hillier gave assurances that he personally would be intimately involved with the work, his company was commissioned to do the design.

The ensuing weeks were especially busy. Aware of the high priority local communities placed on the environment (see figure 14), Hillier and Pearce met with representatives of the Borough of Peapack and Gladstone's Planning Board and learned that traffic, water, sewage, and the scale of the headquarters were major concerns. Conversations with Mr. Caspersen, the Building Committee and department heads reaffirmed the space requirements and established that the Beneficial complex should be a cluster of relatively small structures with a conservative "colonial" appearance. Based on information from all these sources, the architects developed three preliminary concepts: a campus-like scheme, a charming village, and a series of landscaped pavilions. After reviewing the various sketches and models, Mr. Caspersen and the Executive Committee opted for the village theme—a group of low-scale offices and landscaped courts along a corporate street.

FIGURE 14   The Charming Village of Peapack (Photo by Eugene A. Shenesky, Jr.)

The team charged with translating these ideas into reality represented a diversity of talent. Beneficial depended on JMCA to address environmental issues, The Hillier Group to refine design, and Garmen Associates to solve traffic problems. This last consultant was a local firm. It dealt knowledgeably with state and federal authorities and had a good reputation among corporate clients such as Exxon and Bell Labs, and in towns such as Trenton, Paterson, and others in New Jersey. In parallel fashion, the architects established their own partnerships, reconfirming professional ties with highly qualified structural, mechanical, and electrical engineers as well as with a landscape architect. Worth noting is the fact that both Beneficial and The Hillier Group based these relationships on the same criteria: skill, communication, and cooperation.

JMCA also assisted the Building Committee in choosing a construction manager and contractor for the project. It was a crucial decision because this firm would evaluate the cost effectiveness of various design decisions, oversee and perform phased construction of the project and, at some predetermined point, guarantee a maximum price for the entire job. After discussions with about half a dozen candidates, Turner Construction was selected because former clients uniformly felt that the company maintained close control over schedules and consistently made recommendations that resulted in significant savings. This confidence was amplified by the fact that New York–based Turner was one of the largest general contractors in the nation, had a seventy-eight-year building record for corporations such as Polaroid, General Electric, and Standard Oil of Ohio, and could boast in its brochure that "over half our projects are for repeat clients. . . . [an] expression of trust . . . unequaled by any other leading building contractor in America."[8]

In terms of organization (see figure 15), JMCA, Garmen Associates, The Hillier Group, Turner Construction, and Innerplan (an interiors firm hired after the building shell had been designed) reported directly to Beneficial but shared recommendations with the designers. Other professionals, including the engineers, landscape, acoustical, and audio/visual consultants, coordinated their work through the architects. To monitor the project, formal meetings were held biweekly. Key members of the Building Committee, Bob Hillier and John Pearce, Thomas Gerlach (Turner's senior representative), and Jason Cortell (JMCA's principal) were usually in attendance. When important issues such as traffic, mechanical systems, or interiors were under consideration, consultants from those areas were also present. Every six months Beneficial's board was given a status report and any decision that added more than $250,000 to costs had to be approved by the corporation's Executive Committee.

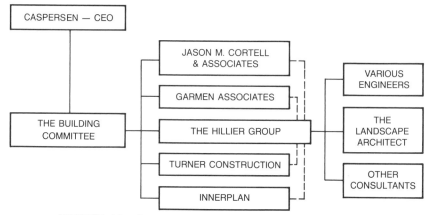

FIGURE 15   Organization of the Beneficial Design Team

Design Development

During the early part of summer, the corporation and the design team renewed their commitment to the village concept and coordinated efforts to resolve large-scale planning and building issues. In its site analysis, JMCA evaluated soils, vegetation, wildlife, topography, water quality, air, noise, visual and historic resources, and land use. The transportation and utilities consultants made their recommendations. Finally, Hillier and Pearce reviewed these reports in order to identify areas most suitable for construction. Of the 150 acres in the eastern half of the site, approximately thirty were needed for the complex itself. Then, by choosing a location south of a small stream, the architects were able to preserve much of the property's natural beauty, create a harmonious relationship between the headquarters and the nearby villages, and reserve the northern parcel for modest future expansion.

Next came the job of translating space needs into specific buildings. After carefully studying many alternatives, ten structures were arranged along a combination of courtyards, gardens, and terraces (see figures 16a and b), and connected by broad underground passages for easy year-round access. This blend of elegance and practicality was evident throughout. The designs for the Beneficial Insurance Group (Buildings 5 and 6) and Beneficial Data Processing Corporation (Buildings 7 and 8) featured handsome arches and Palladian windows and allowed for growth with over 270,000 square feet of space. The executive areas (Building 10) were planned around a dramatic three-story domed octagon and contained thirty-three thousand square feet for offices, meeting, and dining facilities. Beneficial Management Corporation and other subsidiaries were housed in four pavilions near the "village" clock tower (Buildings

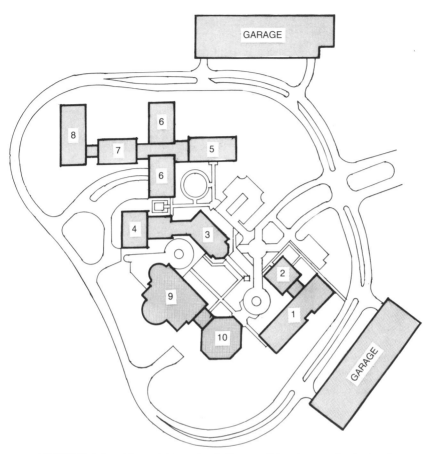

FIGURE 16a   Plan of Beneficial Center (Numbers refer to text)

FIGURE 16b   Architect's Model of Beneficial Center (Courtesy Beneficial
Management Corporation of America)

1, 2, 3 and 4). With dormer windows and colonnaded halls, these two- and three-story edifices had an attractive human scale that belied their aggregate size of almost two hundred thousand square feet. The last oblong structure (Building 9 with sixty-six thousand square feet), had large semicircular bays overlooking the stream and meadows and included the main dining facility and other employee services. A ring road surrounded the complex and was the approach to the four hundred underground parking spaces and to the two large garages off to the sides.

While Peapack and Gladstone officials had been happy with initial presentations on Beneficial Center, they were especially pleased when the architectural details were revealed. The completed project promised to bring economic *and* aesthetic contributions to the borough. Still, euphoria was tempered by concern over three specific items: building heights, sewage treatment, and traffic control. The fire marshall worried that his ladders would not reach the tops of the taller buildings envisioned by the designers, but after Beneficial received a height variance and helped purchase new emergency equipment, this official expressed confidence that his volunteers could handle most problems. To meet the need for increased sewage treatment, the corporation financed flow devices which enhanced the efficiency and capacity of the existing plant so that it more than met the demands of the villages and the company. To minimize congestion on Route 206, and maintain important vistas, Beneficial proposed an underpass at the entrance to the headquarters, even though the traffic consultant noted that an on-grade design would be several hundred thousand dollars less expensive. The company also enlarged a nearby intersection and installed a signal light. Together, these improvements added more than $5 million to costs, and when they were combined with a plan for staggered work hours and van pooling, most residents were reassured that Beneficial would be a good neighbor in every sense of the word.

There was also another critical "people" problem: how to convince Beneficial employees that relocation would be worthwhile. In a 1981 memo to the Executive Committee, Gordon Wadmond wrote: "We are all concerned with the problem of potential loss of personnel when we move to Peapack/Gladstone as well as how to attract new personnel from the general area in view of the strong competitive market." After outlining financial and educational programs calculated to make the transition easier, he commented how the buildings themselves were "both attractive and retentive (enhancing worker loyalty)." He emphasized how luncheon facilities would look out on a panoramic view of the countryside (see figure 17); how exercise rooms, saunas, tennis courts,

FIGURE 17   Beneficial's Gracious Dining Room (Courtesy the author)

ball fields, and other previously unavailable activities would serve the staff's physical needs; and how a small store in the complex, as well as coffee and tea stations near offices, would make work more convenient and pleasurable.[9] In addition, the headquarters would have a barber shop, gas station, check-cashing operation, and an automated mail-delivery system. Finally, there would be the interior spaces themselves, with about 1200 windows providing ample natural light and access to beautiful vistas. Remarkable about the Wadmond memorandum was the broad appeal of the attractions it described. It did not promise Shangri-La or Camelot. It did outline a project where employees were regarded as invaluable assets who made important contributions to corporate success. The memo was, in short, the translation of Beneficial's service-oriented philosophy into concrete realities.

To design offices and work stations and carry out many of the details in this program, the corporation hired a facilities planning expert. Made part of the team during spring 1979, the consultant was known as Innerplan and had a list of clients that included Nieman-Marcus, IBM, and the Sun Company. This specialist reported directly to the Building Committee and was engaged to complement the talents of The Hillier Group. While architect John Pearce lamented that the firm should have been hired earlier to help develop building configurations, the interior designers still managed to devise an effective scheme. After extensive interviews with Beneficial department heads, a two-track approach was adopted. Conforming to a traditional view, senior executive offices were enclosed and located on the perimeter; however, to give all workers the advantages of natural light as well as to preserve views and flexibility, outside rooms were kept to a minimum and staggered throughout the plan. Open offices were provided for mid-level managers, secretaries, and other support personnel. Acoustically treated 72″ panels were used to give privacy and an area for intensive work, while 42″ panels defined spaces where communications were important or where people worked in small groups.

Approval and Construction

With the exception of the interior specifications just described, the design of Beneficial Center was essentially finished early in 1979. It was time, then, for complete presentations to the citizens of Peapack and Gladstone and to the Beneficial board. The Hillier Group prepared an elaborate model and drawings; JMCA completed a voluminous environmental impact statement; Turner drafted a twenty-eight-month construction schedule.

The critical review by the Borough of Peapack and Gladstone's Planning Board came during March 1979. Although different aspects of the project had been discussed at more than a dozen meetings, this session brought the moment of truth to approve or disapprove the proposal. The Building Committee and the design team had been conscientious in their work with town officials and were reasonably confident of support; at the same time, previous experience cautioned them not to count the chickens before they hatched. Representing Beneficial, Charles Hance emphasized how the corporation saw itself as a responsible citizen who had made every effort to preserve and enhance the area's beauty. And in case "persuasion by aesthetics" faltered, there was a potent financial argument: Beneficial Center would represent slightly more than half the borough's real estate tax base. Architect Bob Hillier, pointing out the design highlights of the complex, paid particular attention to matters of scale and building detail; JMCA's Jason Cortell stressed the project's minimal impact on noise, water, and traffic and its harmony with the area's natural beauty. Even more reassuring was the company's pledge to monitor environmental concerns for two years after job completion. Beneficial was not going to ignore unanticipated problems: it was there to stay and staying meant sensitivity to community needs. That final reactions were extremely positive was demonstrated when the Planning Board unanimously recommended to the Board of Adjustment that it, too, give approval. The second review went equally well, especially after a consultant hired by the town of Bedminster reported that this was "one of the best-conceived proposals with which I have had the privilege of being involved. . . . Numerous potential problems were identified and solved before they happened or even had to be debated."[10]

When Beneficial's board met on May 22, 1979, the mood was upbeat. The directors examined site plan and model, budget and construction schedule, and heard Chairman Caspersen's report on the Peapack/Gladstone meetings. Excavation began in July and formal groundbreaking occurred on August 16.

Plans called for construction to proceed on a "fast-track" schedule. Turner immediately started foundations and structural work while The Hillier Group finished drawings and specifications for the building exteriors, public areas and landscaping. Once the construction manager received these documents, experts analyzed them to suggest modifications (changes in finishes, slight adjustments to the design) that could save money without significant reductions in quality. To keep on top of the budget, monthly updates were submitted to Beneficial, and as an added incentive to control costs, after a maximum price had been determined, Turner would receive up to 25 percent of any savings below the specified amount. Within the corporation, a project manager was appointed to make daily site inspections, submit weekly progress reports to the Building Committee, and check drawings and specifications for completeness.

To preserve the carefully cultivated relationship with the community, a Project Coordinating Committee was formed which included Peapack Mayor Mary Hamilton, Charles Hance from Beneficial, and representatives from both the Planning Board and the Board of Adjustment. Able to follow construction activities, review environmental reports, and make sure complaints received immediate attention, this group proved enormously effective. Beyond this *ad hoc* committee, borough officials were given periodic site tours, warned in advance of blasting, and promptly notified of other problems. The building inspector made rounds weekly and the Town Engineering Office shared its reports on such topics as soil erosion, site work, and public access with Beneficial executives. If corrective measures were necessary, the corporation and the contractor responded quickly.

No project ever goes forward without surprises and Beneficial's came at the end of summer 1979 with the discovery of several limestone caverns under the building area. At that point, work was stopped to allow a thorough re-examination of structural calculations and the foundation design. The delay ended in about a week, however, when engineers recommended the extensive use of piles. While the modification ultimately added several months to the construction schedule, what first appeared another setback was, like the Bedminster incident and change of architects, transformed into an opportunity. Especially impressive was the capacity of the design team to deal with the unexpected effectively and efficiently—no mean achievement when it is recognized that surprise often brings frustration and temporary decision-making paralysis. In this case, site preparation and design continued during the pile-driving operation. The Hillier Group completed most of the drawings and specifications and this, in turn, allowed Turner to estimate costs more accurately. Beneficial executives also used these weeks to reconsider their own needs, and the assessment resulted in significantly enlarging the space for the data-processing corporation. Fortunately, this was accomplished at reasonable cost since construction was not too far advanced.

With major problems resolved, the building pace quickened:

- By October 1980 the steel superstructure was up;
- Exteriors were completed by August 1981;
- Interior finishes were done by December;
- Landscaping was in place by April 1982; and
- During May the staff prepared to move.

By late fall 1981 Turner had guaranteed the price of Beneficial Center at $108 million. This was substantially more than original estimates and, while inflation and interest contributed to the increase, most of it was due to other factors. Changes in the foundations and related consulting fees, as well as extra space and computer equipment, were large expenses. But another major reason for higher costs was Beneficial's unwavering emphasis on quality: a wide range of indoor and outdoor athletic facilities, top-grade interior details, an on-site gas station, an extensive road layout, earthquake-resistant design, emergency power generation, and an elaborate safety and security system. Executives believed these items were important, for while they added to the construction total they were also the features that identified Beneficial Center as an extraordinary headquarters.[11] When the final figure came to $105 million, the company was satisfied that it had used its resources wisely and shared a portion of the savings with Turner. Then, because of tax and financing advantages—a consideration understandably part of the corporation's decision-making process—Beneficial sold the complex to a real estate investment trust.

In May 1982, after negotiating a long-term lease with a predetermined rental for the first five years, the company began the long-awaited move. In one sense, psychological preparations for the transfer had begun months earlier when the in-house advertising department distributed the first of four brochures designed to tell employees about their exciting new home. Photographs and a diagram supplemented the written word to convey the organization and architectural character of the center; a second booklet outlined available commuting routes and van pooling arrangements; the third and fourth pamphlets, disseminated immediately before the move, used more pictures and renderings to show the specific location of offices, work station designs, and the project's many amenities. A site tour prior to completion and a series of post-occupancy orientation sessions complemented the selling effort. That the phased relocation during May and June went so smoothly was satisfaction enough to the Building Committee which planned the entire program.

On August 19, 1982, Mr. Caspersen officiated at the dedication of Beneficial Center. The thousand people who had come to celebrate heard former President Gerald Ford refer to the complex as "an example of perfection . . . a meshing of Old World influences with the computer age." Mayor Mary Hamilton gave her personal assessment saying that, "I can't imagine anyone working in these surroundings and being unhappy. It's breathtaking."[12] The comments reflected the excitement of employees who, serving as hosts, gave tours to families, friends, and new neighbors. Senior executives, and especially members of the Building Committee, must have been gratified by the enthusiasm: while there is no place like the old homestead, it is equally true that there is no place quite like a gracious new home.

The Benefits of Design Quality

A year and a half after the dedication, Hance observed that return-on-investment from Beneficial Center had to be calculated from a number of different viewpoints. Economics is one. But others are enhanced corporate identity, greater prestige, and improved morale. Understanding company activities more clearly, workers point to the headquarters as a symbol of business vitality, and such impressions have obvious implications for job security. Since the new facilities opened, both absenteeism and staff turnover have decreased and, in the single location, there are more opportunities to share ideas.[13]

Architecturally, the complex has won a variety of awards, including the county's Land Use Award and the state's Good Neighbor Award. It has been featured in the American Institute of Architects Journal, and the critic for *Architectural Record* applauded the human scale of the offices, stating that this demonstrated "the concern of the company for the comfort of its employees [and] . . . the concern of the community about the impact of a major corporate headquarters on fragile surroundings."[14] Although not intimately involved with the design, David J. Ferris, President and Chief Executive Officer of the corporation's Beneficial Management subsidiary, articulated a conviction common among company managers when he said: "People are proud to work for Beneficial. The staff dresses better and they seem to want to make sure that things are done right, even if that means coming in occasionally on Saturday or Sunday."[15]

In addition, the headquarters project has had an impact on how Beneficial uses design as a business tool in other ways. In 1982, the company hired Lippincott & Margulies, one of the nation's foremost graphic designers, to devise a new logo and provide standard formats for Beneficial's publications and stationery. After more than a year of testing and evaluation, a new symbol was developed and a corporate identification manual prepared to describe its use on letterhead, advertising, buildings, vehicles, brochures, and reports. The design, a rainbow of arches accompanied by the word "Beneficial" (see figure 18), is meant, according to Senior Vice President for Marketing Richard Kotz, to connote quality, warmth,

FIGURE 18 Logos of Beneficial Corporation and of Beneficial Management Corporation of America and the Consumer Finance Subsidiaries of Beneficial Corporation (Courtesy Beneficial Management Corporation of America)

humanness, and modernity.[16] Implementation of this change was completed in 1985 and the concept of better design for better results has had significant returns: the corporate image has been enhanced, customer response has been overwhelmingly positive, worker esprit is strong, and while design quality has improved, design costs have been reduced.

Another significant event was the election of architect J. Robert Hillier to the Beneficial board. As a member of the Strategic Planning and Evaluation Committee, he recommended development of a uniform quality image for company loan offices. Like the Heinz Ketchup or Coca-Cola bottle, the design's purpose was to convey a message: Beneficial benefits customers! In 1983 the prototype (see figure 19) was tested, and 950 nation-wide locations were scheduled for renovation by the end of 1987. The environment for each is a blend of open work stations, a computer area, and a lounge where clients can discuss with privacy their needs and options. Warm colors, carpeting, and comfortable furnishings create a relaxed atmosphere that emphasizes personal contact and service. Even in regions where there was an initial reluctance to renovate because of costs, there is now a sense of enthusiasm among staffs whose morale and pride have risen perceptively. As a result, Jack Carr, Manager

FIGURE 19   Loan Office Prototype (Courtesy the author)

115

of the Fredericksburg office in Virginia, has noticed that since moving to the redesigned facilities, loan volume has increased and customers appear happier and more at ease.[17]

Beneficial's decisions about the headquarters, the logo, and the loan offices are in some ways separate issues requiring different kinds of expertise and talent. At the same time, they coalesced under the leadership of one man—CEO Finn Caspersen—whose sensitivity to quality design made the new building a catalyst for a new corporate culture.

Evaluation

While certainly not unique, what makes the Beneficial story most interesting is that, until just a few years ago, the company had practically no commitment to design as a business resource. The corporation accomplished much in a short time. This was possible for three reasons: (1) strong leadership from a CEO sensitive to design issues; (2) priorities that allowed the firm to pay the premium quality sometimes demands; and (3) the wisdom to look for the return on its design investment over the long term. On the other hand, because it was a neophyte in the field, there were unanticipated costs. The learning curve, although generally positive, included a few downturns. Beneficial began the headquarters project with vague goals and too often depended on *ad hoc* processes to respond to important questions and needs. The results were some bitter first fruits: false starts, lost time, and frustration.

Gradually, however, the company developed the specific design criteria essential to effective decision-making and communications, and this began to reap rewards. One benefit was a sharper identity, especially important during an era of deregulation that has meant increased competition and confusion for financial institutions: banks sell insurance, insurance agents provide financial counseling, Sears handles real estate, and credit card companies ask customers to use their accounts for savings.[18] In such a climate, a corporation that has moved imaginatively to exploit *all* its resources, design included, deserves recognition. For this reason, Beneficial's initiatives should be highlighted because they have enhanced employee dedication and output, strengthened the firm's image among consumers, and helped maintain the confidence of investors. Studying the situation with respect to the following maxims suggests how others can achieve these benefits while avoiding this company's painful experiences.

116

Maxim One: Integrate Multiple Perspectives

The difficulty in evaluating Beneficial's approach to design is that its first headquarters proposal was rejected by the community and abandoned by the corporation while its second was a great triumph. Certainly early efforts must be taken into account; at the same time, since the project was ultimately successful and led to other well-conceived design initiatives, it seems fair to critique initial steps as a learning process. In this regard, Beneficial was slow—but not neglectful—in articulating management's perspective on the headquarters. There was great enthusiasm for the idea, but the rush to get things done combined with inexperience meant that detailed objectives and priorities were developed incrementally rather than at the beginning of the job.

This had two repercussions. First, it was harder to control the budget. Because Beneficial's standards of quality were exceptionally high but poorly defined, additions to the design were made without balancing costs against specific and predetermined goals. Everyone was pleased with the final results, but there may have been alternatives that would have made people just as happy and saved money too. Second, the failure to have, as a top priority, a clear statement of corporate values followed by a thorough discussion of how these should be translated into buildings was a significant barrier to effective communication between client and architect. This information emerged eventually, but besides lost time, the delay may have narrowed the range of options and, without doubt, prompted the company's decision to work with other professionals. In summary, because of the negative consequences and the slowness with which Beneficial clarified its managerial perspective, the firm merits a "below average" rating (3.0 out of 7.5 points) in this area.

By contrast, the corporation involved employees in the project at an early stage. The Building Committee included representatives from key departments; almost every manager was interviewed—some several times—concerning needs, preferences, and the development of efficient interior layouts; most especially, workers were given a complete orientation to the headquarters well before the move. This made for a smooth transition. The staff quickly felt at home since people had already explored the complex and were familiar with its design, amenities, the offices, and various commuting routes. While not extraordinary, this approach to the employee perspective is typical and competent and deserves an "average" score (3.0 out of 5.0 points).

In seeking a compatible architect, it is evident that hasty decisions and poor communication hampered relationships with the first designer. Beneficial, however, learned quickly. By the time the second designer was hired, the company had articulated its aesthetic and functional goals and knew how important it was to work with the local community. Thus, the corporation and The Hillier Group were able to develop a set of common expectations that greatly enhanced the success of their team effort. In addition, as the case study makes clear, the link matured into a larger design strategy that has become the basis for other major undertakings. In this instance, the final client-architect marriage has been fruitful, but because of an initial false start and some friction over the selection of an interior designer, a "superior" (2.0 out of 2.5 points) rather than "excellent" rating is appropriate.

Maxim Two: Emphasize Casting

The major failure in Beneficial's design process was starting a large project without identifying in advance the skills that would assure success. The problem was compounded by tight deadlines, executives unfamiliar with architectural decision-making, and the environmental concerns of neighboring communities. The result was the selection of a design team that resembled trial-and-error. As time passed, the corporation involved dedicated in-house personnel, capable designers, consultants and managers, and supportive municipal leaders. By then, however, costs had started to mount. In coping with the multitude of actors and roles in a building effort, Beneficial's approach was obviously "below average" (1.0 out of 2.5 points).

Although it took a while to assemble, once chosen, the final cast was quite talented. The interior designers might have worked more closely with the architects. But with this exception, the company hired professionals who communicated effectively and got the job done. Indeed, two relationships must be acknowledged as exceptional. In a part of the country where residents are wary of giant businesses and large-scale development, Beneficial is regarded as a sensitive corporate citizen, willing to deal with its own concerns *and* those of the community. The second ongoing partnership is the bond between the architect and chief executive. This dialogue has enhanced understanding of design as an economic resource (evidenced by the redesign of the logo and renovation of the loan offices) and has made substantial contributions to a new and stronger corporate culture. After a rough beginning, then, these achievements indicate that Beneficial ultimately put together a "superior" (6.0 out of 7.5 points) design team.

Maxim Three: Sift for Relevant Facts

If there was a weakness in Beneficial's research, it was the *ad hoc* nature of the process. Rather than following an overall plan, the corporation responded to issues as they emerged: the concern for scale and materials only became critical after Bedminster rejected the first headquarters proposal; a total analysis of subsurface conditions at the Peapack site occurred once limestone caverns had been discovered; most interiors were designed when it was impossible to alter the shape or size of individual buildings. In part, this can be attributed to the fast-track schedule. The pressure to keep things moving meant that certain decisions had to be made before all the facts were available. From another point of view, however, there was no strong technical expertise in-house to weigh recommendations from the architect and construction manager. This inexperience and the dependence on consultants to analyze options limited the consistency and timeliness of Beneficial's design research. Such a methodology warrants a "below average" score (1.0 out of 2.5 points).

The company was more successful in the breadth of topics it explored. Image was particularly well handled and has helped reshape the corporate culture. Building interiors and technology also received much attention. Work spaces were designed in consultation with managers and staff, numerous amenities were thoughtfully integrated within the project, and executives insisted that the complex have the latest computer, communications, and energy-saving equipment. Still, these are the concerns of many firms and this performance, therefore, should be evaluated as "average" (4.5 out of 7.5 points).

Maxim Four: Manage Pluralistic Decision-Making

In design management, Beneficial's strengths were twofold. First, throughout the headquarters development and in the later logo and loan office projects, executives kept their eyes on business objectives rather than on preconceived notions of style or image. In one example, numerous amenities were included at Beneficial Center not because they were fashionable perks but because they helped attract and retain talented personnel. In another illustration, the renovation program was not interpreted as a cosmetic cleaning, but as part of a full-scale effort to reinvigorate the corporate image, and offer new products and services to new customers. Beneficial's second strength in this area was the ability to exploit design as a facet of culture. Strong and consistent leadership from the CEO made this possible and the results, which began emerging

119

only recently, are highlighted by financial prosperity and worker loyalty and pride.

One aspect of design management has not evolved as completely as others, namely, developing consensus. All of the corporation's projects have been conceived of individually, each supported by a unique rationale. While together, they have been responsible for dramatic changes, the process has not been efficient. It would be a significant improvement if Beneficial prepared an explicit business/design philosophy and based decisions on a long-range plan. This would make implementation easier and more coherent. Even without such a process, however, the company certainly has a "superior" record (12.0 out of 15.0 points) in design decision-making.

Conclusion

The Beneficial story is a lesson in hope. It demonstrates that, without a technical background, executives can learn to use design as business tool. The rewards can be great but vision and patience are essential. In addition, to avoid failure, enthusiasm must be balanced with careful planning and analysis.

Building the Company—The Beneficial Design Program

MAXIM		CORPORATE TASKS	MAX PTS	RATING	ACT PTS
MULTIPLE PERSPECTIVES	The Managerial Perspective	Define Objectives and Priorities			
		Establish Standards of Quality			
		Articulate Corporate Values	7.5	BELOW AVER.	3.0
	The Employee Perspective	Seek Employee Participation	5.0	AVERAGE	3.0
	The Architectural Perspective	Look for a Compatible Marriage with the Architect	2.5	SUPERIOR	2.0
		MAXIMUM SUBTOTAL	15.0	ACTUAL	8.0
CASTING	A Multitude of Actors and Roles	Appoint the In-House Players			
		Hire Outside Managers			
		Select the Design Team			
		Work with Key Public Actors	2.5	BELOW AVER.	1.0
	Assembling the Cast	Determine the Mix of In-House vs. Outside Services			
		Stress the CCC Syndrome: Commitment, Communications, and Competence	7.5	SUPERIOR	6.0
		MAXIMUM SUBTOTAL	10.0	ACTUAL	7.0
RESEARCH	Design Research	Turn Facts into Options	2.5	BELOW AVER.	1.0
	Critical Topics	Study Technology, Layout and Image	7.5	AVERAGE	4.5
		MAXIMUM SUBTOTAL	10.0	ACTUAL	5.5
DECISION-MAKING	Elements in Design Management	Emphasize Goals, Not Positions			
		Develop Consensus			
		Integrate Decision-Making and Culture	15.0	SUPERIOR	12.0
		MAXIMUM SUBTOTAL	15.0	ACTUAL	12.0
		MAXIMUM TOTAL	50.0	ACTUAL	32.5

121

6

Herman Miller—Design and the Corporate Culture

HERMAN MILLER INC.
HOLLAND, MICHIGAN

PROJECT INITIATED: 1979
PROJECT COMPLETED: 1980

Summary

IN the midst of the Depression when Herman Miller Inc. had committed itself to a business strategy of innovation and design leadership, the company's principal consultant kept reminding executives, "You're not making furniture anymore. You're making a way of life."[1] For the Michigan-based manufacturer, it was an attitude that has proven economically *and* philosophically fulfilling. Revenues now exceed half a billion dollars and Herman Miller's systems furniture is internationally respected and emulated. This belief also supported the firm's culture—a management style that blends tenets of the local Dutch Reform faith, an emphasis on employee dedication and loyalty, and an insistence on excellence in products, architecture, and graphics.

This reputation for quality is the result of continuous efforts to improve communications and share both rewards and responsibility. In spite of dramatic growth during the past fifteen years, decision-making at Herman

Miller remains personal, a fact that emerges clearly in the area of facilities development. In a highly interactive process, management, staff, and consultants come together as a team to evaluate choices which will satisfy long-term business and planning goals, immediate functional and production requirements, the needs of workers, and the designer's desire for creativity. As the case illustrates, three features contribute significantly to success: (1) precise design objectives; (2) an in-house group to manage an array of ongoing projects; and (3) a participatory approach that involves employees—as well as professionals and executives—in final decisions.

In the minds of many, the words architecture and factory are contradictory. Complexes such as Bethlehem Steel's Sparrows Point Mill in Baltimore and Ford's River Rouge Assembly Plant near Detroit conjure up images of a wasteland—smokestacks and towers, vast and shadowy sheds, sprawling storage areas and dirt. Located in the forgotten corners of cities, they line railroad tracks or the edges of major waterways. And rather than being designed, they just seem to occur, growing spontaneously and haphazardly.

In stark contrast to this stereotype is Herman Miller's Seating Plant in Holland, Michigan, a distinguished manufacturing facility. Its low, spreading profile complements the region's wide plains and open skies; stainless steel wall panels, a curved clerestory, and molded corners suggest a Bauhaus efficiency and order; bright red loading docks and a landscaped entrance provide a joyful accent and an essential human scale.

As the American economy abandons much of its heavy industry, the

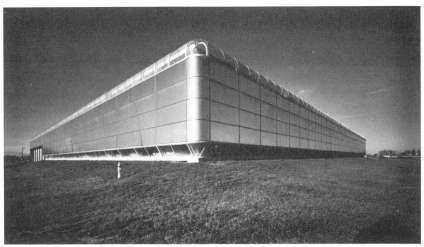

Holland Seating Plant (Balthazar Korab Ltd. for Herman Miller)

construction of light industrial plants is an increasingly important aspect of corporate building. Such structures traditionally lack prestige and visibility. Incentives to invest in quality are further reduced by tight budgets, the need to build quickly in response to changing markets, and the desire for flexibility. Given these parameters, this type of architecture was aptly characterized by one critic as "the architecture of impermanence."[2] Yet as that article about Silicon Valley concludes—and this analysis of the Herman Miller facility supports—it is possible to build production spaces that are cost-effective, responsive to change, *and* architecturally excellent.

Background—The Evolution of a Corporate Culture

The success of Herman Miller in combining efficiency and aesthetics is due to a philosophy that has matured over eighty years. Founded in 1905 as the Michigan Star Furniture Company, the firm produced traditional and period reproduction home furnishings. In 1923 an employee, D. J. DePree, with financial assistance from his father-in-law, Herman Miller, bought controlling interest in the company. The corporate name was changed and the new management placed special emphasis on quality—quality products, quality workers, and quality working conditions.

In spite of this focus on excellence, within seven years the Great Depression, as well as stiff competition from southern manufacturers, pushed Herman Miller Incorporated toward bankruptcy. With little to lose, Mr. DePree decided to abandon his old line of heavy, rather ornate products to enter the sleeker, less detailed, "modern" furniture market. As a first step, he hired Gilbert Rohde, an advertising and display illustrator, whose brash self-confidence convinced the executive to develop a variety of chairs, sofas, and tables more appropriate to the new smaller houses that were beginning to appear across the country. The trick was to provide a sense of style, comfort, and pride to families living in fewer rooms with lower ceilings and simpler detailing.

While many would interpret such dramatic change in production as a last desperate gamble, DePree used the experience to develop a corporate culture where innovation became an essential element rather than simply a fad. " 'What makes Herman Miller different from its competition,' says Max DePree, D. J.'s son and the current chief executive, 'is that it is able to catch the fast ball of America's most innovative designers.' And toss it to the rest of the world."[3] This strategy, plus D. J. DePree's willingness "to abandon himself to the strength of unusual people,"[4] has meant that the company history, traditionally an anonymous chronicle after a description of the founder's initial achievements, continues to stress individual effort. After several years, Rohde's approach proved financially viable and the firm hired others to contribute to its reputation as a design leader.

Since World War II, three personalities have figured prominently in the corporation's success: George Nelson, Charles Eames, and Robert Propst. Educated as an architect, Nelson was managing editor of *Architectural Forum* when he was hired by Herman Miller in 1945 as design director. In this role, he developed a variety of elegant office and home furnishings, but perhaps his most influential contribution was "the wall system"—units which offered an array of innovative interior design options by combining a free-standing structure with flexible shelving, display, desk, and storage space. A year after Nelson's appointment, the company recruited Charles Eames who, in addition to films and exhibits, was known for his experiments with fiberglass and bent plywood. As a consultant, he designed a stackable chair that is used in institutions throughout the country and his famous lounge chair and ottoman are part of the Museum of Modern Art's permanent collection. In 1960 Robert Propst was chosen to head Herman Miller's research subsidiary. An inventor and scholar studying the relationships among people and machines, he investigated white-collar work patterns and efficiency issues and in 1964 introduced Action Office, the first integrated system of panels, work surfaces, and file storage capable of creating an office without walls (see figure 20). Although widely emulated, the corporation has maintained leadership in this area by continuously refining the product and extending the approach to both health-care facilities and factories.

Not surprisingly, when a company identifies excellent products and excellent people as top priorities, one of the corporate culture's chief attributes is a capacity to recognize talent wherever it appears. Relevant is the story told by Max DePree of his father's visit to the home of an employee, a millwright, who had just died. After awkward condolences, the deceased's wife read some poetry written by her husband, poetry so impressive that since that time, executives have wondered, "Did we have a poet who did millwright's work, or did we have a millwright who wrote poetry?" DePree's answer is that "in addition to all of their ratios and goals and parameters and bottom lines, it is fundamental that corporations have a concept of persons . . . , an understanding of the diversity of people's gifts."[5] At Herman Miller the energy, dedication, and commitment of workers are treasured assets.

This philosophy is revealed in multiple ways. Managers define their

FIGURE 20   Herman Miller's Action Office (Susan Wood for Herman Miller)

relationships with employees as a covenant; managing means steward-ship; staff speak of "joining" rather than "working for" the firm. Such respect has attracted wide attention. In 1979, for example, the company received the Walter C. Mason Award for an annual report that stressed "the importance of human resource management to the corporation's overall soundness and success."[6] The 1983 *Annual Report* illustrated how the trend continued when it devoted over half its pages to summaries of employee interviews. Some twenty people, ranging from the vice president for operations to a machine maintenance supervisor to an assembler/packer were asked: "What's important to you?" The response of John Adams, associate director for consulting, Facility Management Institute (the research arm of Herman Miller), was typical: "I think there's a sense that in this company, one ought to do better work. That somehow more is expected of the company and the people in it. I think there's a sense of striving in this community."[7] According to Max DePree, the reason for including these conversations was "not only to report on our sound financial condition, but also to show . . . some of the strengths that are the sources of our vitality."[8]

Inside Herman Miller, further recognition of employee contributions is effected through the Scanlon Plan, a participation process modeled on the theory of Joseph Scanlon, a labor-management consultant in the 1930s. The key assumption is that labor-management cooperation is possible—even in the mass production setting—when executives truly

126

believe that "workers have brains and ingenuity as well as muscles.
. . . Once these conditions are established, people collaborate because
it is to their interest to do so. They don't need to be made to 'feel'
important; they are important and they know it."[9]

Obviously a concept which fitted so naturally with Herman Miller's
outlook was given a warm welcome once it was formally adopted by
firm in 1950. At the time, sales volume was less than $2 million annually
and the work force numbered about 120 employees. By 1985 revenues
exceeded $500 million and four thousand were employed. Still, the Scan-
lon Plan, with some modifications, remains a key ingredient in manage-
ment-employee relations. The system of elected committees encourages
every member of the organization to enhance business performance.
Suggestions are reviewed each month and reports are made on the savings
and/or improved sales resulting from ideas that have been implemented.
Finally, the company measures productivity using a sophisticated formula
that compares production costs to income and pays a bonus equal to
the percentage this figure exceeds expectations. Significantly, between
1950 and 1976 workers have received an average annual bonus of 10.95
percent.[10] In addition, both turnover and absenteeism are dramatically
lower than most American companies.[11]

Interestingly, while collaboration among consultants, management,
and employees has been both innovative and profitable, religious convic-
tions, rather than money, are probably the ultimate forces behind Herman
Miller's designs and culture. The Grand Rapids area is steeped in Dutch
fundamentalism and the corporation's creativity has emerged from an
"unlikely marriage between John Calvin and Calvin Klein."[12] Looking
back, D. J. DePree believes that the shift from period to modern furniture
was essentially an ethical decision: if the heavy details of earlier designs
were immoral chiefly in their pretense, "that pretense hid other immorali-
ties: moldings and carvings were used to conceal sins of sloppy workman-
ship, for instance."[13] Expanding on his father's principles, Max DePree
has urged executives to think of leadership "as a concept of owing certain
things to the institution; as a way of thinking about your institutional
heirs; as a way of thinking about serving as contrasted with being served;
as a way of thinking about stewardship as contrasted with ownership."[14]
These sentiments are the stuff of a biblical ethic and, in a real sense,
the Scanlon Plan bonus system is a way of sharing that reflects the
theology of the Reformed Church in America: "If the enjoyment of material blessings is a good thing . . . , then it is good for all and cannot
legitimately be monopolized by some to the disadvantage of others."[15]

FIGURE 21   Herman Miller's Ethospace Furniture System (Peter Kiar)

It is not unexpected, therefore, that Herman Miller's new "Ethospace" furniture system (see figure 21) would be described in terms that go beyond function and comfort: "Ethospace walls, work surfaces, storage, lighting, filing, and organizing tools can create interiors that express and support the spirit, the values, the work—the ethos—of your organization."[16] The corporate architecture displays similar virtues. The multipurpose campus for sales and marketing in Grandville, Michigan, for instance, has a landscaped entrance that welcomes visitors and employees alike, numerous rest areas so people can really relax during breaks, and a two-story "commons" that is both an exhibition and celebration space (see figure 22).

The Architectural Design Process

If the corporate philosophy is an interesting amalgam of economic, sociological, and theological concepts, the way such concepts are put to work is also interesting—especially in facility planning. Regardless of the project, the design program incorporates eleven objectives that define relationships among the company, workers, and neighboring community. These are worth reviewing because they suggest why the firm's buildings

FIGURE 22   Commons at the Grandville, Michigan, Campus (Balthazar Korab Ltd. for Herman Milller)

are consistently of such high quality. At Herman Miller the following criteria must be followed:

- Our goal is to make a contribution to the landscape of an aesthetic and human value.
- The environment should encourage fortuitous encounter and open community.
- The space should be subservient to human activity.

- Commitment to performance for single functions or needs is to be avoided.
- The facility must be able to change with grace and be flexible and nonmonumental.
- Planning of utilities has to meet the needs we can perceive.
- We wish to create an environment which will welcome all and be open to surprise.
- The quality of the spaces should reflect the company's commitment and reputation in environmental arenas.
- Whatever we do must be constructively involved with the neighborhood and civic community.
- Utilization patterns should allow for future options, for growth and for change.
- We would like a building that permits maximum relation of work spaces to the outdoors.[17]

With overall standards established well in advance of any project, work on a specific facility can begin promptly and efficiently. Because the design team already knows what is expected in terms of quality, managers and consultants can concentrate on the execution and details of a project.

This advantage is singularly important to a company that, since 1976, has experienced such dramatic increases in revenue that some analysts have interpreted the situation as potentially destabilizing.[18] Growth has generated a need for physical expansion and managing the adjustment is a real challenge. The firm cannot afford to overbuild because stiff competition, changes in demand, and downturns in the economy can slow—or even reverse—the pattern. To achieve flexibility and nurture rapport with local communities, the strategy has been to lease facilities until it is apparent that space is needed permanently. Once this decision is made, executives respond quickly. The building criteria are explicit and, based on long-term business objectives and the master plans for plants around the world, a site can be selected, a design developed, and a structure completed and operating in as little as sixteen months.

The efficiency is due, in large measure, to the talent of Herman Miller's in-house design staff. The group is headed by Thomas D. Wolterink, Vice President for Facility Management. Prior to joining the firm in 1975, Wolterink had organized a successful land development company in Portland, Oregon, and also had extensive experience in hospital management. With support from the Human Resources and Finance divisions, he is responsible for coordinating the work of a hundred individuals in the areas of property management, interior design, facility construction, leasing, lodging and food services. To keep on top of his operation, Wolterink asks key people from the various company units to help prepare a

Strategic Facilities Plan. This document, updated at least annually, defines specific building needs three years into the future and outlines general options five to ten years in advance. In addition to responding to production requirements and establishing the optimum balance between owning and leasing, the plan covers issues such as cash flow, product development, distribution, and use of the facilities as a sales and marketing tool. Thus, building decisions are part of an overall business strategy. When the corporation was small, executives could react with greater spontaneity because they were personally aware of almost everything that was going on; however, as revenues expanded to over one half billion dollars annually, a more formal process became necessary.

Importantly—and in keeping with Herman Miller's culture—the transformation in size has not meant the loss of the personal touch. Wolterink's attitude is "can do"; rather than tell people "why not," he and his colleagues strive to meet the many demands placed upon them. To make sure individual managers are heard, the facilities operation is divided into geographic regions. And once there is a commitment to a specific project, senior management and employees are involved in programming and design development, and both collaborate with a team of professionals to assure quality.

Interior office changes (some staff move as often as once every nine months) and the layout of manufacturing equipment are done entirely in-house. Major construction and proposals for showrooms generally require outside consultants. The company uses the services of architects, engineers, contractors and experts in graphics, exhibition lighting, acoustics and other related disciplines. Since the schedule is usually tight, a formal and often lengthy selection process is ruled out. Instead, the Facility Management division chooses consultants on the basis of the skills needed, its own and others' past experiences, and the professional's compatibility with the corporate philosophy. This last point is significant: Herman Miller regards such associations not as contracts but as "covenants." It is not the letter of the law but the spirit of mutual trust that is expected to prevail between client and extern. So competition is avoided not only to save time, but to reinforce shared values and creativity. In this way, the company establishes relationships with regional as well as nationally known firms and takes advantage of their diverse talents and ideas to enhance the flexibility, efficiency, and attractiveness of its facilities.

This means that many architects have contributed to the corporation's design reputation. Houston-based Caudill Rowlett Scott has done several structures in Michigan, including the Holland Seating plant, the Zeeland

Energy Building, and an addition to the manufacturing and office facility in Grandville. Frank Gehry, a Los Angeles architect, recently received a commission for a production building and master plan in Sacramento, California. The Roswell complex in Georgia was developed by Heery & Heery, architects and engineers from Atlanta, and the Ferrell/Grimshaw Partnership in Britain was responsible for the factory on the outskirts of Bath (see figure 23).

To maintain continuity and high standards in different locations and for different types of work, Wolterink has divided facility management activities into three categories: administration, project management, and design. People in the first area handle routine maintenance and support services; the two remaining groups deal with renovation and construction, in some cases, doing the work themselves and in others, serving as project representatives to others, facilitating the exchange of information and monitoring contractors. In these last situations, the team is balanced between outside consultants and knowledgable in-house staff. This combination makes the company a full working partner in the design effort, a hands-on approach that yields many benefits: questions are answered quickly; the final results better reflect the corporate philosophy; and excellence is achieved at a competitive price.

FIGURE 23   The Factory at Bath (Courtesy Herman Miller)

132

The Process in Action

Although procedures for dealing with facilities are constantly being refined, the development of the Seating Plant in Holland, Michigan, provides a good illustration because it highlights specifics that make the program effective. As is the case for all Herman Miller buildings, the need for a new structure emerged from a bottom-up process and not by executive fiat. In 1976, when a price reduction in systems furniture significantly boosted demand, the additional sales strained capacity and the ability to meet shipping deadlines. Space was leased and, in accord with a 1975 master plan, two buildings were opened in 1978 that increased facilities by 145,000 square feet. Still, pressures—especially on support functions—continued to mount. To find a solution, the in-house planning group used the Scanlon Plan to explore options with executives and production personnel. After evaluating the input, a decision was made to move seat manufacturing from the Zeeland headquarters to a yet-to-be-determined location and to recapture the vacated space as offices for sales and marketing personnel and for a new library and cafeteria.

The immediate challenge of finding a site for the seating plant was made easier by the availability of a low-interest $10 million federal loan and by a willingness to decentralize production. In terms of money, like most corporations, Herman Miller was searching for an attractive price. For this company, however, human factors were just as critical as costs—as Wolterink explained: "We like to keep our organization of small groups so that we can communicate openly."[19] With this criterion in mind, he looked for land in communities that had a strong work ethic and that were well-kept, proud, and modest in size. Within a few weeks, it was clear that an eighty-acre parcel in Holland, Michigan, fit the bill. Each spring, the town hosted a nationally known tulip festival, and it had a friendly and diligent population of about twenty-six thousand. The tract was ideal in other respects as well: less than ten miles from Zeeland, it was accessible to workers; it was close to major highways and a small airport; and it was large enough to allow for a three-fold expansion.

In early 1979, not long after a contract for the site was finalized, Herman Miller selected Caudill Rowlett Scott, Inc. (CRS) to design the building. Since one of its principals, William Caudill, was a member of the Herman Miller board, Max DePree was generally familiar with this Texas-based firm's approach to architecture. After this information was amplified by discussions specifically about the seating plant, both companies knew they could establish an effective partnership.

Significantly, what others may have perceived as a conflict-of-interest, DePree saw as a reflection of his covenant philosophy. One reason for this was the way CRS dealt with programming and the early phases of design. For these decisions, the architects requested that Herman Miller convene a meeting where key players could gather to distill and synthesize major issues. Since this complemented the corporation's participatory management and would simultaneously expedite the work, everyone agreed it was an excellent idea.

At this gathering, Caudill and CRS president Paul Kennon served as lead designers. They developed the architectural scheme and coordinated the work of Jay Neyland, their project manager, and Kevin Kelly and Mike Shirley who assisted with programming, estimating, and drafting. Herman Miller also organized the assignments of its representatives. DePree and Wolterink headed the "client group." John Stivers, Manager of Facilities Construction, was responsible for design. Gordon Nagelkirk, a thirty-year veteran with the company, dealt with technical issues and managed contracts and construction. Finally, John Keelen represented Owen Ames Kimball Company, the contractor. Together, these many individuals—from diverse backgrounds and disciplines—became a very creative team.

CRS had used these intensive meetings for some time and had nicknamed the technique "squatter sessions" after ideas promulgated by a founder of the architectural firm, William Pena. Pena believed that the client must be accepted as co-equal in the design process and must participate in partnership with other team members to answer five critical questions:

GOALS	What does the client want to achieve and why?
FACTS	What is the project all about?
CONCEPTS	How does the client want to achieve the goals?
NEEDS	What level of quality and how much money and space are required?
PROBLEM STATEMENT	What are the significant conditions and general directions the building should take?

During the sessions, responses were refined to take into account (*a*) function (people, activity, and relationships), (*b*) form (site, environment, and quality), (*c*) money (initial budget, operating costs, and life-cycle costs), and (*d*) time (past, present schedule, and future needs). To achieve consistency, answers were then reviewed to eliminate contradictions.[20]

Herman Miller's unwavering commitment to the Scanlon Plan made the squatter session particularly appropriate. It was also efficient, in this case, because corporate design principles were clear in advance and because important decision-makers were intimately involved. But there was another element contributing to success—CRS president Paul Kennon's experience as a team leader. This method is a dynamic process. Analysis and conclusions are developed on the spot and conversations move quickly from the general to the specific, from important to minor issues, from design criteria to detailed concepts. In this situation, the team leader's responsibilities are formidable, and Kennon was up to the task. He recognized inadequacies in input and made certain that the whole array of relevant facts was unearthed; he asked the right questions at the right time and reconciled conflicting priorities; above all, he skillfully summarized where the project was headed—and why.

All this occurred during two weeks in early February 1979, when those from CRS and those from Herman Miller met at Marigold, a beautiful early twentieth-century estate near Lake Michigan which served as the company's learning center, guest house, and employee retreat. As an introduction, Max DePree and Tom Wolterink reviewed the corporation's history and philosophy and provided examples of its products and buildings. The next few days were spent analyzing the site and specific objectives for the seating plant. These discussions concluded with the identification of several key factors:

- The site was in a flood plain and water protection would be necessary.
- Prevailing winds were from the west and this needed to be considered since the plant would not be air-conditioned.
- The facility would be used to produce a dozen chair products and space was required for raw materials storage, foam processes, fabric and upholstery shops, raw wood molding and engineering, a final assembly area, and temporary storage before shipping to a warehouse.
- The plant would have a total of 200,000 square feet—30% for raw goods, 60% for manufacturing, and 10% for office and service areas.
- Work stations would have as much natural light as possible.
- The structural system would be flexible to permit easy retooling, as well as circulation for people, fork lifts, and an automated robot delivery system.
- The ceiling would be high enough to allow for a second-story track for the storage and moving of seating components.
- The environment would be attractive and pleasant with acoustics to minimize noise and reverberation.

Not surprisingly, given Herman Miller's concern for its staff, the design team arrived at the foregoing criteria after interviewing machine engineers, production workers, and floor managers. In addition, extensive notes were made on amenities such as a single attractive entrance, nearby parking for both executives and employees, convenient restrooms and break areas, a cafeteria, a nurse's station, and a health-care operation. The budget was also thoroughly reviewed during the squatter session so costs would not exceed the Economic Development Corporation (EDC) funds made available by the federal government. EDC financing is subsidized to help communities maintain their existing manufacturing and economic base. After construction is complete, permanent loans are made at several points below prime; for Herman Miller these arrangements translated into $10 million at 7 percent for twelve years at a time when interest rates were normally more than twice that amount.

At first blush the financial package seemed quite generous for a building the size and nature of the seating plant. Company executives, however, stated that this limit had to include the price of the land and new equipment, interest on the construction loan, the money devoted to research on products to be manufactured in Holland, and a reserve for changes in layout and machinery for the first three years after completion. Subtracting these expenses, approximately $5 million remained for design, construction, and site work. Given the size of the plant and the schedule, the mandate became straightforward: develop an investment grade facility at a cost of $25 per square foot and complete the task within sixteen months.

Since the challenge necessitated careful coordination, the team spent the remainder of the squatter session working out a preliminary design. They established a "footprint" for the plant—a pinwheel composed of three units, none larger than 80,000 square feet (see figure 24). The biggest pod was for materials storage, and the other two were for manufacturing, assembly, shipping and support services. The configuration, responding to the work flow, meant that employees were no more than a hundred feet from a window and occupied spaces that could be subdivided into more human-scaled areas. At the center of the pinwheel a "people place" was planned—the location of a landscaped entrance, several offices, the cafeteria, and a general gathering spot for workers.

Structurally, the engineers selected a 40' by 40' bay; steel columns, twenty-five feet high, supported bar joists and a corrugated metal roof; interior walls were concrete block. On the exterior, tubes formed a framework for stainless steel panels which were filled with styrofoam insulation and were demountable when expansion was necessary. A molded clerestory at the roofline admitted light while at eye level operable windows provided a view and fresh air. The outside base of the building was surrounded by a gently sloping berm to reduce the visual impression

136

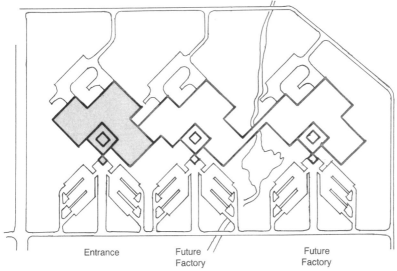

Entrance   Future   Future
              Factory   Factory

FIGURE 24   Site Plan of the Holland Seating Plant

of the plant's size and to act as a dike during floods. The mechanical systems were also designated. Fourteen roof-mounted, gas-fired burners were used for heating; electricity was delivered from above in production areas and with flat wiring (covered by carpet tiles) in office spaces. Loading docks were oriented to the west and in the summer the doors were left open to admit breezes. Four sodium vapor lamps per bay brightly illuminated the facility at night and augmented bountiful natural light during the day.

By the end of the two-week meeting, the steel for the project was actually on order and only the detailed drawings and contract documents remained to be executed. In a very short time, the design team had developed a scheme that balanced efficiency and ease of construction with Herman Miller's desire for a humane and aesthetically inspiring environment. Although the Holland Seating Plant could be built quickly by using standardized elements, its streamlined quality had an air of sophistication and elegance. Its layout was designed to enhance productivity and speed operations. At the same time, long bands of windows provided significantly more natural light than in most plants and, when opened in conjunction with loading bay doors, served as natural cooling devices. The earth berm not only protected the structure but reduced the facility's scale and integrated it with its expansive setting.

137

Construction

In mid-February the CRS people returned to Houston to finalize their work. In the interim, Wolterink and his associates presented the design and preliminary cost analysis to Herman Miller's financial division, to the President's Work Team, and to the community. In-house approval was granted with the stipulation that the budget not be exceeded. Public endorsement was enthusiastic with the City of Holland making only one request: that a street intersection be slightly modified to accommodate increased traffic.

In May 1979, only two and a half months after the Marigold meeting, the design was complete and concrete footings were being poured. To speed construction a fast track approach was used. Drawings and specifications were prepared in carefully scheduled phases and as soon as the documents arrived the contractor, Owen Ames Kimball Company, prepared estimates and performed the work on a cost-plus basis. To supervise this process for Herman Miller, John Stivers and Gordon Nagelkirk inspected the site and monitored expenses. Also, to help stay within the budget, subcontracts were competitively bid and, as an incentive to keep prices below original estimates, 10 percent of any savings were given to the general contractor and 5 percent to subcontractors.

While there were no major changes during construction, by September 1979 it was evident that available funds were insufficient to build the facility as planned. Equally unfortunate was the fact that the budget could not be increased without incurring a large interest penalty. As a result, the design team reconvened to study possible substitutions and changes. After an exhaustive analysis, the choice was made to eliminate the "people place" entry pavilion, a decision that appears to contradict the company's employee-oriented culture. Other strategies, however, required reducing the quality of finishes and interiors throughout. Left with this option, executives resolved to postpone one facet of the design rather than compromise overall excellence.

Production at the Holland Seating Plant began on June 1, 1980. Even without the "people place" the building is airy and cheerful (see figure 25): columns, bar-joists, ducts, and pipes are exposed and painted bright colors; daylight fills the space from the clerestory and eye-level windows; and a variety of shelves, storage walls, desks, and partitions (selected from Herman Miller's own Action Factory line) divide large spaces into areas that one critic referred to as "downright cozy."[21]

The plant has been operating for several years now and during this time workers have suggested ways to refine and improve the design.

138

FIGURE 25   Airy Interior of the Seating Plant (Balthazar Korab Ltd. for Herman Miller)

Most have addressed the layout of equipment, but a few have called for changes in the building itself. In particular, the south, east, and west exposures of the clerestory admit too much light, creating such an annoying glare that shading devices are necessary. Noise is also an issue, especially for offices on the manufacturing floor. Absorbent materials, panels, and walls help somewhat, but the final resolution may only come when the "people place" is built as a quieter place to work. In addition, this space will be a more attractive spot for the snack bar and cafeteria, which are presently located near production equipment.

After the Seating Plant

In May 1981 Herman Miller Incorporated received the coveted American Institute of Architect's Gold Medal. The citation read:

> The American Institute of Architects is honored to confer this AIA medal on Herman Miller Inc. Dedicated to design excellence, this firm has provided an opportunity and a showcase for talented designers spanning a half-century. Through commitment to technical innovation in the service of efficient, humane environments, HMI has profoundly influenced the architectural profession and the spaces in which people work and live.

Yet this analysis should have made clear that innovation at Herman Miller goes beyond the design of products and spaces to include the design of processes. Creative decision-making and an ability to establish, rather than follow, trends remain hallmarks of the corporation. Each project provides a learning experience, and as noted earlier, techniques effective in the development of the seating plant have since been further refined. New construction is now planned well in advance in order to contribute to such business objectives as sales, marketing, distribution, and productivity; and management is divided by region and discipline to enhance communication and consensus. Voices heard are voices listened to—yet final responsibility is clear. Ideally, project leaders orchestrate a process where employees and executives, professionals and consultants share goals and design information, an exchange especially important during the programming, schematic, and design development phases. Squatter sessions continue to be used, but additional reviews take place among senior management, company directors, and staff. There is less spontaneity than the seating plant example, and approval procedures are more time-consuming and involved; nevertheless, increased feedback generates a close relationship between proposals and what actually gets built. Budget estimates are precise, unexpected cutbacks are a rarity, and fewer schemes are postponed or abandoned.

Often corporate philosophies appear to be the product of cautious lawyers or imaginative public relations experts. At Herman Miller, however, these ideals spring directly from a family's values. The company practices what it preaches and firmly believes that business success is the result of a commitment to excellence—excellence as a designer and manufacturer, excellence in services and ideas, excellence as an employer and member of the community.

140

Evaluation

Design, an integral feature of Herman Miller's culture, is obviously a consideration regarding products, facilities, and graphics. More interestingly, it is an important component in the firm's competitive strategy and in dealing with issues such as planning, productivity, and employee needs. Specifically related to building and interior design, several factors enhance this process: (1) decisions emerge from clearly stated design principles reflecting human and moral goals as well as aesthetic and economic concerns; (2) there is a predetermined framework for communication among the design team, senior management and staff; and (3) an in-house group monitors and refines procedures so they meet the increasingly complex demands of a rapidly growing company. An analysis based on the four maxims provides an opportunity to elaborate on these points.

Maxim One: Integrate Multiple Perspectives

This study is particularly relevant to medium-size organizations because it demonstrates that size does not determine how effectively architecture can be exploited. IBM and Olivetti are often cited for their accomplishments in design; Herman Miller is less known yet, as this case illustrates, experts recognize that modest firms can also take advantage of this resource. This is possible when executives initiate a project with explicit objectives, priorities, and quality standards. At Herman Miller, these facts are identified up front and are closely related to general corporate values. In the Holland Seating Plant, function, work environment, community impact, and beauty were carefully analyzed before a detailed proposal was developed. The single weak link in the process was the budget review. In this instance, the "people place" was deleted because original estimates proved overly optimistic. To avoid similar disappointments, operating units now do more advance planning and costs are more thoroughly evaluated. This slows decision-making somewhat but ultimately improves results by helping to fine-tune goals so that changes during construction are minimized. Given this record, Herman Miller merits a "superior" rating (6.0 out of 7.5 points) for its efforts to articulate the managerial perspective.

The company has even greater success involving employees in design choices. The Scanlon Plan, squatter sessions, and most recently, the decentralization of facilities management offer numerous opportunities for workers to participate in the process. At the seating plant and other projects, the staff contributes to programming, design development, and even to modifying and refining structures after occupancy. Such techniques provide valuable models and justify an "excellent" score (5.0 out of 5.0 points) for Herman Miller's thoughtful integration of the employee perspective.

This responsive attitude is also significant in relationships between the corporation and its architects. "Covenants" with talented local, national, and international designers generate the kind of confidence that leads to imaginative proposals. As this type of arrangement suggests, however, consultants must be as willing to listen as they are to advise. The firm's in-house design staff demands high quality at a reasonable price and is an intimate managing partner in projects. It seeks a creative dialogue—a team approach that was highly effective for the seating plant. But this method will not work with architects who insist on their own autonomy. In addition, by using many designers instead of developing relationships with a select few, the company increases the risks of failure and lost time. Even with these drawbacks, Herman Miller deals with the architectural perspective in a "superior" manner (2.0 out of 2.5 points).

Maxim Two: Emphasize Casting

One feature that keeps things on track is that no single perspective is allowed to overwhelm the others. A lesson from this case is that a building represents a blend of expertise. For the seating plant, community officials were consulted; executives, managers, designers, construction specialists, and employees were included as part of an in-house team; the architect's skills were complemented by advice on programming and cost analysis; and the contractor contributed to design as well as scheduling and construction. In general, these actors were brought together at the outset of the project, a process that improved both the quality and speed of decision-making. While there were shortcomings in terms of budget control at Holland, these have been corrected and Herman Miller deserves an "excellent" mark (2.5 out of 2.5 points) for the breadth of talent used in facility development.

In defining roles, few companies participate so completely in the design of facilities. From concept to details, Herman Miller acts as a partner with the architect. Squatter sessions have become showcases to introduce the company's unwavering commitment to excellence, its belief in open communications and the high level of competence it expects from consultants and its own managers. If rapid growth continues, however, it may be difficult to maintain this personal and responsive exchange. Regional subdivisions among the facilities staff may help but it may also lead to uneven performance and unnecessary competition. Still, the corporation's record of excellence and its willingness to refine the way it assembles the cast for a project are certainly "superior" (6.0 out of 7.5 points).

Maxim Three: Sift for Relevant Facts

Due to tight construction schedules, research for individual buildings is handled as a facet of planning and design. Options are evaluated at squatter sessions and subsequently developed by outside professionals or Herman Miller's own experts. Inevitably, with little time to analyze a multitude of criteria and with an expanding number of projects, some issues go unexplored. At the seating plant, for instance, acoustics and lighting needed further study. In the end, the positive and negative aspects of a facility become a checklist for the future where successful strategies can be repeated and problems avoided. While not perfect, such a methodology is "superior" (2.0 out of 2.5 points) in the sense that it provides valuable continuity from one commission to the next.

With respect to specific research topics, these are pursued at two different levels. Image, planned growth, equipment layout, and the quality of space are major concerns during design. Beyond this process, the corporation is engaged in ongoing studies of people and their environmental needs in offices, factories, and hospitals. Technology (computers, communications and mechanical systems), flexibility (the ease of adjusting to new work patterns), and psychological factors (including noise, natural light, and the personalization of space) are investigated in the quest for useful and innovative products. Obviously, when it is building or renovating facilities, Herman Miller itself is a customer for these new approaches. This gives the company an edge, enriching the breadth of research without directly affecting costs. Although not completely tied to particular projects, the two-tiered effort deals with most critical issues and should be rated "superior" (6.0 out of 7.5 points).

Maxim Four: Manage Pluralistic Decision-Making

At Herman Miller excellence in architecture is not an isolated event. Some companies erect a fine headquarters and ignore the rest of their facilities. In the case under review, the corporate culture so emphasizes quality that well-designed buildings become part of the commitment to employees, communities, and sustained business performance. Decisions emerge from a goals statement that is endorsed and interpreted by the many groups involved in a project. Human values and consensus, rather than arbitrary aesthetic judgments or autocratic leadership, hallmark the process. The result is an efficiency and reputation in design management that provides an "excellent" example (15.0 out of 15.0 points) to other corporations.

Conclusion

Perhaps better cost control and more detailed research on individual buildings could enhance Herman Miller's procedures, and these techniques are indeed being refined; but the more significant challenge is to sustain quality in the face of continued expansion. While decentralization and a better definition of design criteria are helping the transition, it is ultimately the creativity and dedication of the facility management group itself that are the best omens for the future. To date, its track record is cause for optimism.

HERMAN MILLER INC.—HOLLAND SEATING PLANT

MAXIM		CORPORATE TASKS	MAX PTS	RATING	ACT PTS
MULTIPLE PERSPECTIVES	The Managerial Perspective	Define Objectives and Priorities			
		Establish Standards of Quality			
		Articulate Corporate Values	7.5	SUPERIOR	6.0
	The Employee Perspective	Seek Employee Participation	5.0	EXCELLENT	5.0
	The Architectural Perspective	Look for a Compatible Marriage with the Architect	2.5	SUPERIOR	2.0
		MAXIMUM SUBTOTAL	15.0	ACTUAL	13.0
CASTING	A Multitude of Actors and Roles	Appoint the In-House Players			
		Hire Outside Managers			
		Select the Design Team			
		Work with Key Public Actors	2.5	EXCELLENT	2.5
	Assembling the Cast	Determine the Mix of In-House vs. Outside Services			
		Stress the CCC Syndrome: Commitment, Communications, and Competence	7.5	SUPERIOR	6.0
		MAXIMUM SUBTOTAL	10.0	ACTUAL	8.5
RESEARCH	Design Research	Turn Facts into Options	2.5	SUPERIOR	2.0
	Critical Topics	Study Technology, Layout and Image	7.5	SUPERIOR	6.0
		MAXIMUM SUBTOTAL	10.0	ACTUAL	8.0
DECISION-MAKING	Elements in Design Management	Emphasize Goals, Not Positions			
		Develop Consensus			
		Integrate Decision-Making and Culture	15.0	EXCELLENT	15.0
		MAXIMUM SUBTOTAL	15.0	ACTUAL	15.0
		MAXIMUM TOTAL	50.0	ACTUAL	44.5

7

Philosophy and Process— United Technologies' Design Audit

UNITED TECHNOLOGIES
HARTFORD, CONNECTICUT

FOUR PROJECTS DEVELOPED DURING THE MID-1980s

Summary

UNITED Technologies' annual budget for new construction exceeds $100 million and, with five divisions, a dozen major subsidiaries, and a product line that includes air conditioners, automotive equipment, military aircraft, and electronic controls, architectural requirements are diverse in size, location, and building type. In 1983, in order to develop corporate-wide standards for excellence and enhance performance, an office of Design and Construction was established which, after a year of intense work, disseminated both a philosophy and process to guide planning and design. Key elements in this effort were threefold: (1) a mandate for high-quality facilities from the CEO, describing the benefits of the policy; (2) long-term planning procedures; and (3) an audit technique addressing immediate needs by analyzing the concepts, details, schedule, and construction of individual projects.

146

Although only five years old and still being refined, the program has resulted in significant financial savings and improved design. An investigation of the method in theory and in practice (four structures are examined—two complete and two under construction) leads to these conclusions:

- Success depends on high-level support, since managers are reluctant to give up autonomy and have mixed reactions regarding the value of audits;
- Planning and audits that occur early in the design process are more effective because this allows time to evaluate and implement specific recommendations; and
- Understanding and cooperation will grow as senior executives, the Design and Construction managers, division leaders and auditors engage in a dialogue to mutually define architectural objectives.

Background

No architectural critic would refer to United Technologies' Optics and Applied Technology Laboratory (OATL) as a "high profile" structure. Nevertheless, its lean silhouette, straightforward detailing, and well-tended landscape suggest pride and accomplishment. The design reflects a balance among several objectives: productivity, flexibility, sensitivity to worker needs, and the desire to create a corporate symbol. While

United Technologies OATL Facility in West Palm Beach, Florida (Courtesy United Technologies Corp.)

these management attitudes are not unique, the facility is distinguished by the way the results were achieved.

Many firms build—or renovate—with a particular function and image in mind and base their decisions on multiyear plans for physical growth and capital spending. For United Technologies, however, these are first steps. Under the direction of the company's Design and Construction office, before any work costing more than $2 million is begun, proposals must satisfy both immediate and long-term objectives *and* undergo an independent third-party construction audit "to reduce overall project costs while maintaining . . . operational integrity and an appropriate corporate image."[1] What is remarkable is that, although the audit process was only initiated in 1984 (OATL was one of the first structures developed with the procedure), benefits are already emerging. This is apparent in two cases that will serve as the detailed focus of this study: in a test tower for Otis Elevator more than $3.5 million in potential architectural, structural, and mechanical savings were identified; and in a Pratt & Whitney production plant in Nova Scotia, possible cost reductions amounted to $2.7 million. Significantly, in both examples, the audit team believed it was possible to take advantage of the recommendations without sacrificing quality.

Historically, the ability to integrate efficiency and excellence has been a hallmark of United Technologies during five decades of growth. Founded in 1934 as one of three companies from the government-legislated reorganization of United Aircraft & Transport Corporation (the two others were to become United Air Lines and Boeing), major sources of revenue for the new United Aircraft Corporation were Pratt & Whitney aircraft engines and Hamilton Standard propellers. By 1970, sales had exceeded $2.3 billion and the company was thirty-seventh in the *Fortune* 500.[2] Still, executives had to struggle with a critical problem: the firm was totally dependent on the boom/bust cycles of the aerospace industry. When Harry J. Gray was appointed president in 1971, then, his mandate was to make acquisitions that would assure steadier profitability. Diversification proved successful. In 1975, the corporation was renamed United Technologies to reflect its broader focus; by 1980, sales had climbed to $12.3 billion and by 1985, had expanded to over $15 billion. Today, the company manufactures a wide range of products in the aerospace, defense, building, and automotive businesses including Pratt & Whitney aircraft engines, Sikorsky helicopters, Carrier air conditioners, and Otis elevators. It employs over 184,000 people, has offices in fifty-seven countries, and operates about three hundred production plants.[3]

With such a large staff housed in many buildings throughout the world, effective facility management is obviously crucial. In 1986, the budget for renovation and new construction was $106.4 million. During the same year, twenty-three different architects, interior designers, and contractors were hired for more than sixty-five projects. To guide and coordinate the effort, a corporate-wide, step-by-step program has been prepared that outlines decision-making from the planning stages to completion and occupancy. In addition to in-house expertise, consultants evaluate architectural choices in order to assure executives that United Technologies is getting the most from its resources. Chairman and CEO Harry Gray noted that

> the appearance of our facilities should reflect the high technology essence of our corporation, an image we want to communicate to the business and financial communities and to the general public. Moreover, we can all appreciate the value that a thoughtfully planned, well-executed working environment has on our own pride and productivity. With these objectives in mind, we have established a systematic approach to managing all the factors involved in the design and construction of United Technologies facilities.[4]

The Process in Theory

The Manager of Design and Construction (D&C) is charged with translating these aspirations into reality. The position, created in 1983 and now a key element in a subsidiary known as United Properties Incorporated[5] (see the organization chart in figure 26), is filled by an individual

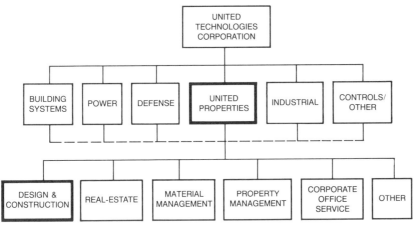

FIGURE 26   Design in the United Technologies Organization

149

who leads a team of four professionals responsible for development of almost all company facilities. The philosophy of the group is straightforward: "We don't just build buildings. We build business."[6] The attitude makes the difference. Obviously the small staff would exhaust itself if it were intimately involved with particular projects (building buildings), so it wisely fosters excellence through leadership and advisory activities (building business).

In this respect, the specifics of a new structure or renovation are appropriately left to the division that needs and will use the space. On the other hand, D&C has prepared certain general procedures to improve accountability, maintain schedules, promote quality, and control costs:

- It requires that divisions have (and annually update) a Master Facilities Plan before expansion programs are approved;
- It helps select trained and experienced construction managers to organize and manage individual commissions;
- In collaboration with the division, it awards design and construction contracts on the basis of competitive bids;
- It oversees the schedule and phases of design and construction;
- For many undertakings, it hires a consultant to perform a formal Construction Audit during the schematic design phase as well as during other points in the process;
- It reviews plans to see that they comply with the corporate design standards; and
- It coordinates a Corporate Construction Council—a body of experts whose task it is to disseminate and help divisions utilize the most up-to-date information concerning building technology, construction systems, energy conservation, computer technology, fire safety, standardized construction documents and construction management.[7]

These tasks were outlined by Jim Stillwell, a facilities expert with Owens Corning, who was appointed United Technologies' first Manager of Design and Construction and given the monumental job of redefining the entire building operation. Before the policies were in place in 1984, executives generally interpreted the physical plant simply as an expense necessary to the "real" work of the company. By contrast, Stillwell was convinced that the corporation's factories, research labs, and offices were important assets, and that he could not only reduce costs by streamlining planning and construction but, in the same process, could design facilities that would contribute to other business goals—improved productivity, enhanced community relations, and greater flexibility. With support from senior management, then, he spent a year defining a methodology to reach this complex array of management objectives.

The mission of the D&C office was clear: "To achieve and maintain a consistent high standard of excellence for corporate architectural design at the lowest appropriate cost and promote efficient operations, employee productivity and positive public impact."[8] But to do this, priorities had to be determined. Thus, to avoid overwhelming the staff, only projects costing more than $2 million come under D&C control (smaller efforts remain in the hands of subsidiaries). In addition, in order to share responsibility and not get bogged down in minute problems, D&C's primary role is to monitor planning, appropriations, design, and construction, rather than to make day-to-day decisions. To this end, the critical tools are the previously mentioned Master Plan and external "audits," each of which merits a brief discussion. The Master Plan includes a comprehensive analysis of a division's strategy regarding existing and future physical needs. Topics covered include:

- annual projections for building and land use;
- architectural, landscape, lighting and graphic guidelines;
- functional requirements regarding circulation, access, parking and utilities;
- environmental issues such as air quality, energy conservation, hazardous materials, radiation, water resources, and solid waste; and
- the concerns of the community with respect to planning and local history, and the impact of United Technologies projects on neighboring recreational, cultural, educational, medical and religious facilities.

Interestingly, the motivation for gathering this information is not only to improve the siting and quality of buildings, but also to serve "as a catalyst for determining the long-range development of the division under study."[9]

Ideally, careful preparation expedites the execution of a proposal. Planning and appropriation can take as little as two months during which managers refine space needs, explore lease-versus-build options, select the site, estimate the budget, and secure preliminary funding. Design follows for three to eight months where first steps include scheduling and the appointment of a project manager. A "Design Criteria Book" is written with information on energy, size, flexibility, technology, cost, image, and taxes. Next an architect/engineering team is competitively chosen and the actual design gets underway. Once final authorization is received, the plans, budget, and construction documents are given a thorough review and, upon approval, are sent out for bids. Generally, construction is completed within a year and a half under the project manager's constant supervision.

The second major feature of United Technologies' facility management program is the "construction audit," an outside project evaluation that takes place up to four times during the design phase (see figure 27). The first can occur as a job begins to study the scope, Master Plan, budget, schedule, and objectives. The second and most common is a concept review where issues such as function, size, aesthetics, engineering systems, environmental concerns, energy, costs, codes, and construction are probed. The third, scheduled when design is 30 to 35 percent complete, investigates specific design decisions including materials and finishes, power and fire protection, insurance considerations, and construction documents. The fourth can be convened just before the proposal goes out for bids, a last check for accuracy and completeness.[10]

The cast of characters in the audit process includes the project manager, architectural and engineering representatives, manufacturing engineers and users, financial officers and special consultants. The documentation required ranges from site soil analyses to the life cycle costs of building systems and recent utility bills. After each meeting, a formal report is distributed to the D&C office, the division head, and the architect/engineering firm for that project. Implementation of changes is mutually determined by these decision makers and, for the most part, timing of the audit is such that adjustments are cost-effective and can be made with relative ease. Fees for the evaluation average about 0.2 percent of construction costs, and the firm that audits United Technologies' buildings estimates that even if only half its recommendations were approved, the corporation's return-on-investment would be $69 for every dollar spent.[11] In addition to the dollar savings, suggestions can also improve space efficiency, maintenance, employee and customer satisfaction as well as image and security.

While in theory the rewards for this effort are great, success depends on cooperation among senior executives, the D&C staff, division managers, facility personnel, the audit team, and numerous architectural, engineering and construction consultants. Not surprisingly, with such diversity, fostering common goals and a shared perspective is a challenge. The manager of design and construction, for instance, reports to the financial vice president, a relationship that emphasizes immediate quantitative rather than long-term qualitative issues. In another illustration, some subsidiary executives remain skeptical of the complex master plan and audit procedures. They note that multiyear projections consume significant resources and, due to changes and inaccuracies, need to be continuously updated and amended; and that auditors, because they

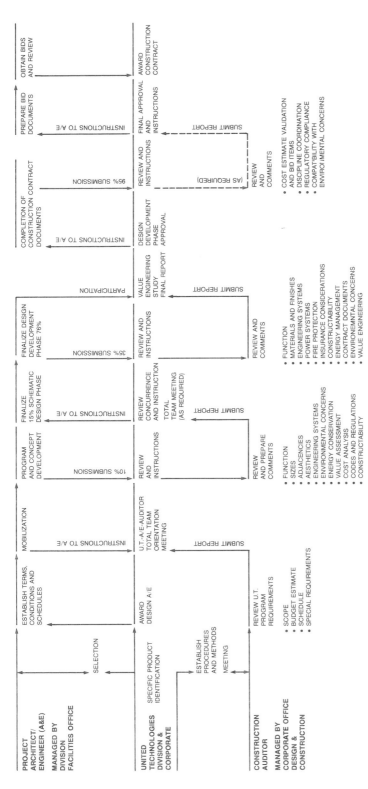

FIGURE 27 Flow Chart of the Audit Process (Courtesy United Technologies Corp.)

are unfamiliar with project details, often make obvious or even counterproductive recommendations.

The reactions can be attributed to several sources. One difficulty is coming up with reliable forecasts: managers like to be positive but not overly optimistic; they want to be prepared for growth but do not want their hands tied. In this sense, facility planning is accepted with caution because it suggests precision in circumstances perceived as uncertain. A second problem has to do with the nature of change itself. In the past, divisions built on a rather *ad hoc* basis. Now, not only did they have to give up autonomy, but also pay for the studies headquarters used to evaluate design performance. A third dilemma deals with the integration of the audit and appropriation processes. To receive preliminary funding for a structure, a division must have a program and budget. However, these proposals are frequently vague and undergo major changes as architects and engineers work out final schemes. When the design audit occurs, ambiguities are occasionally discovered and have to be clarified. Further, the proprietary nature of certain information means that outside consultants may not receive all the facts about the space they are designing. To compensate, professionals tend to enlarge buildings to provide flexibility—but this increases costs which subsequently become a focus for investigation during the design audit.

Smith, Hinchman & Grylls (SH&G), America's oldest architecture and engineering firm (founded in 1853), has worked with United Technologies to make improvements. Originally the corporation selected SH&G in 1983 to assist in developing the design and construction program. With an office dedicated solely to value management and the World Bank, IBM and Owens-Corning Fiberglass numbered among its clients, the Detroit-based consultant had established itself as a leader in architectural analysis. This expertise, which was instrumental in defining policies, was later put to the test as SH&G has gone on to audit more than thirty-five buildings for United Technologies. The practical experience, in turn, has served as feedback for enhancing the facility management effort. Suggestions include:

- Performing an audit during the programming phase to better articulate needs and goals;
- Stressing life cycle as well as first costs;
- Devising a way to calculate the noneconomic and long-term benefits of quality architecture;
- Auditing equipment—in addition to buildings—since in high-tech plants and laboratories, these expenses can easily exceed the cost of the structure itself; and

- Using post-occupancy evaluations as a method of resolving problems in existing facilities and avoiding them in future work.

These refinements are evidence that United Technologies' approach is beginning to mature. Not every manager is enthusiastic about every technique, but all understand that design is a valuable corporate resource and that they have a responsibility to strive for excellence. An advertisement in the *Wall Street Journal* summarized the company philosophy:

> Aim so high you'll never be bored. . . . Get out of the slow lane. Shift into the fast lane. If you think you can't, you won't. If you think you can, there's a good chance you will. . . . Reputations are made by searching for things that can't be done and doing them. Aim low: boring. Aim high: soaring.[12]

And two years after the facilities program was started, there are indications it is beginning to soar: "Space overruns dropped from 10.9 percent the first year to 6.9 percent the second year. And project capital cost savings increased from $2 million to $17.3 million per year."[13] The one quality the numbers do not convey is the pride both staff and executives take in their new buildings.

The Process in Action

Studying projects which have used this process is an alternative way of judging success. From an aesthetic viewpoint, for example, the Norden administration and manufacturing facility at Merrimack, New Hampshire (see figure 28), is a notable accomplishment. While visual attractiveness is a component of United Technologies' overall design commitment, generally this feature has been played down by the corporation's defense subsidiaries due to their limited public exposure and the pragmatic scope of their businesses. The Merrimack office/plant, however, with its warm brick facades, landscaped site, and nicely finished interiors, demonstrates that these structures can be architecturally inviting as well as modestly priced and efficient.

Norden products include airborne and shipboard radar, battlefield command, control and communications systems, and fire control systems, hardly household needs. Yet, despite a low profile and a small group of potential customers, the audit for this Norden building pointed out that the design provided for ease of expansion, flexibility, a pleasant environment for employees and visitors and a sense of quality. It also noted

FIGURE 28   United Technologies Norden Facility in Merrimack, New Hampshire (Courtesy United Technologies Corp.)

that at $47 per square foot, construction costs were well below the $65-per-square-foot average.[14]

Other cases—the Otis Research Tower and the Pratt & Whitney production plant—offer a more complete review of the audit process. For these two projects alone, investigators outlined $6 million in potential savings, reducing estimated expenses by 15 percent. In the end, the corporation did not take advantage of all the recommendations and, in a few areas, there were unforeseen costs and counterproductive changes. Nonetheless, while audit projections may be optimistic, the statistic is an impressive testament to the facility management operation. The stories of the two buildings highlight factors that contribute to this achievement.

Otis Elevator, founded during the mid-nineteenth century, was acquired by United Technologies in 1976. As of 1985, it was first in sales throughout North America, Latin America, and Europe. In the Pacific it ranked fourth (after three Japanese firms), but in 1984 a joint manufacturing venture with the People's Republic of China enhanced its presence in the Orient. Worldwide, it is committed to advanced product design in elevators, escalators and moving sidewalks and competes with smaller, lower-priced independent firms by offering unsurpassed service and maintenance. The strategy has paid off: the market has softened but the company continues to be profitable.[15]

Given this history, the decision to construct a state-of-the-art elevator test tower was regarded as an investment. Otis president François Jaulin referred to the facility as a "focal point for our resources and efforts . . . on quality, field productivity and product excellence."[16] It would replace an older, less flexible structure in Yonkers and would handle elevators operating up to two thousand feet per minute. It would add to corporate prestige as the highest building of its type in North America, and with three low-rise, four mid-rise, and three high-rise shafts, it would serve as a unique marketing tool for Otis equipment. It would also provide a location for testing prototypes, for developing more efficient field installation techniques, and for evaluating reliability. In June 1985, then, United Technologies approved a $14.9 million appropriation to build the 150,000 square-foot tower.

To save time, managers had selected a twelve-acre site for the structure a few months before. The land, located in a light-industrial park near Bristol, Connecticut, was ideal in many respects: (1) its price was less than the $500,000 budget for this purchase; (2) it was large enough for expansion; (3) it was less than thirty miles from the company's research and development campus in Farmington, Connecticut; (4) it was suitably zoned; and (5) a pond on the property and a mountainous background would be a dramatic setting for the tall edifice.

To further speed construction, preliminary design had begun in February 1985. In a competitive solicitation, the team of Hellmuth, Obata & Kassabaum (HOK), architects, and Spiegel and Zamecnik, Inc., engineers, both from Washington, D.C., received the commission. In addition to cost, these professionals were chosen because of their outstanding design reputation, the high quality staff assigned to the project, and the ability to meet deadlines. In-house, United Technologies Project Manager William Tarinelli, and Otis representatives George McRae and Walter Kincaid, Managers for Technical Services and Real Estate respectively, were appointed to oversee the consultants' work. Finally, in May, as details were clarified and as funding seemed certain, New York construction manager Lehrer/McGovern, Inc. was hired to monitor the budget, schedule, and actual construction.

Effective communication among these experts translated into rapid progress. In fourteen weeks, the conceptual design was complete. At this point, the building was 370 feet tall, had twenty-eight levels plus a penthouse, and was sheathed in two shades of reflective glass to give it a high-tech image. Because there was no intention to use most of the upper floors, every third one was omitted and eleven others were unoccupied. The interior contained about 148,000 square feet and included a basement, lobby, escalator testing facilities, shops, work and assembly spaces. Structurally, the tower was designed to act as a normal high rise with a thick foundation mat to counteract uplift pressure from a water table ten feet below grade.

Based on this proposal, a cost estimate of $16.3 million, and other technical data, the first audit took place on June 14. The meeting was convened in Washington under the direction of Stephen Kirk, SH&G's Construction Audit Manager. Having worked with both Stillwell and Rowe, Kirk was well versed in D&C's procedures. After the day's discussion and an analysis of the drawings, budget, schedules, and studies of the site, energy, and geotechnical conditions, he wrote a thorough report recommending that: (1) Otis management quickly fix the scope of the project to eliminate program changes that were causing delays and increasing costs; (2) because of the building's height and poor soil conditions, the company subject the scheme to wind tunnel analysis—a step that might make it impossible to meet a July 1, 1986, deadline for partial occupancy; and (3) the designers reduce the size of the structure and modify certain features to produce savings of $3.7 million.

The last suggestion was subdivided into forty-five specific ideas, each indicating its impact on initial and life cycle costs. Listing a few reveals their nature and magnitude:

Topic	Initial Savings	Life Cycle Savings
MANAGEMENT AND ORGANIZATION		
Because of potential foundation difficulties, hire a geotechnical specialist as part of the design team.	N/A	N/A
To maintain the tight schedule, advance the contract authorization for structural steel and the exterior building skin.	N/A	N/A
TECHNICAL		
Reduce tower area between floors 13–28 by about 22 feet in the N–S direction. This deletes 19,712 square feet at $90 per square foot without adverse effects on function.	$1,774,000	$2,060,000
Delete every two out of three floors to complement structural system.	222,000	351,000
Delete the escalator space as inconsistent with the tower's use since adequate space for this function exists elsewhere (reduces the floor area by 4,579 square feet at $50 per square foot).	229,000	295,000

Topic	Initial Savings	Life Cycle Savings
ARCHITECTURAL		
Explore alternate exterior wall systems which still meet image requirements but minimize cost.	450,000	450,000
Provide a janitor's closet on each level containing toilets.	(+2,000)	slight increase

The precise critique appeared to solve budget problems, improve quality, and identify important scheduling issues. Adopting many of the recommendations, Tarinelli and the construction manager worked closely with the architect and engineers to refine the design. During October 1985 there was a ground-breaking ceremony and by the end of that month contracts had been let for excavation, site work, concrete, and the foundation; around this time, too, bids for the first three phases of steel fabrication were being evaluated and a consultant was synthesizing the results of the wind tunnel studies. In light of this activity, a design development audit was organized for October 30. Again, SH&G's Steve Kirk established the agenda which sought input from United Technologies Design and Construction office, Otis Elevator's facilities team, the architect, various engineers, and the construction manager.

Unfortunately in the weeks prior to the meeting, indications arose that the project still faced significant difficulties. Not including the price of the site (which had risen from $250,000 to $800,000), a September cost estimate was $1 million more than the original $14.9 million appropriation. The bulk of this increase was due to soil conditions that were much poorer than anticipated, necessitating structural and foundation changes. Another concern was schedule. Even at this late date, Otis managers were modifying the program. The adjustments were modest but, coupled with delays in the wind tunnel research, they interfered with completion and coordination of the construction drawings. This, in turn, slowed the advance purchase of materials and made it less likely that the tower could be delivered by the corporation's December 31, 1986, deadline.

The value of the design audit was particularly apparent in this discouraging atmosphere, for although the situation was grim, the process allowed people to find ways of keeping the facility on track. On a large scale, the October report stated that architectural alterations had reduced costs more than $1.5 million, principally through the elimination of 11,300 square feet of space and the substitution of metal panels for

159

the original glass facades. SH&G experts also discovered that their estimates for steel were substantially less than those of the construction manager; instead of 2,954 tons, the audit team believed that 2,170 tons were necessary. This difference, in combination a price that was $200 lower per ton, could save an additional $1.7 million.

An inventory of smaller suggestions improved performance and augmented savings by another $329,000. These examples were typical:

Idea	Initial Savings
Site improvement costs have increased 220% since the schematic stage. Do these fit United Technologies image? Consider more natural setting to reduce maintenance and planting costs.	$100,000
Because of the expense and the requirement for special sprinklers and guard rails, delete the openings on floors 13, 14, 15, 16, 17, 19, 20, 22 and 23.	42,000
If operable windows are solely for the purpose of cleaning windows, then recommend using fixed windows and washing them from the exterior. This is less expensive and will minimize damage to fireproofing.	25,000
For each level air conditioned, consider a floor-mounted unit since the floor area does not warrant duct distribution.	some
Ensure provisions are made for the handicapped.	N/A
Integrate artwork, paintings, photographs, or other objets d'art in lobby to express history and creative linkage of the art and science of vertical transport to the function of the building.	N/A
In toilets hang all fixtures and partitions from walls or ceilings.	N/A
Compile a maintenance manual for the inhouse or contracted operating engineer.[17]	N/A

Ultimately, response to this analysis was mixed. The impressive economic rewards from the reduced quantity and cost of steel were never realized because wind tunnel studies (which were only completed in November) made it clear that, in order to assure stability, the tower's mass had to be increased rather than decreased. While smaller ideas were implemented, the design team was frustrated. Tarinelli, in particular, felt those doing the audit were unfamiliar with the dynamic decision-making that was occurring and wished SH&G had been involved at an earlier stage.[19] Interestingly, the building's schedule and $16.1 million budget seem to be on target (see figure 29), a genuine accomplishment after unexpected foundation problems and continuous adjustments to the program.

FIGURE 29   United Technologies Otis Test Tower in Bristol, Connecticut
(Courtesy United Technologies Corp.)

Thinking about the project in retrospect, the experience taught Otis and United Technologies executives certain lessons. In a survey, each participant in the audit described the ten strongest and the ten weakest features of the project and suggested improvements. The three elements viewed most positively were the satisfaction of functional requirements, the image/marketing aspects of the tower, and the creative structural design. Three important negatives were the site selection process, the constantly changing program, and the building's high cost. The main conclusions were that, while managers were pleased with the utility and high-tech profile of the effort, they would in the future devise more thorough site evaluations, and promptly review and freeze space needs.[20]

In an intriguing comparison, Pratt & Whitney Canada's (PWC) new plant near the Halifax, Nova Scotia, airport was developed almost without a hitch, but even this serene narrative provides opportunities to learn, especially about design's contributions to long-range business objectives. To maximize efficiency and minimize lead time and inventories, Pratt & Whitney wanted to simplify the form and number of operations in manufacturing and be able to produce parts on demand. A Flexible Manufacturing System using sophisticated computers, microprocessors, programmable machines and equipment, robots and automated material handling made this strategy possible. But it also demanded a rethinking of the traditional factory. For three years, an in-house "manufacturing modernization" team studied alternatives and by March 1985 had prepared a detailed program for an engine parts plant. As this document was finalized, negotiations with provincial and local governments in Canada resulted in the purchase of a site, for which PWC prepared a ten-year master plan.

The appropriation for construction and equipment was estimated at $270 million and Dumaresq & Byrne Limited architects from Halifax divided the work into three phases (see figure 30): the first was a 124,000 square-foot structure laid out along an east-west axis; the second and third additions would have a north-south orientation and would expand the facility by 112,000 and 142,000 square feet, respectively. All production areas were based on a 60' by 60' module and would be built at the same level linked by a two-story administrative and service pavilion. The mechanical systems would provide zoned controls for ventilation, temperature, exhaust, and electrical power; unrestricted access to all utilities; and state-of-the-art energy conservation.

This information—amplified by a breakdown of space needs but having few specifics on the installation of manufacturing equipment—was given to a multidisciplinary team with the challenge to have a schematic proposal before the end of June. The group successfully met the deadline due, in large measure, to cooperation and balance between in-house talent and competitively chosen local expertise. Because of its vast engineering background, Pratt and Whitney decided to serve as its own general contractor and to participate actively in the design. For Guy Poulin,

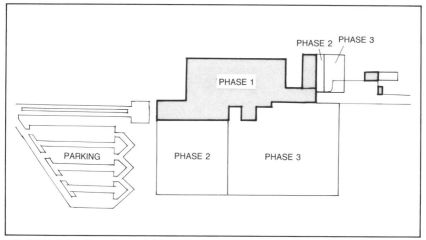

FIGURE 30   Site Plan of United Technologies Pratt & Whitney Canada's New Plant Near Halifax, Nova Scotia

the company's project manager, this was a full-time job. In addition, three others—the director of plant engineering, the manager of plant programs and facilities and the construction specialist for purchasing—devoted most of their time to the project. Beyond the architects, the team's outside consultants were advisors on mechanical/electrical systems, energy, construction management, and cost control.

After several exhausting weeks, representatives from all these areas met for a design audit on June 26 and 27, 1985. As in the test tower, SH&G was responsible for the analysis, and the results of this and the follow-up design development review proved quite beneficial. On the positive side, investigators praised the structure's image created by a clean roofline, facades modulated with attractive metal and textured concrete panels, and interior skylights providing generous natural illumination (see figure 31). They pointed out the virtues of a plan that addressed security needs with a minimum amount of fencing and animated the front of the building with amenities for recreation. Good management procedures were also highlighted, such as requesting an early review by the fire marshall, contracting for maintenance and operations manuals, and involving production staff and employees in the design process.

More immediately useful were the comments and recommendations on shortcomings, which were listed by subject with an indication of their effects on costs. The biggest issue was that phase one construction was $2 million over budget. A $500,000 site preparation subsidy from Halifax County would relieve part of the problem, but other steps

FIGURE 31   Interior Sketch of Pratt & Whitney Canada's New Plant (Courtesy United Technologies Corp.)

were necessary. Fortunately, one of the most obvious was also possible. The building was about fifty-four thousand square feet larger than programmed. While a portion of this added space could not be eliminated, SH&G did identify twenty-nine thousand square feet of reductions that would save almost $1.3 million. A second significant option—the redesign of the production floor using fifty' by fifty' or forty' by forty' bays— would decrease expenses by another $500,000. Finally, there were a

164

series of modest mechanical and electrical suggestions that together produced a dramatic $662,000 in cuts.[21]

In the follow-up audit, hosted by Pratt & Whitney on October 9, 1985, in Montreal, it was apparent that in the brief three-month period between meetings, much had been accomplished. The corporation and its consultants, by implementing over 80 percent of the audit ideas, saved $2.1 million. The project was on budget; its size had shrunk from 179,000 to 140,000 square feet; and construction was proceeding on schedule. The building shell would be completed in early 1986; machinery would be installed during the summer and occupancy would occur no later than November 1. The other item of good news was that bids for the first four contracts (site clearing, building and site services, structural frame and decking, and concrete substructure) had been received and were $200,000 below estimates.

Not content with these successes, the design team continued to search for improvements. It noted that the need to purchase cleaning equipment would increase expenses by $82,000, but simultaneously found $652,000 in potential reductions, the largest of which were to delete an unused service tunnel, relocate a rooftop mechanical platform, and postpone construction of the kitchen. These generated a total of $350,000 in savings. Other proposals were smaller: combine the elevator tower and fire stairs to minimize fire walls (a $5,000 savings); delete windows that will be blocked by later construction (a $15,000 savings); replace tube columns with H-shaped supports (up to $30,000 in savings).[22]

Similar to the Otis test tower situation, however, it was difficult to implement changes at this later stage. For ease of construction, the service tunnel (required for phase two) was left in the plans; safety precautions made the combination of fire stairs and elevators impractical; and environmental and aesthetic considerations mandated that windows and columns remain as designed. The kitchen was delayed with good economic consequences; unhappily, these were offset by higher costs from the suggested modification to the mechanical system.

Conclusion

In summary, while it is evident that the timing and details of the audit must be refined, it is also obvious from the Otis and Pratt & Whitney cases that the process helps solve immediate problems and reinforces the principle that quality facility design can be managed as a corporate resource. Success emerges from thorough analysis done by experts in architecture, engineering, costs, construction, and management. Yet insight and talent by themselves are not enough. A second critical factor in United Technologies' program is the emphasis on consensus decision-making, and the Delphi process used by Pratt & Whitney stands out as an effective model. In this technique, those involved in a project are asked to identify a structure's problems, options, and priorities. As a follow-up, responses are discussed and ranked by the group and the two-step procedure is repeated until there is general agreement. In the case of the Canadian plant, only two rounds were needed before everyone supported the recommendations that became the focus of the schematic audit and subsequent design changes. But whether reached through Delphi or by other means, mutual understanding is crucial to the facility management effort.

A final comment on the audit concerns the fact that during the Pratt & Whitney study, SH&G noted that construction was only 15 to 20 percent of the plant's total appropriation and that other expenses, especially those for computers and manufacturing equipment, were really more significant. Since technology has grown in sophistication and this kind of budget allocation is common, SH&G urged that these additional items undergo an audit similar to the one performed on a building. Interestingly, the company is beginning this type of review, and it is an important move. By analyzing quality, controlling costs and monitoring the schedules not only of buildings but of equipment, the value of design as a business resource is greatly enhanced.

Evaluation

It does not seem a coincidence that during the summer of 1986 United Technologies (in partnership with Fiat) sponsored an exhibition of Futurist art. The retrospective of sculptures and paintings—renowned for their emphasis on modernism, speed, and technology—was an opportunity to explore the interaction between "the economic world and the artistic world, and between entrepreneur and artist as participants in the development of society."[23] United Technologies design and construction program continues to investigate these issues in, perhaps, an even more dynamic fashion. In this case, the corporation is patron; the artists are talented architects and engineers; and rather than simply looking back at history, the company is making enduring contributions to its own future, to the productive and meaningful work of employees, and to the vitality of local communities. These are the goals of the facility management program and an analysis based on the four maxims suggests that: (1) support at the highest level and a philosophy calling for excellence are the foundations for success; (2) correct timing is essential to the effectiveness of corporate-wide design procedures; and (3) to assure understanding and cooperation, objectives and quality should be defined jointly by senior management *and* divisional project teams. These and other themes emerge in the discussion that follows.

Maxim One: Integrate Multiple Perspectives

It is useful to compare Design and Construction policies with the realities of implementation. In theory, they are impressively comprehensive: promoted by the chief executive, they address—in some detail— such long-term concerns as flexibility and productivity and such short-term needs as cost and efficiency. If the research ended here, United Technologies would receive an "excellent" rating for its thorough articulation of the managerial design perspective. The building histories, however, suggest that this praise must be tempered. While the OATL, Norden, and Otis facilities create a uniformly positive image for the corporation, the audit results indicate that division managers could be more involved in decisions. Besides paying for the studies, project leaders could participate in determining the timing and focus of these analyses. At present, certain audit recommendations are generated too late to be of value and, due to lack of information, others duplicate work being done by the design team or are even counterproductive. More input from subsidiaries would help avoid these difficulties, give middle managers a larger stake in the rewards for architectural excellence, and enrich a perspective that is already "superior" (6.0 out of 7.5 points).

Interestingly, while United Technologies has carefully stated the company's expectations, its approach to the employee perspective is only "average" (3.0 out of 5.0 points). In a typical case, a building program is developed by the division needing the structure, and local firms are selected to translate the data into a specific design. Obviously, the procedure allows users to make some contributions, but a more formal technique for soliciting and sharing staff ideas would probably enhance function and the transition to a new facility.

Given the diversity of operations and building types, the corporation has enjoyed remarkable success in the choice of architects. The designers vary, but quality is consistently good. A design/construction company prepared the scheme for the Norden office/plant; the Otis test tower was developed by nationally known architects; and a local firm was responsible for the Pratt & Whitney facility. All were chosen on the basis of competitive bids, but the relationships work because the selection criteria go well beyond costs. Past performance, the talents and schedules of those assigned to a commission, accessibility, the ability to meet deadlines and a commitment to work closely with both the in-house design team and other consultants are evaluated along with price. In the end, winning professionals exhibit a combination of virtues, a balance that pays off in "superior" architect/client compatibility (2.0 out of 2.5 points).

Maxim Two: Emphasize Casting

Reflecting the complex demands placed on modern facilities, United Technologies buildings are the result of partnerships among many experts. Actors in this effort include in-house managers and construction specialists, architects, engineers, a construction manager, cost analysts, contractors, and an outside auditor. Depending on their background and security demands, these individuals can be from within subsidiaries or hired consultants. If there is a unique problem (the Otis wind tunnel studies, for example), other advisors are brought in and, except for the auditor, the group is organized as a team under the direction of a division manager and/or a representative from the Design and Construction office. One skill, however, is missing—a knowledgeable programmer. In the Otis research tower, functions were constantly changing and in the Pratt & Whitney factory, equipment layout was vaguely defined. In both cases, the result was wasted time and money, a fact highlighting the importance of stating needs early and clearly. Despite this deficiency, which is being corrected, the corporation's understanding of who should be in the cast for architecture projects is quite sophisticated and merits a "superior" rating (2.0 out of 2.5 points).

In terms of how these people are assembled, a couple of refinements might be useful. Occasionally, division managers are not qualified to oversee a large undertaking and would be well served by educational programs and opportunities to work with more experienced colleagues. The second issue is the relationship among the auditor, the project team and the Design and Construction group. Presently, subsidiaries pay for audits—but the evaluations are presented to corporate headquarters. In addition, D&C also determines the timing of reviews. Instead of cooperation, this creates an adversarial situation where divisions often feel compelled to defend their choices and play down the value of audit ideas. An alternative would have the auditor report to the project team and then to headquarters. In this way, scheduling and the implementation of recommendations could focus on productive results rather than on who made correct decisions. Overall, United Technologies' building effort effectively blends in-house and outside services. Still, there is room for enhancing training and communications, improvements that suggest an "average" performance (4.5 out of 7.5 points) in the area of assigning roles to players in the design process.

Maxim Three: Sift for Relevant Facts

To remain competitive, research is the norm at United Technologies. Not unexpectedly, this attitude has had an impact on architecture, especially with respect to technical questions. The Pratt & Whitney plant was the outgrowth of a three-year investigation of flexible manufacturing systems; and the slender, high-rise structure of the Otis elevator facility went through several metamorphoses as building functions changed. The company has also devoted considerable attention to image. The striking facades of the OATL and Norden structures suggests quality and efficiency, while landscaping, courtyards and warm materials provide a welcome human scale.

By contrast, innovations in terms of layout seem to have been ignored. Instead of a plan responding to different types of production, for instance, the Pratt & Whitney factory simply uses a 60' by 60' bay because that will accommodate the largest piece of machinery. More generally, buildings often contain more square footage than anticipated, and offices are designed with little regard for new communications equipment and options of open versus closed space.

Because of this dichotomy, it is evident that research is not yet an integral feature of the corporation's design management program. Large-scale engineering and aesthetic alternatives are studied, but significant details go unexplored. Such a combination is not unusual and, although the Design and Construction staff is aware of deficiencies and is trying to find solutions, an "average" score for both methodology (1.5 out of 2.5 points) and the research topics covered (4.5 out of 7.5 points) seems appropriate.

Maxim Four: Manage Pluralistic Decision-Making

In just over two years, the rewards from United Technologies planning and audit procedures are notable. Besides the $17 million savings in capital costs, benefits include a higher degree of flexibility, better scheduling and cost control, reduced maintenance, and an increased emphasis on life cycle costs.[24] This is possible because: (1) process and objectives are outlined in advance; (2) designs are developed by teams representing a critical spectrum of expertise; and (3) decision-making is divided between corporate executives who deal with strategic issues and subsidiary managers who implement actual projects. Still, two modifications would further promote consensus and the focus on goals. The first, which has already been discussed, would make the auditor a member of the team at the division level rather than a watchdog for headquarters. The second would allow Design and Construction more direct access to the chief executive. Presently, the group reports to the financial vice president, which puts the stress on immediate returns rather than long-term quality. If responsibility could be shifted to the executive vice president or the CEO himself, there would be a better balance between the qualitative and quantitative measures of design excellence. Even with these drawbacks, United Technologies facility management techniques are "superior" (12.0 out of 15.0 points) particularly given the magnitude and scope of the operation.

Conclusion

The model described here enriches the thesis of this study because it demonstrates that the value of architecture is universal. It is not limited to special projects. Large as well as small and medium-sized firms can take advantage of this resource. And good results are not dependent on the initiative of individuals but on the integrity of the design process.

Philosophy and Process—United Technologies' Design Audit

UNITED TECHNOLOGIES CORPORATION—FOUR PROJECTS					
MAXIM		CORPORATE TASKS	MAX PTS	RATING	ACT PTS
MULTIPLE PERSPECTIVES	The Managerial Perspective	Define Objectives and Priorities			
		Establish Standards of Quality			
		Articulate Corporate Values	7.5	SUPERIOR	6.0
	The Employee Perspective	Seek Employee Participation	5.0	AVERAGE	3.0
	The Architectural Perspective	Look for a Compatible Marriage with the Architect	2.5	SUPERIOR	2.0
		MAXIMUM SUBTOTAL	15.0	ACTUAL	11.0
CASTING	A Multitude of Actors and Roles	Appoint the In-House Players			
		Hire Outside Managers			
		Select the Design Team			
		Work with Key Public Actors	2.5	SUPERIOR	2.0
	Assembling the Cast	Determine the Mix of In-House vs. Outside Services			
		Stress the CCC Syndrome: Commitment, Communications, and Competence	7.5	AVERAGE	4.5
		MAXIMUM SUBTOTAL	10.0	ACTUAL	6.5
RESEARCH	Design Research	Turn Facts into Options	2.5	AVERAGE	1.5
	Critical Topics	Study Technology, Layout and Image	7.5	AVERAGE	4.5
		MAXIMUM SUBTOTAL	10.0	ACTUAL	6.0
DECISION-MAKING	Elements in Design Management	Emphasize Goals, Not Positions			
		Develop Consensus			
		Integrate Decision-Making and Culture	15.0	SUPERIOR	12.0
		MAXIMUM SUBTOTAL	15.0	ACTUAL	12.0
		MAXIMUM TOTAL	50.0	ACTUAL	35.5

8

Architecture and the Corporation: Approaches to Excellence

The results of this study are captured in oxymorons: silent structures speak loudly; inanimate buildings have a life of their own; motionless details create rhythm and energy; the solitary edifice is the heart of a community. The apparent contradictions summarize a very important historical lesson which business has long recognized almost instinctively, namely, that architecture expresses both aesthetic *and* commercial functions. This is evident in the design of Renaissance palazzos in Italy, of guildhouses in northern Europe, of shopping arcades in Brussels, Paris, and Milan, and of monumental railroad terminals and soaring office towers in the United States.

It was, however, during the nineteenth century that companies deliberately began to exploit good architecture in support of good business. In the 1860s, for example, a boom in the American insurance industry enabled those executives to commission buildings that not only satisfied growing space requirements but also enhanced the image of insurance firms as benefactors to society. The beauty and grandeur of the Equitable, Manhattan, and Mutual Life buildings as well as other New York insurance offices prompted a 1894 guidebook to comment:

172

Beside their benevolent work, these life corporations have been among the prime causes of the city's architectural growth, for the life insurance buildings of New York surpass the office structures of any city in the world. Life insurance is indeed one of the vital features of modern life.[1]

A few years later, as other organizations emulated this approach, the general public, too, came to understand the larger significance of corporate structures. In a telling remark, Oscar Lovell Triggs, an English professor at the University of Chicago, noted that "the daring, strength, titanic energy, intelligence, and majesty evidenced in many of the modern business temples indicate . . . perhaps the dominant feature of the American character."[2]

As often happens, enthusiasm may have resulted in oversimplification not unlike the recent books that describe pathways to management nirvana and financial utopia. While it is comforting to believe that buildings reveal the *Zeitgeist* of an age or are panaceas for business problems, corporate archons and ambitious architects are neither magicians nor medicine men. Nonetheless, as this research demonstrates, they are two very different types of talented professionals who can collaborate to achieve more modest—yet quite meaningful—results. The cases show how, by working together, these individuals have used design as a tool contributing to immediate financial objectives, long-term business strategies, and favorable acclaim by critics.

Such motives are clear in the Beneficial and Hercules headquarters where executives and architects developed the projects to enhance prestige and sharpen corporate identity. In addition, their interior layouts helped to define corporate culture, improve efficiency, and respond to worker needs. Even when function and budget were priorities, the Lockheed, Herman Miller, and United Technologies studies showed how archon/architect teams struck a superb balance between high quality and moderate cost. To illustrate: the energy-saving natural light in Lockheed Building 157 created a pleasant place to work; at the Herman Miller factory in Holland, joyful splashes of color, eye-level windows and a molded clerestory enriched facades made from inexpensive mass-produced panels; for United Technologies, the high-tech features of the Otis test tower and the Pratt & Whitney manufacturing facility not only reinforced the corporate image but also responded to rigorous financial and operational constraints.

The diversity of these structures highlights the principle that excellence can be achieved independent of building type and of either corporate

173

or project size. The cases represent a David-to-Goliath spectrum: Herman Miller's 1984 revenues were $400 million when United Technologies' income was $16 billion; the Otis tower cost about $16 million whereas Hercules Plaza was an $88-million undertaking. Yet whether the figures are in the low, middle, or high range, the histories uniformly describe the many benefits each firm reaped from thoughtful facility development. Based on a thorough audit, the designers of the Otis Elevator test center were able to modify their plans to solve unforeseen foundation problems without sacrificing image or exceeding costs. And despite four years of high inflation, the state-of-the-art Hercules office, already a Wilmington landmark, was completed within its original budget.

Less dramatic examples have been cited to amplify the findings of the detailed case studies. For instance, the lively interiors of the Tower Record stores so stimulated sales and profits that a lesson was reinforced: small corporations, too, can exploit the relationships between architecture and business.[3] In addition, not only new construction, but renovation must be considered an economically rewarding opportunity. Specifically, the rearrangement of several offices on Capitol Hill and the Federal Aviation Administration's Atlantic City operation resulted in measurable improvements in productivity and worker satisfaction.[4]

With this wealth of information, the one point that needs re-emphasis is the fact that there is no single, all-inclusive method for effective design management. The ongoing facilities program at Herman Miller is staffed by a hundred people, whereas Beneficial and Hercules looked to a few capable insiders and several consultants to bring about happy results for their respective headquarters. Between the extremes are United Technologies and Lockheed, whose senior management have combined the talents of both in-house and external professionals. For the optimum outcome, the planning and decision-making technique should respond to corporate goals, the firm's own expertise, the building functions involved, and to whether a project is a repetitive or a unique commission. When these factors are carefully articulated, the finished work will validate the observation made by Thomas Watson, Jr., the legendary chief executive of a legendary corporation, who said:

> In the IBM Company, we do not think that good design can make a poor product good, whether the product be a machine or a building or a promotional brochure or a businessman. But we are convinced that good design can materially help make a good product reach its full potential. In short, we think that good design is good business.[5]

Common Ground

Because of the tremendous variety in building type, the size of a firm and managerial style, successful corporate architecture may sometimes seem a random event, a happenstance rather than the outcome of a careful process. One of the implications of the cases, however, was that the basis for quality was a system of shared beliefs. Executives at these companies understood that:

1. Design could improve the bottom line and that building, therefore, was not an unavoidable expense but a wise investment;
2. The commitment to architecture and interior design, in addition to being sensitive to short-term costs and benefits, had to be concerned with long-range results;
3. Specific goals for each project had to be established and success or failure calculated in light of these objectives; and
4. The decision-making process had to be managed so that design choices were never isolated from other corporate issues or determined by aesthetic or functional preconceptions.

It is worth expanding on these points.

Management's Conviction That Design Is a Resource

Few architects have gone to greater lengths than the Leo A. Daly firm did in its proposal for Lockheed's Building 157. Elaborate lighting and energy conservation experiments, extended interviews with managers and staff engineers, a full-scale interior mock-up, and on-site testing for fire safety just before the structure was completed represent an extraordinary effort. And judging by the results, the time and money were well spent: the working environment is one of the most desirable in the company; compared to traditional offices, the consumption of electricity was reduced by more than 50 percent; and the building symbolizes the corporation's commitment to employee satisfaction and quality products.

Surprisingly, this account has a disappointing conclusion. The Daly firm has never received another Lockheed commission, and the Lockheed divisional vice president responsible for the award-winning edifice took early retirement. The corporate culture seems not to have followed the pace-setting example of Building 157. While these events have been attributed to unexpectedly high costs, the root of the problem may have been a conflict in priorities. Executives closest to the project emphasized

175

the innovative structure's positive impact on maintenance, productivity, and morale, while those at Lockheed's headquarters were primarily concerned with budget. When the total exceeded anticipated expenses, the company's communication network did not effectively convey to senior management the added long-term value the extra dollars were buying. Thus, in spite of the design's success, those who nurtured the project on a day-to-day basis went largely unrewarded.

The lesson is straightforward: the CEO and other corporate officers, as well as the middle managers and consultants in charge of design and construction, must *all* work from common assumptions that outline how architecture can enhance business objectives. Only with such mutual values can decision makers compare and resolve differences in their analyses of short- and long-range goals, cost, and quality. Obviously, if the building team is not guided by a single perspective, or if senior management is unresponsive to design's benefits, progress will be frustratingly slow.

It does not follow, of course, that the CEO has to be involved with minute architectural decisions or even with every project. At Herman Miller, CEO Max DePree enjoys participating in facility design because it is intimately tied to the firm's products and marketing. By contrast, United Technologies' and Lockheed's corporate size and diversity leave little opportunity for top executives to deal with each building. Unlike Lockheed, however, United Technologies' chief executive has established a decision-making process and defined the parameters for development. These guidelines leave the details of facility management to divisions which use in-house experts and consultants to do programming and design and then employ external auditors to monitor the work. While the complex procedure is still being refined, the corporation and operating groups use the same basic principles to review options. Planning is streamlined; communications are good; and audits help to identify improvements.

Cooperation between senior management and those closest to a particular project is also evident in the other cases. At Beneficial, Sandy Hance and Gordon Wadmond[6] acted as high-level liaisons to CEO Finn Casperson, the Building Committee, the architect, and the construction manager. Their role was to keep things moving and foster consensus regarding the headquarters' design, quality, and price. At Hercules, John Greer, Ed Lacy, and Betty Ronat[7] were the company's project representatives who reported regularly to the corporation's chief executive and senior vice president and maintained daily contact with the designers and contractors. When discrepancies between expectations and reality emerged—

176

whether related to schedule, budget, function, or aesthetics—the arrangement facilitated expeditious clarifications and quick resolutions.

The Long-Term Perspective

Besides commitment to design excellence and to the collaboration needed to secure it, architecture is fully exploited only if decision makers have a long-term perspective. This does not imply that first costs need be excessive; superior quality is not synonymous with lavish expenses. What counts is a sensitivity to those building features that make enduring contributions to employees, to customers, to the community, and to routine maintenance. Some elements, such as energy conservation, recreation facilities, and convenience stores, may command a monetary premium. Others may just require thoughtful planning: offices can be so arranged so workers have pleasant views and good lighting; furniture components can be selected to enhance flexibility, control noise, and ensure privacy; space allocations can help define the organization's culture and encourage the exchange of ideas.

When initial price or a quick return-on-investment is the primary factor in a project, it is easy to ignore less tangible issues which tend to surface in a more comprehensive approach to building. Fortunately, the research illustrates that rewards for a conscientious and patient effort are ample. Because Lockheed's Building 157 is generously illuminated by the sun through an atrium, large windows, and specially designed ceilings, expenses for lighting are as much as 70 percent lower than other offices with the same square footage. The structure's raised floors may have cost more initially but ultimately save money by allowing employees to move computers, telephones, and work stations without assistance from electricians and carpenters—a real plus when reassignments occur as often as once or twice a year. Additionally, the architects are convinced that, although precise measurements are difficult, the attractive work environment has improved productivity.

Other case-study companies have also profited by having a long-term outlook. For Beneficial, the agonizing months devoted to rethinking the headquarters' program and the subsequent increases in budget for amenities and local services were, in the end, seen as investments that will pay future dividends. The corporation's identity and culture are stronger than they were in the spread-out Morristown facilities; staff pride continues to grow; and relationships with the Peapack community, even with the campus's large size and work population, remain cordial. In the case of Hercules, decisions to create a park and plaza and to include

177

stores and a landscaped gallery within the building have made their office a landmark in Wilmington. Visitors revel in the tower's beauty and dramatic silhouette; secretaries and support personnel have spectacular views; and the inclusion of high-tech equipment is balanced by an interior design that creates a humane and comfortable as well as efficient environment.

At United Technologies, the audit program strives simultaneously to improve the quality of planning and design and to control costs. Some bottom-line benefits are immediately apparent, but the more significant reward is that the continued use of the technique enables division managers and corporate officers to develop a fuller understanding of how the company as a whole can take advantage of architecture as an economic resource. Herman Miller's facilities can be interpreted in the same way. Although the firm has employed many designers and although its buildings and showrooms vary stylistically, the common thread is a thoughtful combination of modest price, excellent function, worker satisfaction, and community pride. The guiding precept, then, is that effective design management requires a vision that looks beyond short-term costs and profits.

Developing Specific Objectives

A third element for success is the prompt and clear definition of goals, for, as Beneficial and Lockheed found out, vague or ambiguous objectives mean delay and costly design changes. Seeking speedy answers, Beneficial began its headquarters with an incomplete outline of what it wanted and hoped for. Not unexpectedly, when proposals were presented by the design team, it was difficult for senior management to judge their acceptability. In the end, the community decided for Beneficial by rejecting the initial plan. The corporation had learned its lesson the hard way and before starting a second time it carefully established criteria for the effort. Lockheed's problems were caused by a major shift in priorities. When Building 157 began, space and cost were critical; later the architect and a company vice president modified the program to emphasize energy conservation, productivity, and aesthetics. While the added goals were admirable, they were never explicitly endorsed by corporate executives. As the price for the office grew, so did management dissatisfaction. Everyone praised the structure's high quality; no one was happy with how it had been accomplished. A good end was tarnished by poor means.

In more positive examples, facility development at Herman Miller, United Technologies, and Hercules went well because executives and the design team articulated objectives in advance. These became benchmarks for making trade-offs that kept construction on schedule and on budget. An analysis of the case studies indicates that results are best when:

- Standards of quality are made explicit without mandating specific styles and materials—unless these are part of a company's business;
- Relationships of the corporation to employees in terms of hierarchy, privacy, and security as well as the firm's relationship to the community are explained;
- Attitudes toward technology, energy, and flexibility are defined;
- Cost and time constraints are specified; and
- Priorities for evaluating different proposals are identified.

Once this information is available, professionals can focus on their search for creative solutions.

Managing Design as a Resource

A final characteristic common to corporations that effectively use design is an emphasis on managing the process rather than managing results. Since architectural problems, like many professional challenges, are somewhat unique, answers are not found in formulas. Preconceptions have to be abandoned and options explored. The valuable lesson in the Lockheed story, for example, is the benefit of looking at nontraditional methods. In that company, uninspiring offices were built to provide space and security. Given this background, it was a surprise when the vice president in charge decided—with the assistance of a talented architect— to initiate a broader analysis that could, in addition to these goals, improve energy efficiency and interior layout. It was a risk. The executive was letting go of a "sure thing," the standard plan, in favor of a process that would investigate how space could enhance long-term objectives. The answer was a modestly priced, trend-setting design that has contributed to changes in the way Lockheed management and employees think about the work environment.

Other firms have an even better track record. Unlike Lockheed, which treated its project as a unique affair, United Technologies uses a Design and Construction group to promote architecture as a resource throughout

179

the corporation. Although full implementation has yet to be achieved, the technique is interesting because it depends on a handful of high-level employees who spell out overall procedures and then make divisional managers responsible for project details. In this method, those doing the planning are those who will use the building. As the process is repeated, design becomes part of a unit's continuing strategy. While executives and consultants "audit" decisions and make general suggestions, they are not involved on a daily basis. As mentioned earlier, Herman Miller also addresses architecture and interior design on a company-wide scale, but uses an extensive group of in-house experts to assure quality and oversee construction. With regard to Beneficial and Hercules, the approaches were narrower in scope, but this is largely because their respective headquarters were one-of-a-kind commissions.

Even with such differences, there is one critical factor common to all successful projects: regardless of building type or talents involved, companies manage the decision-making process rather than emphasize final results. The style of facility development can vary, but the constant is that, without exception, corporations know that their physical plants are much more than real estate assets and express this through actions consistent with the four principles just discussed.

What is intriguing about this finding is that commitment to architectural excellence encourages better relationships with the arts, education, government, and the community—the essential aspects of corporate social responsibility. The story of Honeywell's part in an urban revitalization program is illustrative. In the late 1960s, the company realized that good business also meant a concern for society and that this belief, in turn, might be translated into good design. Thus, instead of abandoning its headquarters in a run-down section of Minneapolis, the firm renovated old brick factories into expanded offices and donated land for use as a city park. A few years later, the corporation went one step further, providing funds for neighborhood improvement so local residents could remodel their own properties.[8] The activities were beneficial in several respects. Honeywell enhanced the inner-city environment, stimulated growth, and encouraged other firms like Dayton Hudson and Control Data to institute parallel efforts. It thereby protected land values and helped make down-town Minneapolis one of the most lively and pleasant spots in the country.

What is evident is that the corporate dedication to excellence is not restricted to products or sales or even short-term growth. As University of Southern California professor James O'Toole has pointed out, there are four attributes—independent of particular goals—that characterize exceptional performance:

- Stakeholder symmetry—fairly addressing the needs of all corporate constituents including customers, employees, and shareholders;
- High purpose—recognizing that profit is the result and not the motive for corporate existence;
- Commitment to learning—responding openly and honestly to criticism, challenges, and new opportunities; and
- Aiming to be the best in everything—striving to provide the finest products and services with zero defects.[9]

From O'Toole's perspective, then, exceptional performance leads to well-designed buildings. He describes John Deere's Tractor Works in Waterloo, Iowa, for example, as a Piet Mondrian painting—"all color and geometry." More than a compelling aesthetic, however, is the fact that outstanding function distinguishes the facility. On the production line, an extensive system of computers and robots has allowed the company to cut the parts inventory in half and to customize nearly every tractor. And automation has not meant fewer good jobs, for many positions have been upgraded and the staff appreciates "the cleaner, quieter, lighter work environment and the much improved amenities [cafeterias, dressing areas] off the shop floor."[10] These circumstances demonstrate that senior management has perceived long-term value in architecture and prompted former CEO William Hewitt to comment: "Buildings have added a new dimension to our business, an additional pride in what we are about. In many fundamental ways they have raised the sights of all the people both in and outside our community who in one way or another are affected by Deere & Co."[11]

In summary, "vanguard factories and offices serve as constant reminders . . . [of the] dedication to quality in all its physical, social and psychological manifestations."[12] Buildings include works of art, plants, and quiet, comfortable places for employees to gather, and the headquarters of these firms intentionally symbolize the commitment to excellence. Weyerhaeuser's home, located on a 500-acre forest between Seattle and Tacoma, is typical: commanding a view of Mt. Rainier, it is sited on a ten-acre lake populated by swans and geese, and its five-story plan is so open and relaxed that not even the chief executive has a private office. In short, while Professor O'Toole stresses ways other than design to enhance performance, he specifically analyzes architecture as one of the keys to quality and, in this manner, confirms the thesis of this study: facilities make genuine contributions to business success. This is not to say that architecture alone confers vanguard status but, as the case studies strongly suggest, such companies are among the pace-setting firms doing something right.

The Maxims Revisited: Design Management Alternatives

Successful enterprises hold a common philosophy about the importance of building. But overlap is only part of the picture since each corporation must translate this outlook into a program that satisfies its particular situation. There are numerous alternatives in design management and the following issues, as well as the questions they generate, are critical to sound choices:

- ORGANIZATION AND STYLE OF COMMUNICATION: Is there a strong hierarchy or a more open exchange of ideas and discussion? Is decision-making done in groups or by individuals? Is the project team responsible for both design and budget or are these controlled separately?
- MAGNITUDE OF THE FACILITIES PROGRAM: What is the annual facilities budget? How frequently does the corporation build? How is long-term planning and programming used to guide development? Do the responses to corporate decisions require frequent renovations and interior changes?
- BUILDING TYPE AND SCHEDULE: Is the project unique or similar to other company structures? Does design involve proprietary or classified information? Are unusual outside approvals necessary prior to construction? Is the schedule realistic?
- PRIORITIES: In addition to function, what are the other key parameters (budget, timing, aesthetics, flexibility, environmental quality, culture, communications, efficiency)? How will trade-offs be made? Is compromise possible or are certain aspects of the program absolute?

How the queries are answered determines the appropriate mix of in-house professionals and hired consultants; the relationships among executives, managers, employees, and consultants; the person or group coordinating the design team; and the criteria for making difficult judgments. These arrangements may not only differ company to company, but also within a single firm. A business may use its own staff for the detailed design of labs and production plants and call on outside expertise for a headquarters. In another instance, interior modifications may be so common that a facility management division takes care of the work; on the other hand, if new construction is rare, programmatically diverse or innovative, independent designers and engineers might be called in.

The list of hypothetical models could continue, but the cases themselves offer more practical instruction. An interesting summary of management options is developed by recalling the maxims outlined in chapter two as analytical categories and by relating these to actual performance. An inductive method moves from specific examples to general guidelines.

Maxim One: Integrate Multiple Perspectives—
Alternatives in Assembling the Design Team

Although obvious, it is still crucial to select a design team that knowledgeably addresses project challenges. In arriving at the optimum combination of skills, the important criteria are building type, construction experience and goals. The research shows how these factors influence alternative approaches.

For example, a headquarters is special because it represents that rare moment in corporate history when architectural flair and function can be blended in equal amounts. It is a structure that welcomes visitors and impresses customers, that serves the needs of employees and enhances the decision-making processes of senior management. It provides a fitting image and its beauty enriches human lives. In the sense, then, that a headquarters affords a once-in-a-lifetime opportunity to combine prestige and pragmatism, both Beneficial and Hercules did what came naturally: they articulated objectives and contributed management skills but, having no background with the building type, wisely involved outside experts. For Beneficial, which up to this point had leased facilities, the decision was easy; for Hercules, it was slightly more complicated in that the company had an in-house staff skilled at developing chemical facilities. Its executives realized, however, that consultants knew far more about the design and construction of offices than their own people.

While such division of labor should be second nature, it cannot be taken for granted. Lockheed thought it had the solution to its space problem and only gave the design to outsiders when the architect proved that it was better prepared than the company to deal with energy conservation and innovations in the workplace. At United Technologies, which allows subsidiaries to commission buildings independently, managers now recognize the merit of systematically hiring specialists in programming, design analysis, and construction management. Security precautions sometimes limit these joint ventures, but potential cost savings and improved quality are benefits unlikely to emerge with less rigorous procedures.

Design teams at Herman Miller illustrate an additional way of blending outside talent with corporate resources. The firm produces top-of-the-line furniture components and strives to maintain a reputation for quality and innovation. To do so, it has to rearrange offices on a regular basis, redesign showrooms, and build new factories to meet growing consumer demand. This continuous flow of work (with characteristics that are often repeated one project to the next) and the desire to have greater control over process and aesthetics mean that the corporation can support a large facility management group. Architects are hired to enrich the effort with original ideas but are in constant touch with the in-house team and employees as proposals are developed and go to construction.

In a related aside, the experiences of Data General Corporation in Massachusetts deserve mention. Like Herman Miller, the company wanted a strong voice in the evolution of its office and consequently prepared much of the design itself. However, because its goals were different so, too, were the results. The high-tech firm purposefully sought to convey an image of frugality, so the building was functional and cheap; its attitude was simple: "There's no reason in our business to have an ostentatious display. In fact, it's detrimental."[13]

Without arguing for or against a particular aesthetic logic, the message is clear: project success depends on how well corporations complement the abilities of managers and staff with outside professionals. Consultants should be chosen to respond to precisely defined needs, and organizations doing most of their own work should apply this standard with special care because, as Lockheed discovered, in-house personnel may not have adequate information and skills. Even in those situations where there are exceptional employees, such individuals occasionally require the stimulation of outsiders, and competent architects and builders make excellent tutors.

Maxim Two: Emphasize Casting—The Leadership Alternatives

An effective design team requires effective leadership. Since traditionally architects have been in charge, they often assume the responsibility is theirs. While this is productive in some cases, new patterns are increasingly evident, and designers can no longer be certain that the past is prologue. An emphasis on costs, complex choices regarding computers, communications and technical equipment, and an array of methods for managing construction have shifted the focus toward other experts. In addition, beyond aesthetics and prestige, executives demand that new facilities contribute to productivity, company culture, community relations, and planning flexibility. In this context, quality is the outcome of a dedicated team effort and can be measured by several yardsticks. Deciding which yardstick is the most significant and who should coordinate design and construction evolves, as the building studies show, from a corporation's priorities.

At Beneficial the architect took the lead and once consensus was reached regarding the headquarters' main features, the process moved smoothly. To some degree this can be attributed to the fact that schedule and cost were not driving forces behind the project. Although the community of Bedminster, New Jersey, rejected the first proposal and a second was delayed because of foundation problems, the company pushed forward. Over a five-year time span, it patiently defined goals and the means to achieve them:

- To retain experienced employees, it searched for a site near its former location;
- To better define corporate culture, it constructed a beautiful campus of smaller buildings rather than a single, less costly structure, and to reinforce the effort, it developed a new logo and renovated over seven hundred loan offices across the country;
- To respond to the needs of staff and the neighboring townships, it included automatic banking, a convenience store, an expanded water treatment plant, and a highway overpass as services and amenities;
- To accommodate the future, it constructed space for anticipated growth and erected its own generating station to produce electricity.

Examining these choices, Beneficial clearly interpreted design as an investment—a component of its commitment to workers, clients, and the community as well as to the identity and long-term strength of the corporation. Since these are areas where the architect can have great impact, selecting that professional to lead the project team made sense.

By contrast, Lockheed gave the designer an equally influential role and was disillusioned. The consultant was talented and innovative, and cooperated closely with executives from the Missiles and Space subsidiary to prepare a scheme that was energy-efficient, productive, and attractive. Staff engineers were delighted and the architect was proud. Unfortunately, corporate officers were less pleased. Although costs were moderate for a building of this type, they were more than budgeted. In addition, there were troubles with the construction process. Ultimately, the design was modified slightly, funding was increased, and a construction manager hired—all of which put things back on track. But it was apparent that, with headquarters' concern for money and efficiency, a specialist in building and estimating—rather than the architect—should have been in charge.

This does not mean, of course, that vigilance about finances, management, and schedule comes at the expense of creativity. The Herman Miller seating plant demonstrates that a building can be architecturally distinguished *and* be developed within rigorous time and budget constraints. To achieve these objectives, the company started with a realistic budget and made an in-house management team responsible for the project. This group collaborated with an outside architect to prepare the proposal but followed through by detailing certain aspects of the design, by monitoring costs, and by overseeing construction. In this instance, consultants generated new ideas whereas day-to-day implementation was in the hands of the firm's own experts.

For businesses whose facility requirements do not justify such an intense operation, Hercules' example offers an alternative for monitoring expenses and quality. Following a thoughtfully planned sequence, the corporation depended almost entirely on external talent:

- First, a planner was engaged to outline space needs and optimum functional configurations.
- A construction manager and cost consultant were then hired to determine quality standards, an appropriate price range, and contracting arrangements.
- Finally, various designers and engineers were brought on board to come up with concepts that responded to this pre-established framework.

The only staffing Hercules contributed were three executives whose full-time jobs were to ensure that decision-making went well, that people communicated, and that goals were met. Initially, this approach concentrates on defining needs and objectives, and then translates these into required management and design skills. Hercules' office tower in Wilmington indicates that the results can be outstanding. For unique commissions (or for companies that build infrequently), this process has proven to be both an effective and efficient use of resources.

By combining architectural guidelines and policies from the highest corporate levels with the dedication of those in divisions and with the expertise of outside auditors, United Technologies illustrates yet another way of addressing the leadership problem. The technique is, in a sense, a hybrid of the Herman Miller and Hercules methods. Internally, an understanding of design's value is nurtured throughout the firm and paths are identified that allow managers to take advantage of these benefits. Externally, audits suggest specific modifications to reduce costs, maintain schedules, and enhance performance. As each subsidiary completes several buildings, the program increases awareness of critical issues in facility development and gives senior executives information to decide which employees and which consultants are needed on the design team.

By way of summary it need only be said that, just as there are decisions involving the mix of talents on a project, so there are options regarding who should be in charge. When human and aesthetic concerns are paramount, an architect is probably the right person. When time and money are priorities, an experienced construction manager may be the wiser choice. The individual can be staff or outsider, depending on the type of structure and the company's volume of work. What is important is to avoid leadership by default, which too frequently leads to costly mistakes and costly solutions.

Maxim Three: Sift for Relevant Facts—
Alternatives in Communication

A good marriage is characterized by good communication. The union between a corporation and building consultants is no different. Stories abound (and courts constantly hear arguments) about the architect who never listened, the contractor who never let people know what was going on, the client who was unreasonable and indecisive. Management advisor David Maister noted that difficulties arise when designers see complications where laypersons see none and when executives, who are accustomed to accomplishment, authority, and respect, are "forced to place their affairs for an uncertain period of time [and even more uncertain cost] into the hands of a practitioner of an impenetrable art." This perceived loss of control can also be amplified by a clash in values. Business virtues include organization, discipline, lines of authority, and planning. The creative consultant appears to dwell on "ambiguity, lack of structure and the unconstrained contemplation of nuance."[14]

In view of this potential conflict, taking actions to enhance the effectiveness of the corporate architectural process is an absolute necessity. One step is to make sure the project team speaks a common language. A strength in the Lockheed case was that executives, employees, and the designer were well versed in research (unfortunately, their dialogue did not extend to other critical topics). For Beneficial, the vocabulary focused on the headquarters as a long-term commitment to staff and community. At Hercules, United Technologies, and Herman Miller, the discussion had a mathematical orientation since function and aesthetics were seen in such quantifiable terms as budgets and schedules. While no one language is better than another, sharing definitions is the key to successful interaction.

A second avenue for facilitating communication is to so organize the design team that it complements the corporation's normal decision-making procedures. As an illustration, Herman Miller uses its interactive Scanlon Plan to deal with business problems, and expanding on that technique calls on a similar participatory approach to solve design problems. Officers and factory employees, construction managers and contractors, plant engineers and the architect are all invited to contribute. Everyone is kept up-to-date and asked for advice when major changes are contemplated. And once the structure is finished, the corporation encourages recommendations for post-occupancy refinements. An equally open network between Lockheed Missiles and Space staff and its consultants resulted in the innovative Building 157. As noted, however, frictions emerged between top management and the architect because the exchange did not include the necessary construction management experts, and because it was impossible to integrate the relaxed, matrix-type organization used in the design effort with Lockheed's otherwise formal hierarchy.

The last comment explains why many project teams are arranged in layers. In hierarchical corporations, the convention is to treat architecture as a business issue: state the problem, gather facts, explore alternatives, and seek approval. This is the model adopted by Beneficial, Hercules, and United Technologies. In these cases, one or two consultants were selected as conduits into the decision-making ladder; other outsiders presented ideas to these leaders who synthesized information and then passed it to executives. Architectural choices were thus evaluated in ways that paralleled regular company channels and, since the talents of the team were well balanced, consensus was reached with minimum effort. This was especially true at Beneficial and Hercules, where proposals were made directly to vice presidents and the CEO. At United Technologies, where auditors reported at the corporate level while the design team worked with subsidiaries, the greater distance among decision makers increased the possibilities for misunderstanding. Still, with support from a chief executive who firmly believes that architecture is a long-term resource, the aims of officers, managers, and consultants are beginning to converge and communications are improving.

Maxim Four: Manage Pluralistic Decision-Making—
An Abundance of Tools

The case studies indicate that contemporary corporations are showing a distinct interest in architecture, interior design, construction, and facility management. Some companies (including IBM and John Deere in the United States and Olivetti in Italy) have long been convinced that buildings contribute much more than prestige to corporate success. For others, however, the conviction is a recent phenomenon, brought about, in part, by the energy crisis, rising real estate and development costs, changing technologies in offices and factories, and declining productivity. These challenges and an array of architectural responses have been the substance of feature stories in such nondesign publications as the *Wall Street Journal, Business Week, Fortune, Forbes, Time,* and *Newsweek.* The articles have drawn attention to the economic and strategic benefits of excellence and highlighted the ways forward-looking managers and designers can reap those rewards.

One of the most powerful tools in facility decision-making is the computer. There is, for example, a $285,000 software package available that easily handles voluminous data on equipment, maintenance, and property records and can "also equitably allocate and distribute office space among tens or even hundreds of thousands of employees at a time."[15] While expensive, the system is a window to the future. In addition to inventory and design alternatives, this and other less costly programs can assist with strategic planning and growth forecasts, budgeting and energy conservation, depreciation and tax accounting, and the preparation of presentation and construction drawings.[16] Inevitably, as prices come down and users become more sophisticated, small and medium-size firms will seize opportunities in this field that the large corporation has already exploited.

Improving the efficiency of mechanical systems is another area where computers contribute to building design and performance. Heating and cooling can be so controlled that, regardless of outside conditions, temperatures are comfortable when employees are present and energy consumption minimized when a structure is empty. Related devices can also monitor for fire and help contain hazards by turning on sprinklers and by changing air pressure. Other computerized options include solutions to security, circulation, and lighting concerns. Movement through a facility can be made difficult with entrances requiring special access codes or speeded up with elevators that anticipate demand. And since lights are one of the biggest energy users, sensors can be installed that dim fixtures in daylight and turn them off when rooms are unoccupied. Finally, owners can install private telephone systems that save on line fees and add flexibility in the transmission of voice and data.[17]

On a more personal level, the human resource conclusions of this research establish that good design requires team effort. Engineers and architects are needed but so are professionals in space planning, cost analysis, zoning, transportation, energy, lighting, interiors, acoustics, office and communications equipment, financial and legal matters. Construction management talent may also be useful—especially in the early phases of a project to deal with feasibility, programming, selection of the architect and engineer and later, to address cost control, bidding, contracting, and scheduling.[18] Imitating United Technologies' construction audit, so-called "value engineering" should be included on the list of important tools. In this technique, independent cost and function analyses are prepared to identify changes that reduce expenses while maintaining quality.[19]

A last and indispensable vehicle for exploiting design is to designate specific in-house responsibility for facility management. A 1983 *Harvard Business Review* study calculated that American companies held real estate valued around $1.4 trillion and that this represented at least 25 percent of the average company's assets.[20] With so much at stake, corporations have actively begun to manage properties, trying to measure more precisely the quantitative and qualitative return on these investments. But if they are to avoid certain casual attitudes of the past when many architectural judgments were based simply on aesthetics and cost, then the commitment to excellence must be initiated from within. For a small enterprise, this may be the knowledgeable interest of a senior executive; in a large organization, it may be the mission of a facility management division; in the most elaborate cases, it is among the duties of an extensive real estate subsidiary. Whatever the form, there is no substitute for in-house leadership. ARCO property manager Ben Culber, who is in charge of more than $1 billion in holdings and employs a multitude of consultants, stated emphatically that no one manages projects "nearly as well as our own people."[21]

Concluding Note

In an unorthodox but useful interpretation of engineering, David Billington profiles that discipline as an ally of the arts and an exciting expression of the human spirit. Referring to the Brooklyn Bridge, the graceful viaducts of Swiss designer Robert Maillart, and the Hoover Dam as grand illustrations of his thesis, the author quotes Robert Fulton to the effect that the engineer's real task goes well beyond technology. Fulton wrote that engineering professionals "should sit down among levers, screws, wedges, wheels, etc., like a poet among the letters of the alphabet, considering them as the exhibition of his thoughts, in which a new arrangement transmits a new idea to the world."[22] In this sense, Billington relates engineering ideals to those of the social sciences, claiming that "the worth of engineering artifacts . . . [can be] measured in terms of their benefit to society."[23]

This same thought can be applied to corporate architecture because the organization's offices, stores, laboratories, factories, and warehouses have a tremendous impact on the American landscape. These structures should enrich their communities even as they serve the business functions of management, marketing, production, and research. Perhaps the Draper Company (a textile machinery firm) had these objectives in mind when, between 1856 and 1916, it developed the village of Hopedale, Massachusetts. Workers there rented two-bedroom homes with gardens and indoor plumbing for five dollars a month (about 13 percent of a machinist's pay); they enjoyed a marina, library, town center, tennis courts, and extensive parks. And, of course, the benefit to Draper was a cadre of experienced and loyal employees who rarely quit.[24]

This tradition has been continued in the post-war era by companies like Cummins Engine in Columbus, Indiana. The corporation not only sets an example with its own offices and plants, but also has a foundation that pays the architectural fees for public edifices as well. Established in the mid-1950s with the intention of creating an environment that would lure top executives to the area, Cummins' support has been so effective that Columbus has become a center of extraordinary architecture. Each year sixty thousand visitors come to the city to see structures designed by I. M. Pei; Eliel Saarinen; Skidmore, Owings & Merrill; Mitchell-Giurgola; and other internationally respected firms. But more important than any single project is the fact that, as a local high school teacher put it, "the architectural program has taught this town to dream."[25] Great dreams are the stuff of life and fortunately today great dreamers are found in corporate suites and architectural offices.

It is clear from the case studies and related developments that a heritage of corporate building excellence exists in America; indeed, it is a proud and increasingly rich tradition. To older motives for quality (prestige, visibility, and return-on-investment), new ones can be added (improved productivity, reduced costs, better definition of a business's culture, employee satisfaction, enhanced flexibility, and good corporate citizenship). These goals can be reached regardless of company size or building type. All that is required is a commitment to excellence implemented by a thoughtful approach to organization, leadership, communication, and tools (see table). When this is done well, the benefits accrue to corporations, employees, and society. And the resulting architecture stands as

Motives for Architectural Excellence	
Prestige	
Visibility	Traditional
Return-on-Investment	
Productivity	
Cost Reductions	
Definition of Culture	New
Employee Satisfaction	
Flexibility	
Good Citizenship	

Required Qualities

Conviction That Design Is a Resource

Long-Term Perspective

Specific Objectives

Design Management

Management Options

Maxim	*Management Corollary*
Integrate Multiple Perspectives	Assemble the Design Team to Reflect Goals and Needed Talents
Emphasize Casting	Be Certain Design Leaders Respond to Corporate Priorities
Sift for Relevant Facts	Seek a Common Language to Evaluate Problems and Possibilities
Manage Pluralistic Decision-Making	Organize the Process, People, and Programs

a quiet but powerful response to American designer Louis Sullivan's probing question:

> How shall we impart to this sterile pile, this crude, harsh, brutal agglomeration, this stark, staring exclamation of eternal strife, the graciousness of those higher forms of sensibility and culture that rest on lower and fiercer passions? How shall we proclaim from the dizzy height of this strange, weird, modern housetop the peaceful evangel of sentiment, of beauty, the cult of a higher life?[26]

Appendix: Resources in the Area of Facility Management

Not unexpectedly, as corporate leaders recognize the importance of facility management, the resources available to decision makers in the field continue to grow. As with any new discipline, however, the search for tools requires patience and persistence. In this sense, while the following lists are not comprehensive, they do outline pathways to further expertise and information.[1]

Degree Programs

Cambridge College (New Jersey)—Graduate Program
Cornell University (New York)—Undergraduate and Graduate Programs
Grand Valley State College (Michigan)—Undergraduate and Graduate Programs

Organizations

Association of Physical Plant Administrators of Colleges and Universities (APPA—Alexandria, Va.): A membership organization supporting the unique facility management needs of institutions of higher education.
The Building Owners and Managers Association (BOMA—Washington, D.C.): An organization of managers and proprietors of office buildings and developers and agents of commercial properties. Activities include educational programs in property management and lobbying.

Design Management Institute (DMI—Boston, Mass.): An organization of corporate and independent designers committed to the principle that quality design is a business resource. The focus tends to be on product and graphic design although facility issues are also addressed.

Environmental Design Research Association (EDRA—Washington, D.C.): An organization promoting design research including studies of the work environment. Most members are academics or academic institutions.

Institute of Business Designers (IBD—Chicago, Ill.): A membership group of professional interior designers who specialize in the design of business facilities.

International Association of Corporate Real Estate Executives (NACORE—West Palm Beach, Fla.): A membership organization of corporate executives responsible for functions related to the acquisition or management of real estate.

International Facility Management Association (IFMA—Houston, Tex.): A professional organization supporting the informational and educational needs of corporate, government, and health-care facility management executives.

Publications

The library of facility management titles is expanding rapidly. Categories of particular interest include: Facility and Real Estate Management, Technical Handbooks (e.g. Lighting, Energy, and Acoustics Manuals), Space Planning, Programming, Environmental Design Evaluation (Post-Occupancy Evaluation), Office Automation, Ergonomics, Management and Organizational Development. Many of the professional organizations have recommended reading lists. In addition, these are a few of many periodicals that deal with the subject:

Building Design and Construction
Business Facilities
Contract
Corporate Design
Facilities Design and Management

Computer Software

There is a broad range of facility management computer software. Most of it addresses post-construction management concerns that vary from scheduling and record-keeping to sophisticated space planning and forecasting. Prices and hardware requirements also vary significantly and expert advice is needed to match user needs with the capabilities of various programs. In addition to the graphic options available through separate Computer Aided Design (CAD) programs, facility management software can assist with these tasks:

- Furniture and Equipment Management
- Lease Management
- Maintenance Management
- Project Management
- Space Forecasting
- Space Management
- Stacking and Blocking

Notes

Preface

1. S. Pfeiffer, "Different Breeds," *Science 86* (January/February 1986): 24–26.

Chapter 1.   The Rationale for Rational Design

1. Philip Johnson, quoted in Paul Heyer, *Architects on Architecture: New Directions in America* (New York: Walker and Company, 1966), 292.
2. This term was used by David Fenn, *The Corporate Oligarch* (New York: Simon & Schuster, 1969).
3. Leo Marx, *The Machine in the Garden* (New York: Oxford University Press, 1964).
4. Carl B. Kaufmann, *Man Incorporate: The Individual and His work in an Organized Society* (New York: Doubleday & Co., 1967), 11.
5. James W. Rouse, "Cities That Work for Man," in *Man in the City of the Future,* eds. Richard Eells and Clarence Walton (New York: Macmillan, 1968), 147–148.
6. Charles N. Glaab, *The American City: A Documentary History* (Homewood, IL: Richard D. Irwin/Dorsey Press, 1963), 66–67.
7. Kaufman, op. cit., 178.
8. Richard Eells, *The Corporation and the Arts* (New York: Macmillan, 1967), 80–114, esp. 82.
9. Walton H. Hamilton, "On the Composition of the Corporate Veil," *Publications of the Brandeis Lawyers Society* (Philadelphia, 1946), 4.
10. Johann Friedrich Geist, *Arcades: The History of a Building Type,* trans. Jane O. Newman and John H. Smith (Cambridge: The MIT Press, 1983), 217 and 221–222.

11. John Welborn Root, paper delivered at the Chicago Art Institute, June 1890. Quoted in Sigfried Giedion, *Space, Time and Architecture: The Growth of a New Tradition,* 5th ed. (Cambridge: Harvard University Press, 1967), 382.

12. Montgomery Schuyler, "The Economics of Steel Frame Construction," in Lewis Mumford, ed., *The Roots of Contemporary American Architecture* (New York: Grove Press, 1959), 234.

13. Richard A. Goldthwaite, *The Building of Renaissance Florence* (Baltimore: The Johns Hopkins University Press, 1980), 86.

14. The Tribune Company, *Tribune Tower Competition* (Chicago, 1923; reprint ed., New York: Rizzoli, 1980), 1:3.

15. Thomas Walton, "The Sky Was No Limit," *Portfolio,* April/May 1979, 82–89.

16. The Rouse Company, *The Shopping Place,* Corporate Brochure (Columbia, MD, n.d.), 6–10.

17. Gurney Breckenfeld, "The Rouse Show Goes National," *Fortune* 27 July 1981, 49.

18. "Architecture as Corporate Asset," *Business Week,* 4 October 1982, 124–125.

19. Ibid., 125.

20. Ibid.

21. Craig Unger, "Tower of Power," *New York,* 15 November 1982, 42.

22. Joseph Giovannini, "The Grand Reach of Corporate Architecture," *New York Times,* 20 January 1985, Business Section, 1, 28.

23. A. S. Dewing, *The Financial Policy of Corporations,* 5th ed., (New York: Ronald Press, 1953), 1:17.

24. Ronald Goodrich, "Seven Office Evaluations: A Review," *Environment and Behavior,* May 1982, 354.

25. Lyndall Urwick, *The Golden Book of Management,* (Salem, NH: Ayer Company, 1956; reprint ed., Alfred D. Chandler, ed., 1980), s.v. "William Leffingwell" and "Harry Hopf."

26. John Naisbitt, *Megatrends: Ten New Directions Transforming Our Lives* (New York: Warner Books, 1982), 39.

27. New York Stock Exchange Office of Economic Research, "People and Productivity: A Challenge to Corporate America," November 1982, 47.

28. National Office Products Association, "The Future of the Office Furniture Industry," quoted by Arthur R. Williamson, "Detailed Study Forecasts 10 Year Changes in Office Furniture Industry," *Designer's West,* January 1984, 164.

29. Buffalo Organization for Social and Technological Innovation, "The Impact of Office Environment on Productivity and Quality of Working Life," Research Summary (Buffalo, 1983), 9.

30. Terrence E. Deal & Allan A. Kennedy, *Corporate Cultures: The Rites and Rituals of Corporate Success* (Reading, MA: Addison-Wesley Publishing Company, 1982), 3–19.

31. Thomas J. Peters and Robert H. Waterman, Jr., *In Search of Excellence* (New York: Harper and Row, 1982), 11.

32. Alexander L. Taylor, III, "Striking It Rich," *Time*, 15 February 1982, 39.
33. See the original case study prepared for this book on pages 97–121.
34. This scenario and the quotes are taken from Gurney Breckenfeld, "The Odyssey of Levi Strauss," *Fortune*, 22 March 1982, 110–124.
35. Daniel Yankelovich, *et al.*, *Work and Human Values: An International Report on Jobs in the 1980s and 1990s* (Aspen: Aspen Institute for Humanistic Studies and the Public Agenda Foundation, September 1983), 7.
36. William H. Whyte, Jr., *The Organization Man* (New York: Simon & Schuster, 1956).
37. D. Quinn Mills, "Bridging the Corporate Generation Gap," *New York Times*, 7 April 1985, Business Section, 3.
38. Yankelovich, *et al.*, *Work and Human Values*, 21–24, 79–92.
39. Thomas F. O'Boyle, "Loyalty Ebbs at Many Companies as Employees Grow Disillusioned," *Wall Street Journal*, 11 July 1985, sec. 2, 27.
40. "More Companies Send New York a Message—'Goodbye'," *Fortune*, May 1976, 272.
41. Kent R. Student, "Cost vs. Human Values in Plant Locations," *Business Horizons*, April 1976, 14.
42. *Design Process: Olivetti 1908–1978*, Exhibition Catalogue, Nathan H. Shapira, Curator (Ivrea, Italy: Olivetti, 1979), 20.
43. Ibid., 28–29, 224–227.
44. Building Programs International, "Procter & Gamble: An Analysis of Its Organizational Climate with Implications for Design," unpublished report, New York City, September 1980.
45. Daniel F. May, "You'll Get Even Better Service," *Republic*, August 1985, 71.
46. For details see the original case study prepared for this book on pages 122–145.
47. Gary Hall, "Wired for Change," *Architectural Technology*, Spring 1984, 14–23.
48. The original case study prepared for this book on pages 50–73 adds specifics to the Lockheed story.
49. Thomas Fisher, "Waste Not, Want Not," *Progressive Architecture*, April 1985, 81.
50. James B. Gardner, "Daylighting Cuts Energy Use to 19,600 BTU per Sq. Ft. per Year," *Architectural Record*, January 1984, 139.
51. Alan Windsor, *Peter Behrens: Architect and Designer* (New York: Whitney Library of Design, 1981), 129.
52. Phil Patton, "When Your Company Leaves Town," *United*, May 1983, 94.
53. See the original case study prepared for this book on pages 122–145.
54. Archiris, Letter to the Author, September 20, 1982.
55. John Maurice Clark, *Economic Institutions and Economic Welfare* (New York: Knopf, 1957).
56. Clarence Walton, *Corporate Social Responsibilities* (Belmont, CA: Wadsworth, 1968), 48–52.

57. Ibid., 141.
58. John deButts, Press Release, AT&T, New York, 30 March 1978, 1–2.
59. Philip H. Bess, "Beyond Irony: Can Religion Point the Way to Architectural Renewal?" *This World,* Fall 1985, 106.
60. Alexander Giacco, videotape of Dedication Ceremonies, Wilmington, Hercules Corporation, 28 June 1983.
61. Alfred D. Chandler, Jr., *Strategy and Structure: Chapters in the History of Industrial Enterprise* (Cambridge: The MIT Press, 1962).
62. James Sloan Allen, *The Romance of Commerce and Culture: Capitalism, Modernism, and the Chicago-Aspen Crusade for Cultural Reform* (Chicago: University of Chicago Press, 1983).
63. Alvin H. Reiss, "Satisfying Symbiosis," *American Way,* September 1983, 70.
64. Christopher B. Leinberger, "Your Greatest Asset May Be Your Own Backyard," *Wall Street Journal,* 28 November 1983, 30.

Chapter 2.   Maxims to Maximize Results

1. *Webster's New 20th Century Unabridged Dictionary,* 1958 ed.
2. Joseph Schumpeter, *Capitalism, Socialism and Democracy* (New York: Harper and Brothers, 1942), 61.
3. Ludwig Wittgenstein, *Philosophical Investigations,* trans. G. E. M. Anscombe (New York: Macmillan, 1953). Interested readers will also find Wittgenstein's study, *Culture and Value,* of great relevance to the theme of creativity and rationality; trans. Peter Winch (Chicago: University of Chicago Press, 1980).
4. For a popular description of this momentous debate see the article by John Gliedman, "Einstein Against the Odds: The Great Quantum Debate," *Scientific Digest* 91 (June 1983): 74–83.
5. Fred Alan Wolf, *Taking the Quantum Leap: The New Physics for Nonscientists* (New York: Harper & Row, 1981).
6. Jane Jacobs, *The Death and Life of Great American Cities* (New York: Vintage Books, 1961), 4.
7. Wolf Von Eckardt, *Back to the Drawing Board* (Washington, DC: New Republic Books, 1978), 62–63.
8. Quoted in Robert McLean, III, *Countdown to Renaissance II: The New Way Corporate America Builds* (Pittsburgh: Urban Marketing Associates, 1984), 47–48.
9. Craig Unger, "Tower of Power," *New York Magazine,* 15 November 1982, 45.
10. Thomas J. Watson, Jr., "Good Design Is Good Business," in *The Uneasy Coalition: Design in Corporate America,* ed. Thomas F. Schutte (Philadelphia: University of Pennsylvania Press, 1975), 62.
11. Ronald Goodrich, "Seven Office Evaluations: A Review," *Environment and Behavior,* May 1982, 360–361.
12. Building Programs International & Interior Facilities Associates, "How People Perceive Their Office Environment," for Citicorp, New York, November 1979, 12–13.
13. David B. Hattis and Thomas E. Ware, *The PBS Performance Specification*

for Office Building (Washington, DC: National Bureau of Standards, 1971).

14. Philip Langdon, "Building for Business," *Metropolis,* March 1983, 18.

15. Samuel C. Johnson, "Mr. Wright and the Johnsons of Racine, Wis.," *AIA Journal,* January 1979, 65.

16. "IBM: In Real Estate and Construction," *Corporate Brochure* (Armonk, NY: IBM, n.d.).

17. Based on a discussion with Terence Ainscow, Director of Corporate Facilities Planning at Syntex Inc., Palo Alto, CA, 1 March 1984.

18. David L. Armstrong and Joan B. Dent, "Facility Management: The Growing Importance of Place," *Concepts,* Autumn 1981, 5.

19. This example comes from a conversation with John Glass, design center executive at Ewing, Cole, Cherry, Parsky, 20 November 1985.

20. Tom Wolfe, cited in Thomas Hine, "A Spunky Critic Gives Architects Reason to Pause," *Philadelphia Inquirer,* 16 June 1985, sec. G, 16.

21. Fay Horton Sawyier, "A Service Model for Architects," *The International Journal of Applied Philosophy* 1 (Spring 1983): 55–66.

22. Kevin McKean, "Decisions, Decisions," *Discover,* June 1985, 22–23.

23. Case described in a 15 July 1985 letter to the author from Robert L. Miller, an architectural consultant in Washington, D.C.

24. Thomas Fisher, "Opposites Attract," *Progressive Architecture,* August 1984, 82–89.

25. Interview with Lee S. Windheim, Vice President of Leo A. Daly/San Francisco and head architect for Lockheed's Building 157, 6 March 1984.

26. Leo A. Daly Company, "Going Beyond the Perimeter with Daylight," *Lighting Design and Application,* March 1984, 33.

27. Passive Solar Industries Council, "Passive Offices Performing Even Better Than Predicted," *Passive on the Move* 2 (August 1982): 1–2.

28. U.S. Army Corps of Engineers, Construction Engineering Laboratory, "The Use of Habitability Research to Design Office Environments," *Information Exchange Bulletin* R5 (June 1982).

29. Quotes taken from Andrea Oppenheimer Dean, "Corporate Contrast in the Suburbs," *Architecture,* February 1985, 66, 68.

30. Henri Fayol, *General and Industrial Administration,* trans. J. A. Conbrough (Geneva: International Management Institute, 1929).

31. Alfred D. Chandler, Jr., *The Visible Hand: The Managerial Revolution in American Business* (Cambridge: Harvard University/Belknap Press, 1970).

32. See for example, the books by J. M. Jones, *Introduction to Decision Theory* (Homewood, IL: Richard D. Irwin, 1977); also L. Ackoff, *The Art of Problem Solving* (New York: John Wiley, 1978); and H. E. Frank, *The Managerial Decision-Making Process* (Boston: Houghton Mifflin, 1975).

33. Two older but excellent articles on this topic are M. A. Wallach, et al., "Diffusion of Responsibility and the Level of Risk-Taking in Groups," *The Journal of Abnormal and Social Psychology* 68 (1964): 263–264, and D. G. Marquis, "Individual and Group Decisions Involving Risk," *Industrial Management Review* 9 (Fall 1968): 69–75.

34. Roger Fisher and William Ury, with Bruce Patton, ed., *Getting to Yes: Negotiating Agreement Without Giving In* (New York: Penguin Books, 1983), 13.

35. Robert McLean III, *Countdown to Renaissance II: The New Way Corporate America Builds* (Pittsburgh: Urban Marketing Associates, 1984), 33.

36. Paul Goldberger, "Embracing Classicism in Different Ways," *New York Times*, 30 June 1985, sec. H, 25.

37. Victor H. Vroom, "A New Look at Managerial Decision Making," in *Readings in Management*, 5th ed., ed. Max D. Richards (Cincinnati: South-Western Publishing Company, 1978), 105–121.

38. William M. Evan and John A. MacDougall, "Interorganizational Conflict: A Labor-Management Bargaining Experiment," *The Journal of Conflict Resolution* 11 (December 1967): 398–413. Also see Hans Georg Gemunden, "Coping with Inter-Organizational Conflicts: Efficient Interaction Strategies for Buyer and Seller Organization," *Journal of Business Research* 13 (1985): 405–420.

39. See the original case study prepared for this book on pages 74–96.

40. See the original case study prepared for this book on pages 50–73.

41. J. Patrick Wright, *On a Clear Day You Can See General Motors* (New York: Avon Press, 1979), 25.

Chapter 3. Building 157—The Lockheed Story

1. Robert A. Fuhrman, "An Introduction . . . Building 157," Corporate Brochure, (Sunnyvale, CA, March 1983), ii.

2. James B. Gardner, "Daylighting Cuts Energy Use to 19,600 BTU per Square Foot per Year," *Architectural Record*, January 1984, 138–143, highlights the innovative approach to natural lighting in the Lockheed office.

3. Leo A. Daly, "The Challenge Continues," Corporate Brochure (Omaha, NE, n.d.).

4. Lee S. Windheim, attachment in a letter to the author, 8 March, 1984.

5. U.S. Department of Labor, Bureau of Labor Statistics, Table 78, under "Transportation Equipment," *Handbook of Labor Statistics* (Washington, DC: Government Printing Office, December 1983), 182–183.

6. Michael D. Shanus et al., "Going Beyond the Perimeter with Daylight," *Lighting Design and Application*, March 1984, p. 33.

7. R. J. Riegel et al., "Case Study: Lockheed Building 157—An Innovative Deep Daylighting Design for Reducing Energy Consumption," *Advances in Energy Cost Savings for Industry and Buildings*, Proceedings of the Sixth World Energy Engineering Congress (Atlanta, 29 November–2 December 1983), 148.

8. Buffalo Organization for Social and Technological Innovation, *The Impact of Office Environment on Productivity and Quality of Work Life* (Buffalo, n.d.).

9. R. J. Riegel, 149.

10. James B. Gardner.

11. A. Kent MacDougall, "More Office Workers Are Getting a Little Sunshine in Their Lives," *Los Angeles Times*, 19 December 1982, sec. 6, 1.

12. Dale Bryant, "Lockheed's Secret Garden," *San Jose Mercury News*, 1 March 1984, sec. D, p. 1.

13. A. Kent MacDougall.

14. "Employees Respond to Lockheed Building 157," *The Professional Energy Manager,* August 1984, 3.

Chapter 4. A First New Home—The Hercules Headquarters

1. John Morris Dixon, "Buttressing Downtown," *Progressive Architecture,* October 1983, 76.
2. "A Brief History," Corporate Brochure (Wilmington: Hercules Powder Company, 1962).
3. "The Fortune Directory of the Five Hundred Largest U.S. Industrial Companies," *Fortune,* 5 May 1980, p. 282.
4. John L. Andriot, ed., *Population Abstract of the United States* (McLean, VA: Andriot Associates, 1980), 116.
5. John E. Greer, "Goals for Headquarters Building," Memo, Hercules Incorporated, 2 January 1980.
6. A modest excursion into the significance of the "language game" illustrates why it may have paid off for the New York designers. An analysis called Neuro Linguistic Programming (NPL), developed by Richard Bandler and John Grinder, suggests that "sellers" adjust their communications style to those they seek to influence. NPL practitioners divide people into auditory, visual, and kinesthetic types. If the auditory type asks: "Are you reading me?" a "yes" response is far less effective than a "loud and clear" answer. When a visual person asks if "you see the problem?" the preferred response is: "I get the picture." Finally, the kinesthetic type tends to converse in terms of sense reactions: "I have a feeling it is time to act." In this case, to sell its talent KPF skillfully used the language of models—an essential feature of the Hercules vocabulary— over the language of words and drawings. Richard Bandler and John Grinder, *Frogs into Princes: Neuro Linguistic Programming* (Moab, Utah: Real People Press, 1979).
7. Alexander F. Giacco, quoted in "How Hercules Stole the Show in Wilmington," *Corporate Design,* January-February 1984, 56.
8. Alexander F. Giacco, videotape of the dedication ceremonies, Hercules Plaza, 28 June 1983, Wilmington, Delaware.
9. "First Year in a New Building Reviewed," *Hercules Horizons,* 1 June 1984, 2–3.

Chapter 5. Building the Company—The Beneficial Design Program

1. *Standard and Poors' Register of Corporations, Directors and Executives* (New York: Standard and Poors, 1985), 314.
2. Stanley Abercrombie, "Sturdy Set of Traditional Forms," *AIA Journal,* May 1983, 222.
3. *Annual Report 1982,* Beneficial Corporation, 59, and *Standard Corporation Descriptions: A–B* (New York: Standard and Poors Corporation, July 1985), 9870.
4. Interestingly, within the corporation, this orientation to young people

was evident in a publication initiated by Mr. Caspersen, *Susan, Jon and the Company Without a Factory: A Beneficial Corporation Report to the Younger Generation* (Wilmington: Beneficial Corporation, 1979). The short book was designed to answer children's questions: "Dad, how come you work for a company that doesn't have a factory? . . . If your company doesn't have a factory, how will it have anything to sell?" and responds with imaginative sketches and dialogue to explain concepts such as service, insurance, financing, credit, profits, and free enterprise.

5. Albert E. Winkler, quoted in David Forgione, "Beneficial Corporation to Purchase Land from Allan-Deane for \$9-Million," *The Bernardsville News*, 6 October 1977, 1.

6. Doug Wilhelm, "Bedminster or Bernards, Beneficial Wants to Build," *The Bernardsville News*, 1 December 1977, 9.

7. J. Robert Hillier, quoted in Vic Kalman, "Architect Gives Rise to Dreams," *Newark Sunday Star-Ledger*, Section 2, 28 November 1982, 1.

8. "Turner: Turner Builds on Its Reputation" (New York: Turner Construction, n.d.), 4.

9. Gordon L. Wadmond, Memo to the Beneficial Corporation Executive Committee, 30 July 1981.

10. Richard D. Goodenough, Consultant, Pottersville, NJ, *Summary Report*, 24 May 1979, 3.

11. Beneficial CEO Finn Caspersen's rather free-wheeling management style is also evident in reports that his decision to enter the reinsurance business has cost the company over \$450 million. However, here too, the chief executive may be able to make the best of a bad situation. By putting the corporation up for sale, he caused the price of the stock to jump from the mid-\$40s to more than \$70 a share, and one analyst noted that the move could "make Caspersen go out like a hero." (Laurie Hays, "Beneficial Corp. Flooded with Inquiries from Potential Buyers as Its Stock Soars," *Wall Street Journal*, 25 August 1986, 4.)

12. Danial P. Jones, "Former President Ford on Hand as P-G Officially Greets Beneficial," *The Bernardsville News*, 26 August 1982, 1.

13. Charles E. Hance, Beneficial Management Corporation, Discussion with the author, 16 January 1984.

14. "Traditional Motifs Meet in an Up-To-Date Office Village," *Architectural Record*, April 1983, 113. See also Stanley Abercrombie, "Sturdy Set of Traditional Forms," *AIA Journal*, May 1983, 220–225.

15. David J. Ferris, Beneficial Management Corporation, discussion with the author, 16 January, 1984.

16. Richard Kotz, Beneficial Management Corporation, discussion with the author, 7 February, 1986.

17. Jack Carr, manager, Beneficial Office, Fredericksburg, Virginia, discussion with the author, 11 March 1986.

18. A sense of how the winds of change are sweeping through the financial services industry is seen in these articles: Michael Stuntz, "Growing Competition: Pressures Mount as Business Enters the 80s," *The American Council of Life Insurance Review*, April/May 1980; Doris Fenske, "The Agency System at the Crossroads," *Best's Review*, February 1983, 14–

19; and Peter van Aartrijk, Jr., "The Treat to the Agent's Turf," *Best's Review*, April 1984, 14–16, 96–97. See also *The Financial Services Industry of Tomorrow* (Washington: National Association of Securities Dealers, 1982).

Chapter 6. Herman Miller—Design and the Corporate Culture

1. Gilbert Rohde, in Ralph Caplan, *The Design of Herman Miller* (New York: Whitney Library of Design, 1976), 27.
2. Frank Viviano, "The Architecture of Impermanence," *San Jose Mercury News*, 5 February 1984, *West* Magazine, 10–15.
3. Ann M. Morrison, "Action Is What Makes Herman Miller Climb," *Fortune*, 15 June 1981, 117.
4. Max DePree, in Ralph Caplan, op.cit., 18.
5. Max DePree, "The Prepared Professional," a presentation at the International Design Conference in Aspen, 15 June 1982 (Zeeland, Michigan: Herman Miller), 2.
6. Cheryl Grazulis, "A Look at People in Annual Reports," *The Personnel Administrator*, August 1978, 21.
7. John Adams, *Annual Report*, Herman Miller, 1983, 14.
8. Max DePree, *Annual Report*, Herman Miller, 1983, 1.
9. Douglas McGregor, "The Scanlon Plan Through a Psychologist's Eyes" in *The Scanlon Plan . . . A Frontier in Labor-Management Cooperation*, ed. Frederick G. Lesieur (Cambridge: The Technology Press of MIT and John Wiley & Sons, 1958), 89.
10. Richard S. Ruch, *The Scanlon Plan at Herman Miller* (Zeeland, Michigan: Herman Miller, August 1976), 36.
11. See Richard S. Ruch and Ronald Goodman, *Image at the Top* (New York: The Free Press, 1983), 117: "Herman Miller had an employee turnover average of only 8 percent for 1980–82, compared with a 25 percent national average. The company's absenteeism is also low: 1.3 percent in 1982 versus the national average of 5.7 percent."
12. Robert J. McClory, "The Creative Process at Herman Miller," *Across the Board*, May 1985, 10.
13. Caplan, op.cit. 27.
14. Max DePree, "What Is Leadership?" *Theology, News and Notes*, December 1983, 4.
15. Reformed Church in America, "Biblical Faith and Our Economic Life," *Christian Action and Theology Reports from the General Synod of 1984*, n.p.
16. "Offices That Make Room for the Human Spirit," Promotional Literature (Zeeland, Michigan: Herman Miller, 1985), n.p.
17. These were enumerated by Max DePree in a brochure that beautifully illustrated the Herman Miller assembly plant in Bath, England: "A Statement of Expectations," *Corporate Brochure* (Zeeland, Michigan: Herman Miller, 1978).
18. See David G. Santry, "Why Herman Miller Seems So Enticing," *Business Week*, 6 March 1978, 104, and "Space Systems: That's What Herman

Miller Sells to Its White-Collar Customers," *Barron's*, 23 November 1981, 54.

19. Tom Wolterinck in Andrea Oppenheimer Dean, "Streamlined Shapes Enclose a Splendid Workplace," *AIA Journal*, Mid-May 1982, 201.

20. William Pena, *Problem Seeking: An Architectural Programming Primer* (Boston: Cahners Books International, 1977).

21. Dean, op.cit., 201.

Chapter 7. Philosophy and Process—United Technologies' Design Audit

1. "Construction Audit Procedures Guide" (Washington, DC: Smith, Hinchman & Grylls Associates, Inc., May 1984), 1–1.

2. "500 Largest Industrial Corporations," *Fortune*, May 1971, p. 172.

3. See the *1985 Annual Report* and the *Fact Book 1985* (Hartford: United Technologies, 1985) for these statistics and other details concerning the company and its subsidiaries.

4. Harry J. Gray, *Design and Construction Manual: Phase One* (Hartford: United Technologies, May 1984), p. 1.

5. During 1987, Design and Construction and its related divisions were made part of United Technologies Corporation rather than a subsidiary of the United Properties real estate group. The change is notable because it integrates facility management even more closely with the highest levels of executive decision-making.

6. Drake Rowe, in a letter to the author, 19 May 1986.

7. *Design and Construction Manual: Phase One*, 3.

8. *Design and Construction Manual: Phase One*, 8.

9. *Guidelines for Facilities Development Planning* (Hartford: United Technologies, October 1985), ii.

10. On two occasions, United Technologies has used a fifth "audit" procedure that occurs about a year after completing a building. Referred to as "post-occupancy evaluation," this procedure investigates such attributes as job satisfaction, environmental comfort, circulation, flexibility, life cycle costs and capital costs. The analysis has been well received by both senior management and divisional staff, who use the results to measure the degree to which goals have been met, as guidelines for modifying existing structures, and as feedback on the criteria for future projects.

11. Smith, Hinchman & Grylls Associates, Inc., "Quality Design," in their quarterly *Newsletter*, Spring 1986, Economics Section.

12. United Technologies, advertisement, *Wall Street Journal*, 14 August 1986, 18.

13. Smith, Hinchman & Grylls Associates, Inc., "Quality Design."

14. *Construction Audit Report—Norden Systems Administration/Manufacturing Facility, Merrimack, NH*, Unpublished Report (Washington, DC: Smith, Hinchman and Grylls Associates—Value Management Division, March 1984), ES-1, ES-2, 2–3.

15. *Fact Book 1985*, 18–19.

16. François Jaulin, "370-Feet-High Otis Research Tower Under Construction in Connecticut," United Technologies/Otis Press Release, 23 October 1985.

17. *Construction Audit Report—Otis Test Tower Addition, Bristol, CT—Schematic Design Review,* Unpublished Report (Washington, DC: Smith, Hinchman and Grylls Associates—Value Management Division, June 1985), 4-1 through 4-6.

18. *Construction Audit Report—Otis Test Tower Addition, Bristol, CT—Design Development Review,* Unpublished Report (Washington, DC: Smith, Hinchman and Grylls Associates—Value Management Division, November 1985), 4-1 through 4-14.

19. Interview with William Tarinelli, United Technologies Design and Construction Office, 19 August 1986.

20. *Construction Audit Report—Otis Test Tower Addition, Bristol, CT—Design Development Review,* 1-5.

21. *Construction Audit Report—Pratt & Whitney New Plant, Nova Scotia, Canada—Schematic Design Review,* Sections 3 and 4.

22. *Construction Audit Report—Pratt & Whitney New Plant, Nova Scotia, Canada—Design Development Review,* Unpublished Report (Washington, DC: Smith, Hinchman and Grylls Associates—Value Management Division, October 1985), 4-1 through 4-16.

23. John Golding, "The Futurist Past," *The New York Review of Books,* 14 August 1986, 18.

24. Smith, Hinchman & Grylls Associates, Inc., "Quality Design."

Chapter 8. Architecture and the Corporation: Approaches to Excellence

1. Quoted in Kenneth Turney Gibbs, *Business Architectural Imagery in America, 1870–1930* (Ann Arbor: UMI Research Press, 1984), 25.

2. Quoted in Gibbs, op. cit., 1.

3. See chapter 2 for a more complete description of this example.

4. See chapter 2 for a more complete description of these examples.

5. Thomas J. Watson, Jr., "Good Design Is Good Business," in Thomas F. Schutte, ed., *The Uneasy Coalition: Design in Corporate America* (Philadelphia: University of Pennsylvania Press, 1975), 79.

6. Charles E. Hance is litigation counsel for Beneficial Management and Gordon Wadmond (now retired) was the company's executive vice president.

7. John Greer (now retired) was Assistant Vice President for Administration and Public Affairs; Ed Lacy was a mechanical engineer and had a background in construction management; Betty Ronat was an electrical engineer with computer expertise.

8. James O'Toole, *Vanguard Management: Redesigning the Corporate Future* (Garden City, NY: Doubleday & Company, 1985), 357–358.

9. O'Toole, op. cit., 41.

10. O'Toole, 190–198.

11. Quoted in O'Toole, 232.

12. O'Toole, 232–233.
13. Tracy Kidder, *The Soul of a New Machine* (New York: Avon, 1981), 9.
14. David Maister, "Lessons in Client Loving," *Architectural Technology*, Fall 1985, 47–48.
15. Robert Teitelmann, "Electronic Building Blocks," *Forbes*, 21 October 1985, 156.
16. Michael L. Sena and Eric Teicholz, "Computers: Facility Management Is Fertile Ground for Automation," *Architectural Record*, February 1986, 35–39.
17. Bea Sennewald, "Smart Buildings—Facts, Myths and Implications," *Architectural Technology*, March/April 1986, 21–35.
18. George T. Heery, AIA, *Time, Cost, and Architecture* (New York: McGraw Hill, 1975), 48.
19. For a history and summary of this component of construction management see Larry W. Zimmerman, and Glen D. Hart, *Value Engineering: A Practical Approach for Owners, Designers and Contractors* (New York: Van Nostrand Reinhold, 1982).
20. Joanne Lipman, "Unfixed Assets: Real Estate Is Turning into Big Source of Cash for Many Companies," *Wall Street Journal*, 1 July 1985, 1.
21. Quoted in Ann Nydele, "Comes the Facilities Manager," *Architectural Record*, May 1985, 53.
22. Quoted in David P. Billington, "In Defense of Engineers," *The Wilson Quarterly*, New Year's 1986, 94.
23. Billington, op. cit., 92.
24. John S. Garner, *The Model Company Town: Urban Design Through Private Enterprise in Nineteenth-Century New England* (Amherst: University of Massachusetts Press, 1984).
25. Quoted in Patrick Barry, "Columbus Discovered," *Discovery*, Summer 1986, p. 15.
26. See reprint of article by Louis Sullivan, "The Tall Building Artistically Considered," *Progressive Architecture*, June 1957, 204.

Appendix: Resources in the Area of Facility Management

1. Much of this information was generously provided by the International Facility Management Association in Houston, Tex.

Index

About the Author

THOMAS Walton, Ph.D., is associate professor in The Catholic University of America's Department of Architecture and Planning. He teaches both design and history and has particular expertise in American urbanism and corporate architecture. In addition to his teaching and research, he is the mid-Atlantic regional representative of the National Endowment for the Arts' (NEA) Design Arts Program. Prior to serving as a representative for the NEA's program, he coordinated *The Competitive Edge*, NEA's corporate design initiative.

PROGRAM FOR STUDIES OF
THE MODERN CORPORATION
Graduate School of Business, Columbia University

PUBLICATIONS

———

SEYMOUR MARTIN LIPSET and WILLIAM SCHNEIDER
The Confidence Gap: Business, Labor, and Government in the Public Mind

IRA M. MILLSTEIN and SALEM M. KATSH
The Limits of Corporate Power: Existing Constraints on the Exercise of Corporate Discretion

KENNETH G. PATRICK
Perpetual Jeopardy—The Texas Gulf Sulphur Affair: A Chronicle of Achievement and Misadventure

GUNNAR K. SLETMO and ERNEST W. WILLIAMS, JR.
Liner Conferences in the Container Age: U.S. Policy at Sea

GEORGE A. STEINER
The New CEO

GEORGE A. STEINER
Top Management Planning

FRANK TANNENBAUM
The Balance of Power in Society

The colophon for this book as for the other books of the Program for Studies of the Modern Corporation was created by Theodore Roszak